My Sister's Mother

My Sister's Mother

*A Memoir of War, Exile,
and Stalin's Siberia*

Donna Solecka Urbikas

The University of Wisconsin Press

The University of Wisconsin Press
1930 Monroe Street, 3rd Floor
Madison, Wisconsin 53711-2059
uwpress.wisc.edu

3 Henrietta Street, Covent Garden
London WC2E 8LU, United Kingdom
eurospanbookstore.com

Printed in the United States of America

This book may be available in a digital edition

Library of Congress Cataloging-in-Publication Data
Names: Urbikas, Donna Solecka, author.
Title: My sister's mother: a memoir of war, exile, and Stalin's Siberia /
Donna Solecka Urbikas.
Description: Madison, Wisconsin: The University of Wisconsin Press, [2016] | ©2016
| Includes bibliographical references and index.
Identifiers: LCCN 2015038427 | ISBN 9780299308506 (cloth: alk. paper)
Subjects: LCSH: Urbikas, Donna Solecka—Family.
| World War, 1939–1945—Deportations from Poland.
| Forced migration—Poland—History—20th century.
| Deportees—Poland—Biography. | Deportees—Soviet Union—Biography.
| Polish people—Soviet Union—Biography. | Polish Americans—Biography.
Classification: LCC D810.D5 U735 2016 | DDC 940.53/14509239185—dc23
LC record available at http://lccn.loc.gov/2015038427

Whosoever takes the child by the hand
takes the mother by the heart.

—old proverb

_____

For

Father

who took Mira's hand and won Mother's heart
_____

Contents

Part 2
Russia and Siberia

Part 3
Choices and Destiny

Part 4
Bittersweet Lessons

Epilogue

Preface

This book is a nonfiction account of my family's experiences in pre–World War I Poland and during the years prior to and during World War II in Poland and the Soviet Union, the Middle East, India, and Britain, as well as the United States following World War II.

Before the fall of Soviet-style Communism in Poland in 1989 and in the Soviet Union in 1990, the atrocities committed by the Soviets in the prisoner-of-war camps such as those that my father, a Polish Army officer, witnessed or in the labor camps to which my mother and half sister had been deported, were essentially unknown. It was my aim to bring those events to light when I first began writing their story in English in 1985. Years later, I expanded their story to include the impact of their experiences on me growing up in America after the war.

This account of my mother, Janina, and my half sister, Mira, is based on interviews with them and with my father, Wawrzyniec, who was one of the few hundred Polish Army officers who had not been murdered in the Katyń Massacres. He had met my mother and half sister in the Soviet Union after their escape from the labor camps in 1941. All quotes are either taken verbatim from recorded interviews, from their written notes, or from memories of my life growing up with them. Thoughts and emotions ascribed to them have been reconstructed from these interviews and my memories. Details of war events were taken from historical documents, documentaries, oral histories of survivors, and autobiographies such as *An Army in Exile* by General Władysław Anders, and from reputable historical sources such as Norman Davies's *God's Playground*. All sources of information used can be found in the references section. I also benefited from interviews in 1988 with local Chicago experts on Polish history such as Jan Krawiec, an underground Polish soldier during World War II, historian, journalist, and former editor of the *Dziennik Związkowy (Polish Daily News)*, and John J. Kulczycki, professor of history emeritus at the University of Illinois, Chicago. Professor Kulczycki provided valuable insights into the perspectives of the various ethnic groups in what was then eastern Poland at the outbreak of World War II.

Events that I directly experienced are narrated in the first person, while stories collected from my parents and sister are written in third person to distinguish the time period being described. When I first began writing their story more than thirty years ago, I wrote in a new style of writing intended to show, not just tell, the reader what was then little-known Polish history. Narrative or creative nonfiction was not yet a recognized genre at that time, but thankfully, today it is an accepted form that makes it possible to bring true historical accounts to life with a novelist's eye.

Both older and current names of places, which changed before and following both World Wars are used, depending on the period in which the events being narrated took place. For example, the city of Grodno is no longer in Poland but is part of Belarus, Persia is now Iran, Bombay is now Mumbai, and Palestine is now Israel. Some Poles, including my mother, referred to those inhabitants of eastern Poland, following World War I, as *Białorusi*, or White Russians (today known as Belarusians). Poles often referred to all Soviets, Belarusians and Ukrainians included, as "Russians" though not all would have been, and the reference to "Russian" or "Moskal" was regularly used in colloquial conversation. Similarly, when Europeans found themselves in such foreign lands as the Middle East, they referred to Persians and others as "Arabs," as the distinctions between different groups in the Middle East would not have been clear to them.

Polish history is very complicated, and there is debate and some controversy about what should be considered Poland—there is occupied or partitioned Poland, the Polish Empire, or the Polish-Lithuanian (or Lithuanian-Polish) Republic or Commonwealth, depending on one's point of view. For the unique generation of Poles raised between the World Wars, such as my parents, who were educated in Poland's history throughout its 123 years of occupation by the Germans, Austrians, and Russians and who had a patriotism instilled in them that is largely missing from subsequent generations, there was no debate. Because I absorbed much of their point of view, I have strived to separate that from the known historical record while still keeping their voice. I have worked as a scientific researcher, and so I have attempted to approach these historical events with the same objectivity I came to value through that work.

First names often have various forms in Polish depending on the emphasis of endearment; my name, for example, is formally and officially Danuta, which translates as Donna in English, but I was also known as Danusia, Danulu, Daniusienko, and so forth. Last names also change with gender, so that my father's name, Solecki, becomes Solecka for my mother and me. Finally, though Mira is my half sister, I never thought of her as such and refer to her only as "my sister."

I must thank my parents, Janina and Wawrzyniec, and my sister, Mira, who so generously shared their difficult stories with me over the course of many years while I pressed them with unrelenting questions. I thank my husband, John, for his infinite patience and tireless numerous readings and many helpful comments of early versions of the manuscript while I was still trying to find my writer's voice. I wish to thank Gwen Walker of the University of Wisconsin Press for her recognition of the value of the story and her tireless promotion of the book. The University of Wisconsin Press staff were especially wonderful, and copyeditor M.J. Devaney provided valuable, critical comments.

I thank various friends who have contributed to the project over the years with their helpful comments on structure, writing, and historical details—Elizabeth Redmond of Publishers Group West, Margaret Zalewski, well-traveled Polish history buff, Kinga Rzyska, political scientist, linguist, and Polish history expert, and Leslie Keros, editor. Wesley Adamczyk, Polish deportee, son of a father murdered at Katyń, and author of *When God Looked the Other Way*, and Leonard Kniffel, former editor of *American Libraries Journal* and author of *A Polish Son in the Motherland*, both spent hours and hours reviewing and commenting on later versions of the manuscript. Wesley's clever suggestion for the title is especially appreciated. To them I will be forever grateful. Richard Gross kindly created a first detailed map of my parents' and sister's journey.

Fellow writers and teachers of the University of Chicago's Certificate Writing Program—Paula Peterson, Tim McNulty, Sandi Wisenberg, Dina Elenbogen—were instrumental with their reviews during my two years of classes and workshops there.

My family in Poland—Darek, Marysia, Mietek, Zbyszek, and their families—especially provided me with a deeper understanding of the war experience and its aftereffects as they struggled to regain their lives under Communism. To them I am humbly grateful. My other half sisters in Poland, Luta and Krysia and their families, also welcomed me and shared their struggles, for which I am deeply grateful.

I wish most of all to thank my children, Darius, Justine, and Anton, for their contribution to the book—patiently listening to my oral presentations, reviewing the final work, and Justine's expert editing—and for just being here so that I could be a mother.

My Sister's Mother

"My mother," my sister continued, "was a hero."

I reeled back from the comfortable embrace of our mutual recollections and thought to myself, what do you mean *my* mother? Wasn't she *our* mother?

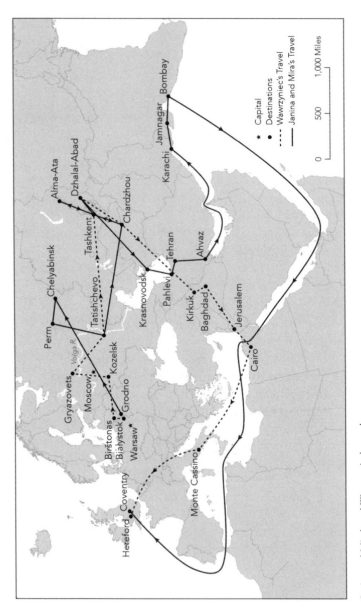

Janina and Mira's and Wawrzyniec's travel routes, 1939–47

Introduction

Somewhere during the years of World War II turmoil, across the fertile plains and snow-covered mountains of Europe, a turning point came in the lives of people like my mother. *Wojna* (the War), as it was referred to during our family gatherings, left a lifelong scar on them, and it was a favorite topic of discussion during my childhood growing up in America—what they did before the War, what happened to them during the War, how and why they came to America after the War.

My mother's stories emerged with little or no provocation— the grainy taste of a piece of coarse rye bread like the scarce ones in the Soviet labor camps in Russia and Siberia, or a quiet walk in the woods at our Wisconsin farm like those in which my mother had worked sawing tree limbs, maneuvering heavy logs in ice cold Russian rivers, or a salvaged spool of sewing thread like the unraveled cloth she once used to mend a barely repairable coat, or the constant hunt for wood ticks in my hair that reminded her of the lice that she had relentlessly battled. Mostly, though, it was the cold—like the cold of the Siberian winter that caused the frostbite that necessitated the amputation of her toes—that brought on more stories. Her memory was acute. Her stories seemed to fall from her lips endlessly, as if they had just been lived. I grew to know them as if they were my own.

When I was twenty-one, newly married and just graduated from college, I had asked my mother to let me write down the stories. We were having dinner at the farm, and she was in the middle of one of her stories, when I realized that I had stopped resenting her constant reminders of the War. She declined without any explanation, and I was too timid then to pursue the request. I asked her again when I was thirty, just out of graduate school, still childless, and again she said no. I was disappointed but assumed that the telling would be too difficult for her. I dropped the idea for a time, but it taunted me like some forbidden fruit, the thought always just beneath the surface of my consciousness whenever another story emerged.

Finally, after I had my first baby, she agreed. She was in her seventies by then and in poor health. I sensed that she felt I could be trusted to understand her journey. And so, some four decades after the War, in 1985, as Solidarność (the Solidarity movement) in Poland was trying to oust the repressive Communist government, I began writing down my mother's stories. With a newborn baby boy and being about the same age as my mother had been when she was arrested and sent to that labor camp with my sister, Mira, in 1940, I felt confident I could capture her story.

When I first began writing my mother's story I thought I could write it like a journalist, like an unemotional third-party observer. It didn't work. After organizing all the notes and doing extensive research with my father's help—he was a well-read and self-educated historian who had met my mother and sister in the Soviet Union when he was a Polish Army officer—and listening to my mother's voice on the audio tapes I had asked her to record, I spent the better part of the next year crying and procrastinating. My sister, on the other hand, was oddly not able, or willing, to recall many details of her experiences.

Then, one day in late summer during a visit to the farm with my baby, I began writing. Immediately, as if I had been thrown back in time, I became immersed in my mother's story, as if I were hearing it for the first time. At times, I felt as if I were there, back in 1940, back in rural Poland at my mother's farm near Grodno, back in the Siberian wilderness with the sound of howling wolves breaking the numbing silence. More than once, as I shopped for groceries for my family, I would put my mind on hold so not to become distracted by the modern-day world of 1980s America. I would glide through the grocery store aisles, making as little eye contact as I could with others. In everything else I did, I tried not to lose the feel of those war years.

During that trancelike period of my life, I came to realize that old age is a time for reflection, a chance to teach lessons, to become immortalized. It was an insight that made me think about my mother in a way I never imagined. Ironically, as she recalled her troubled, desperate times, trapped in the physical immobility of an aging body, she endured those past traumas again for me as if she were reliving them. This time I listened with the compassion learned as a mother. Just as the last weeks of pregnancy make life so unbearable that a woman rushes joyfully into the pain of labor and delivery, so do the last weeks of life in old age prepare one for death.

Over the course of some twenty years, I tried again and again to finish writing her story. Each time I could see how these stories had affected me, but I resisted delving into that unknown. I feared becoming emotionally unglued. If I were to put myself into her story, would it still be her story? I had convinced myself that this was only going to be my mother's story. It was only when I began to revise the story again, when I was almost an old woman myself, with my children all grown and my mother gone, that I felt strong enough, compelled enough, to seek the truth, that no matter how I tried to deny it, our stories were intertwined.

I've asked myself on many occasions—why this story, why now? Would writing about her experiences help me understand my mother and why she had behaved as she did when I was growing up? Would I understand why I was struggling to be so different from her in the way I was raising my own children? Being different from her meant that I would be in control of my emotions. I would not talk to myself in mirrors. I would not live in the past. I would do what? What would I be as a mother to my own children?

It took becoming a mother myself with all its selfless transformations to even begin to understand my mother. I came to realize that the turning point in her life, that fateful day of her arrest and deportation in the winter of 1940, became my fate and had directed the course of my life and that of my children, as her parenting affected me more than I cared to admit. Though I didn't recognize it then, I was writing my mother's and sister's story in an attempt to capture their mysterious closeness, to become a part of it, to satisfy a longing that seemed to never be quieted in my mind.

"When you grow up . . . ," they would say when I asked about some detail as a child. It seemed that my mother only wanted to talk about such things when she needed mental relief. My sister was dismissive, as if she didn't want to be reminded of any of it. Yet there were constant reminders that I had not gone through the War as they had, and that set me apart. These were small things that seemed to surface by surprise, like things my sister never had when she was growing up—a variety of clothes, numerous books, new toys, my own room, my education—my "advantages" as they were called.

"Look what you have," my mother would say. "You're so spoiled. Mira never had it so good. Don't complain. Be grateful." Then they would nod toward each other as if I were not present. I envied their knowing glances and even felt guilty for not having endured what they had gone through together. I wanted my mother to talk with me the way she talked with my sister, as if we too had some deep dark secret that could be revealed with a mere glance.

In her mind, it seemed to me, my mother was always dying, so as a child, I learned not to be afraid of death. "When I die . . . ," she began on more than one occasion. "I don't want to go on living," she would say at other times, when she was frustrated. At first such thoughts frightened me, but as she repeated them I came to realize that my mother embraced death because death had been a constant in her life. At one time or another, she had held in her arms her dying mother, father, sister, brother, and two children. During the War, she witnessed many deaths. At the time of her arrest, there remained no one else but Mira, and it was only to save Mira from any and all danger that she clung to life.

Attuned to each remaining moment of her life, my mother collected these memories and presented them to me as distilled episodes from a lifetime of accumulated wisdom, as a gift, a sacrifice, and I had to garner those lessons: I had to come to terms with growing up and living with a mother and sister who had endured such a desperate journey.

Part I
_____

The Generation
between the Wars

The Haunting Past

My mother furrowed her brow in what had become a familiar prelude to a long and pitiful story. She began in her lulling voice, captivating me, crushing me, evoking the cold darkness of that February night in the countryside in 1940, the small, barely lit Polish farmhouse near Grodno, the sudden angry knock on the heavy door, the stampede of armed Soviet soldiers, the harsh orders to gather her belongings quickly. Within one hour she would leave her home, the birthplace of my sister, Mira, for the forced labor in Russia that was to "free" them. I stopped eating my dinner and stared at her. I was fifteen years old and just beginning to comprehend the impact of those events on my family.

My mother, Janina, was one of several hundred thousand civilian Poles deported from eastern Poland during 1940 and 1941 by the Soviet Communists. She worked in timber operations, in the dense forests of Siberia and Russia, a prison that required no walls. Mira was five years old at the time and had to be left alone in the camp to fend for herself while Janina worked. She and Mira's father had separated before the war, and so he was not with them in the camp. He was later sent to prison, as were most Polish Army soldiers.

Though I was born many years later, in a very different part of the world, I grew up learning of their experiences at family dinners and holiday gatherings. I often felt as if I had been dragged through it all with them, and I began to think my mother was crazy. Who would keep talking about this horrible stuff over and over again, if they weren't crazy?

Then she continued. "*Czegoś mi brak* (Something is missing)."

We were having one of our regular Sunday afternoon dinners prepared by my mother, but it was not our usual Polish cuisine. I was enjoying the meat loaf, creamy mashed potatoes, and sweet cooked peas and carrots in my mother's special buttery sauce when her remark made me flinch. Oh, here we go again, I thought. Another war story is about to take over our otherwise pleasant meal.

It was 1965 and I was immersed in the American culture of the times, except on Saturdays, when I attended Polish school and Polish Girl Scout meetings in Chicago, where I displayed my completely Polish persona. I was growing up in America, the land of ultimate freedom! I had any opportunity I wanted, which like most American teenagers, I took for granted. What my mother had to say was tainted by reliving the distant past, and I naïvely found it irrelevant. Only much later did I realize that although I was growing up in an era of peaceniks and Vietnam War protests, war never really ends; if we are not preparing for or engaging in war, we are recovering from one or trying to avoid the next one.

"What's missing, *Pani* Janina?" my father teased in Polish by referring to my mother using the very formal *Pani* (Mrs.). He sat up tall in his chair, and his wide shoulders seemed to embrace us all. He spoke in a sing-songy voice, very different from his usual husky masculine tone, trying to sound interested and not too serious. He had a mischievous look on his face, and his kind blue eyes smiled at us from behind round eyeglasses that were planted on his rather large nose, which my mother liked to call a "trunk."

"Oh, nothing. It's nothing," she replied. She sounded nonchalant, but I recognized that she was waiting for an invitation to go on with her story.

"Now, Mother, if you're going to say something, then finish telling us," my sister insisted. My sister, who by then was about thirty, always seemed to say the right thing in this mysteriously quiet, confident manner. I admired her composure, her coiffed hair styled neatly into a French twist, her impeccably tailored clothes.

"Well, I was just thinking about that time I had to go dig potatoes in Siberia," my mother began. "Do you remember, Mireczko?" she asked, using an endearing form of my sister's name.

I noticed my mother was poking at her portion of potatoes on her plate with a fork. My sister nodded knowingly toward her. Then they both fell silent as I waited for the rest of the story that I had heard dozens of times before, but nevertheless wanted to hear again. In spite of all the repetition, I was easily engaged by my mother's storytelling. She could make any mundane story come to life with her lulling voice, timely pauses, and expressive face. My father and I stared at her, waiting to hear more.

The conversation we were having reminded me of similar ones my parents often had with their friends. One time, my parents invited several new American friends to our Wisconsin farm during one of our vacations there, and as usual the conversation turned to the War.

"Why couldn't you just fight them or refuse to go?" asked one guest naïvely.

"Wasn't Poland a free country then?" asked another.

My mother grew very grave, narrowing her full, arched eyebrows and wrinkling her forehead, making herself look old and anguished. I sat still, bracing myself for an outburst and anticipating the embarrassment I expected to feel in front of our new guests.

"Free? Do you think *you* know what freedom is?" she asked, her voice rising. "I know what freedom really is, because I know what it's not!"

We all stopped eating and stared at her.

Like the weight of a thousand pounds of potatoes upon her back, my mother carried with her the collective remorse of an entire nation, the regrets of a whole generation that had been teased by a short-lived freedom in their beloved country. Poland had been erased from the world's maps for over a century prior to World War I and had reappeared for only a few short years between the World Wars, long enough for a stubbornly patriotic generation to grow up knowing freedom, and then quickly losing it. It was a generation persecuted by the savageness of Stalin and the ruthlessness of Hitler.

My mother laughed, an exaggerated howl, repeating their questions as if in mockery. My father, sister, and I sat quietly. I looked at our awestruck guests as they stared at my mother.

"Why didn't I resist arrest?" she asked. Without waiting for our guests to speak, she followed with more questions, spewing words in rapid fire. "Why was it so difficult for me, while some-how others survived better? Why can't I forget?"

She shrugged her shoulders, raised her eyebrows and stared past us, the corners of her mouth turned downward, her head moving slowly from side to side in disbelief.

"I had no husband," she answered, referring to my sister's father. Then, she glanced at Mira and realized she'd referred to a family secret, so she quickly added, "He was sent to prison." I sensed my sister's growing discomfort as she shifted in her seat.

My mother continued, and her voice rose, becoming almost piercing. As she rambled on, she spoke faster and faster. Like the roar of a speeding train, the sound of her voice pounded on me until one deep breath after another, I was caught up in her story, unable to let loose.

"Yes, the crime of being a landowner was fabricated. Free human labor, you know," she said, her voice growing shrill. "Resist? How? With what? Me? A lone woman with a small child against a bayonet pointed at my chest?"

She was almost shouting, challenging her guests to dispute what she was saying. Then, she paused and uttered that word, "crazy," with the sound of the *r* rolling melodically, and gave an ironic laugh that seemed more forced than real. She would often use the word "crazy" in odd moments.

There was silence after that, as we all sat recovering. I felt my breathing become shallow until I needed to gasp for air. I snuck a deep breath. At that point, my sister calmly interjected, "Now, Mother, enough," and proceeded to ask some blatantly boring question of one of the guests, just to change the subject. We all shifted in our seats, looked down at our plates, and resumed eating.

Uneasy Peace

When Warszawa (Warsaw) was attacked by the Germans on September 1, 1939, Janina was tending to her many chores on the fruit farm she owned in eastern Poland while five-year-old Mira played among the baskets of newly picked apples. A late summer sun sent colorful lazy rays of light through orange clouds as it set into the distant hills of the Niemen River valley. "*Mój Boże, jaki cud!* (My God, what beauty!)," recalled Janina.

With the last rays of light disappearing, the river valley's green horizon appeared like the rolling waves of a distant ocean. She knew that the gently flowing waters of the Niemen River belied its many perilous whirlpools, where more than one peasant had drowned, a demise she herself had almost met years before. In the dry late summer, an intoxicating mellow mood had befallen neighboring farmers as they tried to go about their daily lives in their secluded corner of the world. It was that dryness that enabled Hitler to move his armies quickly from the west, north, and south into Poland and to hasten its devastation. Unbeknownst to Janina and her neighbors, this dryness also allowed the Soviets to quickly advance onto Polish soil from the other direction shortly after Hitler's attack, as part of a secret Russian-German pact signed earlier that year to divvy up Poland.

On Janina's plot of land, fruit trees were weighed down with apples, plums, and pears. Their thick branches lay low with the precious crop, sweeping the ground like fine crinoline skirts. She had nurtured the trees to maturity, and they stood ready to provide their first abundant crop. "The harvest will give us enough food for the winter ahead," she assured Mira. Remembering the constant threat of starvation as a child during World War I, Janina said she refrained from eating the fruit herself, preferring to save it for Mira and the market.

The farm had twenty-three chickens, two pigs, and a milking cow, all of which were housed in a small stable next to a pond near the woods that abutted the farm. Janina stored several baskets of apples in her four-room chalet-style farmhouse. It was one of forty identical houses built by the Polish government in an area called Rokitno to reward the Polish Freedom Fighters who had secured Poland's independence during World War I. Janina's brother, Walenty, had received it for his heroic deeds during those battles, and she inherited it when he died. After over a century of foreign occupation, Poland had finally become a free, independent country. "I was proud to own such a large and historically significant piece of land," she boasted years later.

The new borders of Poland as established by the Treaty of Versailles in 1919 were not readily accepted by the mostly Belarusian inhabitants in that part of eastern Poland. When Soviet Russia attacked on September 17, 1939, Belarusian peasants, encouraged by Communist propaganda against the Poles, plundered and ravaged Polish farms and villages in retribution. Once peaceful neighbors, the invasion quickly changed the dynamics of life between Poles and Belarusians. As part of the educated *intelligentsia*, Janina considered Roman Catholics to be Poles and members of the Eastern Orthodox Church to be White Russians (Belarusians), but the Belarusian peasantry, influenced by Communist thought, sought to eradicate this social order.

One day, a neighbor drove up to Janina's farm on his horse-drawn hay wagon. "Mrs. Janina," he said. "Did you hear what happened at a village up north? Sixteen of our farmers were murdered! I am leaving here. I advise you to do the same!"

"I've worked too hard for this land," she answered. "Let lightning strike them down! I will not leave all this."

He pleaded with her. "But, you are a woman alone here. Who will protect you if they attack? What about your child?" he asked.

Janina looked down at Mira, who was staring wide eyed at them both.

"I don't know what I will do. I will pray. I will pray that they will leave us alone."

Most of Janina's neighbors escaped these groups of undisciplined bandits, Communist Reds, and NKVD commandos, finding shelter in the nearby city of Grodno. The abandoned surrounding lands became eerily quiet, for a time.

Janina had dreamed of creating an idyllic life for herself and Mira after she left Mira's father, Rudolf. As a landowner, she was an independent woman relying on her own resources and trying to navigate the business world of a very male-dominated culture.

Janina rarely spoke of Rudolf, especially not in Mira's presence. When his name came up, it was as if it were something too terrible to mention. Out of Mira's earshot, she would say, "He neglected us." However, he had once given Mira a small black terrier dog that she named Figa, and Mira never forgot this. "It was the only time my father was *my father*," Mira said years later with a pointed look of regret. "He had given me the dog, and it was the only time in my life I felt that he was *my father*," she repeated, as if hoping to believe it herself.

Figa was joined by a husky-like dog named Moja. Mira played with both of them, often sneaking into Moja's doghouse during games of hide and seek with Janina. Once, Mira was ill with the stomach flu, and Janina forbade her to eat anything. "I was so hungry, I snuck into the doghouse and ate the dog's whole dinner of potatoes smeared with bits of bacon grease, and Mother never knew it," she later admitted in her shy, playful manner.

On certain days in the summer of 1939, Janina stopped working briefly to enjoy Mira's company as she played with the ducks and geese in the courtyard between the house and the stable. One of them was a fearsome old gander who often chased Mira onto the porch. Janina recalled with delight that "all Mira could do was point helplessly and squeal, 'Afraid of *ga-ga*, afraid of *ga-ga*.'"

Deep into the woods behind the farm, gentle summer breezes swept through the silvery leaves of white birch trees flickering against a fading sunset. Tall, narrow poplar trees on one side of the road to Grodno swayed in the warm breeze on many afternoons as Janina walked with Mira. She told Mira the story of Napoleon marching on the same road, embellishing her story with large arm gestures and by varying the intonation of her voice, as if she were on the stage of a theater. Mira listened, mesmerized as they walked together to the Niemen River, picking wild raspberries along the way. When they arrived at the river, they stood on the steep bank watching the rolling waves and were swept into quiet contentment. There was no bridge to cross over to the inviting sands that merged into small dunes on the other side. The only bridge over the river was the one into Grodno. Later, escape from the invading Soviets depended on access to this bridge.

While the war raged in the west with Hitler and in the east with the Soviets, Janina tried to ignore the sporadic stories of plundering. One day as she tended to an old wound in her leg that had become infected, she heard a thunderous roar of planes overhead. She looked out her window and saw that they were Russian military planes. "The sky was blackened from so many of them," she recalled.

Janina hobbled over to a table and fumbled to tune in her radio. Only static and unintelligible words filled the room. "Mira, stay in the house!" she yelled as she ran out, limping to a neighbor's abandoned house, where she turned on the radio just in time to hear one of the many addresses of Stefan Starzyński, mayor of Warsaw. In the echoes of his sad but strong voice, she stood numbed by fragments of the words she recalled later.

"My countrymen, our army is defeated. . . . There is no army. . . . There is no police force. . . . There is no more government. . . . You are on your own. Try to save yourselves as best you can. . . . Oh my God, what's happening here . . . ?" Suddenly, the sound of a bomb cracked over the airwaves and the radio went silent.

"I will never forget those words. I felt as if I were standing in a murky swamp, slowly sinking," she said years later.

Mira, gather your clothes!" Janina yelled when she returned to her house.

She hid several baskets of apples and potatoes in the cellar and sacks of dried foods—beans, barley, buckwheat—throughout the house. Hoping she'd return soon, she collected warmer clothes into a large wooden box, wrapped it in oilcloth, and buried it in the soft soil behind the chicken coop.

"We're going to Grodno like our neighbors," she told Mira.

Grodno was five miles away from Janina's farm, and she had hoped to catch the night freight train that passed by each evening. Walking with a group of peasant women, she pulled Mira along a gravel road to the nearest railroad crossing. It was a dark night and impossible to know whether the train would be carrying Polish citizens or Soviet soldiers bound for a siege on Grodno. Marauding soldiers roamed the countryside shooting Poles along the way, so it was dangerous to walk along such roads. The women and children hid in a field of tall grass whenever anyone approached along the road, waiting until they were certain it was safe to venture out.

Janina could hear the whistle of the freight train approaching fast, but no one in the group moved from their hiding place to flag down the train. Then, she stood up and marched up to the tracks.

Mira shrieked, "Mama, Mama," but Janina continued forward, ignoring Mira's pleas. Swinging her lit naphtha lamp high into the air, she stepped onto the tracks as the old freight train slowly rattled its way toward her. It stopped only a few feet in front of her. With trembling hands, everyone boarded the train, and barely able to see each other in the dark boxcar, they rode in silence to the city.

The Interview

One of the last times I remember sitting with my mother doing something pleasant together was during Christmas break in seventh grade when I was sewing clothes for my Barbie doll. My mother bought the patterns and showed me how to cut out the pieces and sew them together on our old Singer sewing machine that she had brought from England when we came to America. It had no motor and had to be pumped by foot, could not go in reverse, and required my full attention. While I sewed, she worked on some garment for me or my sister, who by then was working full time as a chemist. We spoke little to each other during those times, but we were content together.

When I began writing this narrative, I recalled that fleeting, warm feeling of togetherness from my childhood and tried to capture it. I sat nervously on a creaky chair near her as she lay resting on an old couch in the enclosed farmhouse porch in Wisconsin. Bracing myself for the next pieces of a story, I listened and jotted down notes like a good reporter, trying to hold back tears. A cool summer breeze whisked through the house, gently lifting loose strands of her long fine gray hair, which she had long ago given up dyeing black. She was weak from heart disease, and several other ailments were sapping away her energy. I sensed her tiredness with life. My baby was taking his afternoon nap, and it was so quiet outside that I almost missed the noise and clatter of my comfortable Chicago home.

I did all I could do to sit still and wait for her to allow me into her secret world, the world that would reveal the causes of her erratic behavior, from which I was still recovering at age thirty-five. I had made this special trip to visit, to interview her, to be the good researcher I had become during my graduate school scientific studies. My mother slowly laid down a historical novel about Poland and blurted out in Polish, "*Głupie życie!* (A foolish life!)" I had heard her utter that phrase before, but I wanted to under-stand it, to understand her. She sat silently for what seemed a long time, and I began to wonder if she would continue telling me the story or launch into another soliloquy.

"Oh, how they maltreated me!" she cried and then fell silent. I didn't know what to say. I braced myself for more of her dis-turbing comments, which I dared not question. Her outbursts often left me wary. I puzzled over how to react, trying to evaluate her mental state. I remembered how hurt I had once felt as a child after I had committed some minor transgression and she railed at me in Polish, "Why are *you* maltreating me?" It seemed as if some demon had possessed her and she worked herself into a frenzy, all the time spewing curses in Polish like, "You, you bastard, let lightning strike you down!" and "dog's blood, cholera!" At that point, I suspected she was no longer directing such venom toward me, but toward some unknown figure from her past. I was never sure.

In the silence, as I waited for her to calm down, I lost myself in more recollections from childhood. Once, at the age of five, I was about to dash past my mother's bedroom (which was really the dining room) to the kitchen of our third-story walk-up apartment on a noisy street on the north side of Chicago, when I noticed her sitting at her dressing table. I stopped in the open doorway, but she didn't see me. The tall mirror of the dressing table towered over her, and she stared into her reflection as she applied dark red lipstick to her thin lips, unaware of my presence. Then she began talking to that unknown figure from her past. "What did they want from me? What could I do?" The stark red of her painted lips contrasted harshly with her pale skin and the dyed blackness of her hair, which was pulled back into a large bun gathered low at her neck. I did not like her made up like that.

I wanted to shout, "Stop it!" but I was afraid to invade her secret world, the world that plagued her spirit and invaded mine. I retreated to the safety of my room, yelling in Polish at her as I tried to find a way back into the game I had been playing by myself. She stopped for a moment only to return to another incident from her past. I yelled again, "Stop, stop it, stop talking to yourself!"

but not too loudly for fear that her anger might come crashing down on me again. I so longed to know who "they" were and what "it" was that they wanted. Who was she talking to anyway? Who was taking her away from me?

I returned to her room, having finally mustered the courage to confront her.

"Mama? Who are you talking to?"

Startled, she replied, "Nothing, it's nothing." But I didn't believe her. Then she tried to distract me. "Would you like some vanilla ice cream? I just made it this morning and it should be frozen by now."

These tirades of recalled maltreatment taught me to be cautious. She wasn't quite crazy, I thought, but close enough. Craziness was not something from which she shied away. She would often use the word "crazy" in detached moments, and I had long given up trying to get her to explain.

I waited for my mother to resume her story. My baby would soon be waking from his afternoon nap, so I asked as gently in Polish as I could, "*Mamusiu, co dalej?* (Mama, what happened next?)" I was hoping to bring her back into the present, treading lightly so as not to spark some new upset that would derail her recounting of the complicated chronology of events. She began again with a deep breath as if preparing to embark upon some strenuous mountain climb, her eyes growing distant as she stared out at the fanned orange and yellow rays of the setting sun.

Hiding

When they arrived, Grodno seemed deserted. Janina saw a few expressionless faces, like those of the white corpses of family members who had died within a few years of each other. She saw faces with a kind of blankness she had not witnessed since World War I, when she was a child. She limped quickly along the deserted streets of the once bustling city. Mira could barely keep up as Janina rushed to find a safe haven.

"We have to get inside before the fighting starts!" Janina shouted at her.

She was counting on staying with her good friend, who was also Mira's godmother. When they arrived at her house, she pounded on the door, but no one answered.

"What do you want?" asked the next door neighbor woman, as she slowly opened her door. "Oh, it's you, Mrs. I'm so sorry. It's all so frightening, all this shooting, the artillery. Here is the key to Mrs. Holska's rooms. She left for the country," she added, her hands trembling.

"So, what's been happening here?" asked Janina.

"Who knows? I hear that our Reserve Army is organizing outside the city, but whether they'll get here in time . . . The police are ready. The Boy Scouts want to join the rest of the civilians preparing to fight."

An artillery shell fired near them down the street. Janina grabbed the key from the woman and pulled Mira inside the house. She pulled her into a small room that contained only a toilet and a sink. "Mira, please listen," she said. "You must stay here, do you understand? I will be back. Don't worry. I have to get medicine and try to find some food for us." Janina's voice was frantic, imploring in tone. She kissed Mira on the forehead. Mira tried to protest as Janina locked the door behind her. Artillery was detonating in the distance, and Mira was terrified to be left alone.

Janina ran outside in search of an apothecary only to find the Red Army marching in ominous columns up the street. They followed a procession of armored tanks, their expression cold and bayoneted rifles in hand, while the sky turned black from the hoard of Russian bombers poised for attack. In the distance, she heard gunshots reverberating within the gray, cavernous streets that amplified the noise and sent shivers of fear through her. She wanted to return to Mira, but she was determined to find treatment for the worsening infection in her leg. She expected that this would be her last chance for proper care as she hobbled into the center of the city in a feverish stupor, managing to avoid the troops.

In the commercial district of Grodno, Janina was surprised to find more people wandering the streets. Not believing that the impending march of the Red Army threatened their fragile freedom so recently gained, Poles passed stiffly by her, eyes cast downward, lips held tightly shut. With their country's leaders arrested or in exile, fewer than twenty short years of independence had come to an unbelievable halt. The most ordinary man in the street now knew that he would need to fight again to regain that fleeting freedom.

Janina crossed the wider central streets to a Red Cross post, where she waited for a long time for a nurse to clean and bandage her leg. The nurse sent her to the Jewish pharmacist Janina knew from childhood. She was not surprised to find his place of business open. Medicine would be needed for the approaching battle.

He greeted her in Russian. "Good day, Madame. May I help you?"

Janina stared at him and retorted, "I see you have already forgotten your Polish!"

She handed him the prescription. In a few minutes, he gave her the medicine. She paid him and thanked him pointedly in Polish. He nodded with a weak smile as she left the store.

With the sulfa medicine in hand, Janina walked back along gloomy, deserted streets. As she searched for an open food store, she thought of her childhood during World War I and the recurrence of this struggle seemed a terrible irony to her. With this new siege, a handful of boys, untrained civilians, and a few policemen were again ill-equipped to fend off an unabating aggressor. Though preoccupied with her leg and trying to avoid Soviet soldiers, Janina grew more concerned for Mira. She bought a sausage and some hot tea and hurried back, limping along the narrow streets. As she walked, artillery fire shook nearby buildings. She smelled decades-old dust as it drifted in thick waves through the air. With each detonation, the ground shook and acrid smoke permeated her senses. Janina stopped several times to rest, but fear for Mira overtook her. She stumbled along, her leg now burning with pain.

As she turned down the last street to the house, she hastened her steps. "It had been nearly five hours since I left and I could not stop thinking about Mira. My chest muscles tightened and burned as if a vise had gripped me," she recalled.

When she reached the door, Janina called out, "Mireczko, Mireczko!" She burst into the small room she'd locked Mira in to find her face covered in dried tears, a piercing, abandoned look in her eyes. It was the first time Janina had seen such terror in her child's face, and its memory haunted her for the rest of her life.

As soon as Mira saw her mother, she burst into another flood of tears and screams. For the next hour, Janina tried to comfort her. Finally, pale from exhaustion, Mira took the sausage and tea, and in between quieting sobs, she calmed down. It was their first meal in two days.

"Why are they shooting, Mama?" she whispered as she rocked in Janina's lap. Janina tried to sound reassuring as she held Mira, but there was a gnawing uncertainty in her mind. Soon, Mira fell asleep in her arms.

For several days, Janina and Mira hid in the cubbyhole, as artillery fire from the tanks continued intermittently. Soviet soldiers ravaged the city of Grodno; they were looking for any excuse to shoot civilians, so it was certain death to venture out. Across the street a Jewish woman lived alone with six small children. On the second day of fighting, the woman stepped out of her door, searching for a quick escape, no doubt so she could buy some milk. Instantly, she was shot through the head.

For safety and to muffle the sounds of the battle outside, Janina dragged an old mattress into the tiny bathroom. Barricading herself and Mira in those confining quarters, she developed an uneasy sense of security. After all, she had lived through similar hardships as a child of Mira's age during World War I. Her father's early lessons on the former greatness of Poland had instilled a patriotic fervor in Janina. Marshall Józef Piłsudski had been revered as a hero in her family, for under his leadership Poland had gained independence after World War I. As a young adult, she had married one of his dedicated soldiers, Mira's father.

"Where were my dead hero's followers then? Piłsudski would have saved us from that new siege," she would say years later.

Lost Lives Regained

It was the summer of 1967. Mira and I had arrived around noon at my parents' Wisconsin farmhouse after an early start out of Chicago to avoid traffic and the heat. Having gotten very little rest the night before, I immediately went to my room on the second floor and fell into a deep sleep.

"Mirka, Danusiu," I heard my mother call from outside. Her voice sounded distant in my heavy head, irritating, and nudging me out of my slumber. It was strained, as if she were trying to be pleasant and inviting, something to which I was not accustomed. The last thing I wanted to do was to start acquiescing to my mother's wishes, but hoping to avoid an argument, I dragged myself off my bed in the sweltering heat and ambled downstairs, where it was at least twenty degrees cooler.

After my parents' retirement and move to the farm, I lived in Chicago with my sister. After a year without my mother intervening into every little aspect of my teenage life, I had become accustomed to being my own person. It felt strange being in her presence once again. We had parted on rather poor terms the summer before, as I was entering my senior year in high school and wanted nothing more than to spend the summer with my friends in Chicago. Instead, my parents had insisted that I spend that summer with them, mostly with my mother, as my father was returning to work in Chicago. In retaliation, after my father left, I spent most of the time ignoring my mother, sleeping during the day and watching old movies late into the night on our ancient black and white TV with its poor reception and limited channels in the remote dairy farmland community.

I didn't realize it then, but it would be the last summer of what I had known as our family life together. My mother did not return to Chicago with me in the fall that year. My father soon followed her to the farm when his retirement from his factory job became official. After fifteen years in America, my mother was happy for perhaps the first time in her new life. I was happy to be left without her, to be in Chicago with Mira.

In a move that both my sister and I thought was insane, my parents had begun a dairy farm in their so-called retirement. At first they had six large black-and-white Holstein cows that had to be milked twice daily, a barn that had to be kept clean, and fields that had to be sown and harvested for hay. They added another four cows and a dozen chickens to this adventure and then two piglets that grew to be giant, fierce sows. "This is how it was on my farm in Poland," my mother told us happily. "If I could take care of things then, I can do it now!" she assured us.

"*Córy, córeczki* (Daughters, my little daughters)," my mother called again, trying to sound endearing. "You'll miss this beautiful sunset!"

She had abandoned wearing dresses in favor of three-quarter-length pants and sleeveless blouses. It seemed that country life suited her. Then in her late fifties, she had slimmed down and seemed unusually healthy and robust, unlike the frail person I had known her to be, always reminding me how old and sickly she was getting, how much the War had damaged her.

The move was the culmination of my parents' American dream—retirement on the farm they bought when I was seven, the place they scrimped and saved for, the dilapidated house my father had devoted years of his summer vacations to turning into something livable. The summer before, when I was extremely bored and couldn't force myself to sleep anymore, I worked on the house too—insulating, tiling, varnishing. I learned to become a good "handyman," as my father liked to say.

"Bring the lawn chairs, Danusiu," she ordered. I obeyed, too tired to argue. I went outside and set up the chairs. Then I plopped down and watched. Mira did the same.

"Just like the Niemen River near Grodno," my mother said in a melancholic tone. "Now, watch," she commanded us from her chair. "What beauty God has created!"

The War had not destroyed my mother's belief in God, and she saw all the natural beauty around her as the work of God. We sat watching this enormous orange ball in the sky hover on the horizon. "Look at the size of that sun. Just like at the farm in Poland. Do you remember, Mira?"

Mira nodded without saying anything. I looked over at her and wished that I could have known the farm in Poland too. I wondered if she could remember her five-year-old self back there before the camps, before the hunger, the disease, and the fear. We sat in silence looking out over the horizon of darkened trees in the thick woods, beyond the rolling fields. Barn swallows hovered low over the fields, catching their last meal of the day.

"Rain tomorrow," my father said as he joined us on a rare break from his work in the barn. He wore high black rubber boots that tracked fresh sweet-smelling cow manure and a white T-shirt that was damp from sweat. In my world, my father was a saint, a hero. He made me laugh, gave me advice I felt I could take, told interesting stories from his childhood about his dogs and his adventures without bringing up the War at every turn like my mother.

"How do you know that it will rain tomorrow?" I asked, grateful that he had arrived to rescue me from my mother's presence.

"The birds are flying low," he assured me.

When the last rays of yellow-orange light from the big orange ball on the horizon disappeared and mosquitoes started buzzing around our ears, we gathered our chairs and went inside.

My mother called us to watch sunsets almost daily during our short visit. She made us stop whatever we were doing and look out over the horizon, beyond the round grain storage silo and the field where dozens of brown-and-white milking cows just released from the neighbor's barn were grazing. I grew to anticipate those sunsets, sometimes running to a west-facing window in the house with the excitement of someone who was hoping to catch a glimpse of a passing celebrity. In Chicago, the tall buildings prevented me from seeing such sunsets.

Early on, my father had planted birch trees in the yard around the house to remind him and my mother of those they had left behind in Poland. The trees blended seamlessly into the fields and nearby woods behind the house and barn, where an unpaved road led to a secluded pond. Whenever we took a family walk on the road to hunt for mushrooms or in the hope of catching sight of a herd of deer grazing at sunset, my parents were quick to point out the small treasures of nature—leaves flickering like snowflakes or turning brilliant colors in the autumn, songbirds calling to their mates, or a rabbit or red squirrel scampering through rustling dried leaves and creaking branches. Wisconsin reminded them of Poland with its dense forests of pine, birch, poplar, maple, and oak trees.

My father was an educated man, a forestry engineer, and he longed for the woods he had known in Poland during his youth. Wisconsin was like Poland in climate as well—cool and crisp in the fall, biting cold and snowy in the winter, bearably hot in the spring and summer. Its topography of rolling meadows, neatly plowed fields, and large expanses of forests abundant with game satisfied some inner yearning for the land that he and my mother had been afraid to return to in the face of Communism.

The road to the woods in back of the plowed fields reminded my mother of the road near her farm on the way to Grodno. As we walked, she recalled the story she had heard about Napoleon's army marching on that road. I didn't think much about those reminiscences of hers back then, but her unusually calming story-teller's voice relaxed me, and I began to enjoy the natural beauty around me. Along the road, wild raspberries grew between bushes of wild forest nuts similar to hazelnuts. My mother loved hazelnuts.

"We had these by the farm in Poland," she said. Our nuts, however, were very small, not like the ones she bought to make her special nut cake, and most of them had small holes where some bug had made its nest. She still tried to eat them right there on the road, taking two together and squeezing, trying to crack open the hard, thick shells. The nuts seemed to be one of the few pleasant memories she had from the time before the War.

We then edged toward the back field, which abutted a forest where two dozen white-tailed deer could sometimes be found grazing in the twilight, flicking their tails like tiny beacons of light. My father squatted down and raised his binoculars. "Look, there's a mother with her fawn," he said as he handed the binoculars to me. Soon the deer noticed us, though we were several hundred feet away, and in one quick simultaneous jump, they disappeared into the dark woods. That ended our excursion for the evening, as we made our way back to the house on the shadowy gravel road.

My parents had bought the abandoned farm of eighty acres in 1957 because it was in the middle of Wisconsin, bordering on government-owned forests, far away from any large cities. I was taught that this was the safest place, where bombs would not likely be dropped, where food could be grown and stored for leaner times. They were always preparing for war. Within the year, they amassed a cellar full of food. My mother had prepared green beans, pickles, marinated chicken, beets, and relishes of various kinds in glass jars that were stacked on wooden shelves filling half the cellar, while the other half was stuffed with potatoes, onions, and beets stored in wooden bins. In another part, muslin bags with fermented milk hung drying. It took more than five gallons of milk to make a pound of the pure white farmer's cheese my mother then used to make sweet cheese blintzes. The cellar was cold and damp, and I liked to go down into it to retrieve a jar of something during the summer in order to cool off. I imagined it was like the one my mother had left in her hasty escape from her farm in eastern Poland at the onset of the war and like the one in the house of her parents' farm near Warsaw where she was born.

Birth into War

Born in 1912 in Russian-occupied Poland, Janina lived on her family's farm until the start of World War I. It was a quiet place atop a small hill overlooking the nearby village of Kaszewo some fifty miles south of Warsaw. She was one of three surviving children, fifteenth of sixteen born to her petite mother, Anna, and her father, Jan. At the time of her birth, her sister, Natalia, was ten years old and her brother, Walenty, was sixteen. These were the only ones to survive what was likely the incompatibility between their Rh-positive blood and her mother's Rh-negative blood.

Jan was tall and at forty-five still had a head full of thick, dark hair. He was a dreamer, a farmer-intellectual. He read extensively but also knew the names and songs of all the forest birds. He could recite from memory the long lyrical poem of Adam Mickiewicz's *Pan Tadeusz* (*Mr. Thaddeus*). Its patriotic sentiment appealed to his sympathetic good nature: "Lithuania, my country! Thou art like health; how much thou shouldst be prized only he can learn who has lost thee. Today thy beauty in all its splendor I see and describe, for I yearn for thee." Lithuania and Poland shared over five hundred years of history, and many people, including Mickiewicz, regarded themselves as being as much Lithuanian as Polish. Polish was spoken in Lithuania in the cities and universities, so he spoke Polish.

Jan was a devoted patriot of Poland, though Poland did not technically exist at that time. *Moskale* (Muscovites), he called the Russians with scorn. Under their occupation, open study of the Polish language and the teaching of Polish literature and history in schools were forbidden. The observation of Roman Catholic religious holidays was severely restricted. Subservient to Russia, Prussia, and Austria for over a century, the people who considered themselves strictly Poles stubbornly clung to hopes of a free country someday, a stubborn patriotism that would serve them well during World War I.

Rebellion permeated the consciousness of most discontented Poles, and Jan was no exception. The squelching of education and requisitioning of Polish land by the Russians during the years prior to World War I infuriated him. He was committed to teaching his children all that was forbidden under Russian rule. At every family gathering, he recounted the historical battles through which Poland earned its place as a European power and a defender of Christianity. He was well read, and Janina was his favorite student.

Through risky and clandestine lessons taught by clergy in obscure church cellars, many determined souls sought the forbidden education of their heritage. Older children attended special church meetings to learn Polish. As the children held open their prayer books, nuns and priests passed out lesson books that the children then concealed within the covers. The punishment for teaching and reading such books was hard labor in Siberia, but many people braved exile for their children's sake. The Russians called these patriots *buntovshchiki* (seditionists) and relished in uncovering them.

Without Anna or Jan's knowledge, Walenty began to build a secret library in their house. Using money donated from the richer landowners, he procured booklets printed with large letters in Polish for the semiliterate peasants. He called it the Free Public Library of Kaszewo. In between pages of booklets on crop rotation, dairy cattle care, and butter and cheese making, he inserted passages from the forbidden literature and history of Polish poets and writers. He organized group lessons at his school, but he eventually was discovered, thrown out, and threatened with imprisonment. To keep him out of trouble, Anna and Jan sent him far away, to a farming school in Austrian-occupied Poland to study the making of Swiss cheese and butter. Walenty was barely at this new school one week when he joined an underground youth group for riflemen. Encouraged by Józef Piłsudski's growing success in forming a legion of soldiers to free Poland, Walenty organized his fellow students under the code name *Gołąb* (Pigeon). The students began crossing the border and attacking units of Russian soldiers. Walenty was eventually arrested, however, and sent to prison in a nearby town.

In the meantime, on the brink of World War I, the uneasy stillness of the Kaszewo farm district was broken by activities of the underground movement, which Anna and Jan, like hundreds of other people, supported in whatever way they could. They hid important documents in their house, the contents of which neither of them knew. The documents would be dropped off late at night and a few days later someone would pick them up. The Russians were aware of such conspiracies and regularly sent groups of soldiers to inspect suspicious households. Known as *rewizje* (domestic raids), these could occur at any hour of the day or night.

One moonless summer night when the air was thick with moisture, Jan, Anna, and Natalia were awakened by a commotion outside.

"Lights! Lights!" shouted men.

Anna quickly pulled the cloth-wrapped documents from under her pillow and stuffed them into her ample bloomers. Jan fumbled to light a candle as shattered window glass flew into their room. Janina awoke screeching.

"Make diversions!" whispered Jan firmly to Anna. "Someone has betrayed us."

Anna began shrieking hysterically as a Cossack soldier barged into the house waving a bayonet in her face. Outside, several soldiers circled the house. Anna ran to Janina and scooped her up into her arms trying to quiet her. The Cossack eyed her suspiciously and began turning up the mattresses and bed linens. He turned over the table and chairs and pulled books from the well-stocked shelves. After about fifteen minutes of searching, he left the house.

Four months later, Anna received word that Walenty had been jailed. She gathered three hundred rubles, a small fortune that could have bought several good cows, and bribed the jailer. Walenty was released, on condition that he work on a farm in Russia. So he returned home only briefly, and after a tearful embrace with the family, he left for a Russian milk farm in Omsk as World War I was about to begin.

Polish School

Milwaukee Avenue is one of a few diagonal streets in Chicago, and just north of Division Street at its intersection with Ashland Avenue was the heart of the old *Polonia*. During the days of my childhood in the 1950s and 1960s, it was filled with Polish churches and schools, restaurants, banks, and shops of every kind. The iconic Polish newspaper building for *Dziennik Związkowy* stood prominently on one corner. As a Polish Girl Scout, I marched with my troop up Division Street west to Humboldt Park, cheered and waved on by the Polish community who came out by the hundreds to celebrate with us Poland's Constitution Day of May 3. I often attended Catholic Mass, given in Polish and Latin, and other events at the venerable baroque-style Holy Trinity Church on Noble Street just south of Division Street. By then the neighborhood was already changing, as wealthier Poles, who had immigrated a generation before us World War II political refugees, began moving out northwest along Milwaukee. They bought up two-flat buildings, lived in one apartment, renovated the other for renters, and then sold that and moved on to another building, reaping significant income.

My parents' "new" generation of immigrants descended on the area hungry for anything that reminded them of the home they would not return to while it was in the hands of the Communists. When I was six years old, my mother began taking me every Saturday morning on the long train ride from our Edgewater apartment on the far north side to this enclave of Poles. A high second-floor meeting/dance hall over a shop served as one of the first Polish schools, and thus began my years of learning the language and history of Poland from war-displaced Polish college professors and teachers. By then I had learned to read and write a little Polish at home with my father, so I was put into a class of first graders. For two or three hours every week I tried my best to keep up reading from the crudely produced lesson books and to understand the high-spoken Polish, all of which seemed far removed from the America in which I was growing up. My mother sat in the back of the hall reading or chatting with the other mothers.

"Piłsudski," said my mother on the way home one day. "You must learn about Piłsudski. He was my hero," she added and then fell into deep thought. She never elaborated more than that, but it was a name I grew to know well. To please my mother, I would listen intently during class as the history teacher, a slender man well into his sixties with a bad set of dentures, expounded through the distracting whistle of his fake teeth all the details of the greatness of the Polish empire of earlier centuries and compared it with Communist Poland. I was always confused by the juxtaposed chronology and soon stopped paying attention, but I humored him by looking intently at him, trying to be as polite as I could. I sensed these teachers' great love of Poland, individuals who were donating their time to the mission of educating the next generation of patriots.

Reading the official non-Communist-produced Polish history book in later years proved a great challenge for me. Mastering pronunciation of some of the absurd combinations of letters in Polish was also difficult. Slight differences in the sounds depend on a diacritic of a dot or a stroke above a letter or on subtle differences in the sound of combined letters like *cz*, *dz*, *sz*, or *rz*. My teachers told me that Polish was easy because every letter in a word is pronounced, no matter how illogically combined, with no silent letters as in English. But it seemed to me that tying my tongue into a knot and trying to speak would have been easier. Nonetheless, I became fluent in speaking, reading, and writing Polish, and this ability has served me well throughout life.

Slowly, I began to master the complicated history of Poland during Polish school and later during Polish Girl Scout meetings and summer camps. The main goal of all this effort on the part of our elders was not only to forge a bond between us and the Polish community at large but to teach us what could not be taught in Poland during those repressive Communist years. I began to learn my family's own history in the context of Poland's, and I became fascinated by it.

The First World War

Following President Woodrow Wilson's famous speech on January 8, 1918, proclaiming that Poland should be a free, independent nation, changes began to happen almost overnight. As the war neared its end by the fall of 1918, Polish partisans stopped the Germans from exporting food products, and food suddenly appeared on store shelves. Janina was ill with the measles and lay in bed recuperating. For the first time that she could remember, her mother's face was bright when she returned from a shopping expedition.

"Poland is free! The Germans abandoned the city of Radom during the night. Józef Piłsudski is here!" she proclaimed. Immediately, she opened up her large, long apron and a dozen freshly baked rolls tumbled onto the kitchen table. As their fragrance filled the room, Janina breathed in deeply to savor that happy moment. For a long time, she looked into her joyful mother's tired face, whose beauty still shone from beneath layers of wrinkles. "My beautiful mother," she would repeat years later, recalling this moment as one of the few happy times of her childhood. It seemed that she wanted to have happy stories to tell.

The following day, Janina was feeling better and left the apartment to fetch water from the city well. Swinging a blackened teapot, she skipped happily along sunny streets. As she filled the pot at the well, she looked up at marching feet and noticed a familiar tune. It was "My, Pierwsza Brygada," the Polish Legion's song, which began, "We, the First Brigade, Riflemen's group, onto a pile, we threw our life's lot . . . ," and it was being sung by the newly formed Polish Army. They were the battered liberating units of Piłsudski's Legions. Their feet were tied with rags, for their boots had worn out long ago. Their clothing hung dirty and ragged and their rifles were strapped to their backs with old knotted ropes. In spite of their shabby appearance, they marched with pride and confidence, singing joyfully.

Poland's existence had not been officially recognized for generations and the acceptance of it as an independent country at the end of World War I was not widespread. Various ethnic groups who had lived in the former lands of Poland remained fiercely nationalist, and frequent fighting dampened the paper peace that marked the end of war. With the rise of ethnic consciousness and the anti-Polish policies of Germany and Russia during their long occupation of Poland, much Polish culture and loyalty had been lost in the distant parts of the once large and strong Polish-Lithuanian Commonwealth.

Once the defender of the Christian world against such massive invaders as the Turks in the seventeenth century, the newly established and weakened country now stood hobbled by continuous border disputes. The Ukrainians, supported by the Germans and Austrians, took over the city of Lwów, among other cities. In response, almost every Pole stood in its defense. After many bloody battles, the city was taken back from the Ukrainians. Similarly, the Germans occupied the region of Górny Śląsk (Upper Silesia) and would not relinquish the lands that were naturally rich in minerals. After two bitter battles, the people there were given the right to choose whether to belong to Poland or to Germany. During one of the plebiscites ordered by the Treaty of Versailles, words from patriotic songs, such as "Jak Długo w Sercu Naszym (As long as in our hearts)" written in about 1920, rang in their ears:

> As long as in our hearts,
> flows but one drop of Polish blood,
> As long as in our hands,
> shines one fervent sword,
> United will stand our country,
> strong will stand King Piast's fortress.
> The White Eagle will triumph,
> the Polish people will prevail.

Many Polish-speaking inhabitants, who had been taught by Polish priests and nuns as their ancestors had been taught, voted to belong to Poland. Eventually, in 1921, the territory of Upper Silesia settled into peaceful existence as part of Poland.

On the Russian border, there were continual disputes. Janina's family, who profoundly distrusted the Russians, wondered if Russia would ever respect the Treaty of Versailles. In response, Poland escalated its rebuilding efforts, focusing in particular on assembling an army that would be stronger than ever, in the anticipation of further attacks. Though economic conditions were abysmal and there was discord among several political factions, the struggling Polish government began feeding the masses of undernourished citizens. Janina remembered how her mother bought soup made from beans or potatoes with a few meaty bones thrown in for taste. From her young perspective, this new Polish government, in whatever political form it existed, was her "savior."

However, the best shipments of aid came from America. Saliva gathered in her mouth as she recalled how she skipped along with her small bowl and spoon to one of the many temporary shelters. American white rice with its aromatic cinnamon and white sugar was dispensed to the many starving children. Years later, it was a dish she prepared frequently.

"*Oj, jakie to było życie!* (Oh, what a life it was!)," she would say of her childhood days.

Janina's mother often stared out of the window of their apartment hoping to see Walenty returning home. "Is he still alive?" she asked out loud. "I pray that he will come home to us." Janina was saddened to see her mother longing for her brother.

Mothers

I picked up a long blond strand of my hair off the page upon which I was writing notes and dropped it to the floor, watching it float downward as it caught a glimmer of light that made it sparkle, though only fleetingly—how strange it was to be in the moment of that otherwise inconsequential event as I sat listening to my mother telling me another war story. My mother spoke in halting sentences, gasping breaths, uncharacteristically searching for words. She had just finished the story of her mother, her beautiful mother, and how she had missed her brother, Walenty, growing up in the squalor of World War I.

"I didn't really know him then, you know," she said, much to my surprise. Lost in her story, I had not realized that he had been away at war the whole time of her early childhood. She knew him only from the stories her mother told her, which she repeated to me that first summer when I interviewed her.

I caught my mother staring at me. She smiled. I played with my hair often when deep in thought, running my fingers through it, twirling strands around my index finger, calming myself as I had done many times as a child.

"Bambino," my mother laughed, launching into a different story of one of my childhood antics and teasing me with the Italian word for "baby." I stopped playing with my hair, slightly embarrassed to have been caught in the act, hoping she would stop the silly story and resume the war story. It seemed that I provided much amusement for her when I was a child, as if I had been a reprieve from her otherwise sad thoughts. As a child such endearments annoyed me because they seemed contrived. I so wanted to be taken seriously. I had not heard that comical name in years, and it seemed strange for her to be calling me that then, as I too was a mother. However, it made me realize that we were sharing a special, though brief and uneasy moment together, one I had always longed for.

Who did I say I would become when I began my journey into motherhood? Not like my mother, I said, not ever like her! Strangely, not even a parent like my father, whom I cherished, longing to spend whatever time I could with him. Yet I was stubbornly defined by the rearing forces that carved in me both desirable and not so desirable characteristics. All my high-minded education did not prepare me for what I had to face as a mother. My children tugged at my heart like nothing else in this world. I feared for them, and I feared nothing else. I feared that my effectiveness diminished as they grew older and more independent. I feared that I would fail them. Were these the same fears my mother had for me? That her mother had for her children?

I suspect this was the journey I embarked on within the odyssey of my mother's war stories. In them I thought I could come to understand her finally, come to terms with her, and to know the family I had never known. I had hoped to secure that connection with the past that defined my life through my immersion in it daily as a child and that came to haunt me during my parenting breakdowns with my own children. Unlike me, though, my mother did not have the luxury to analyze such things during her daily struggle for the basic necessities for survival. She rarely displayed any ability to explain emotional, psychological things, if she even had that ability—her life had been shaped in a completely different way from mine. I didn't understand that, and once I did I still could not accept it, for my expectations of her were of a mother in modern-day America, not the refugee mother whose full attention was at times given to no more than the acquisition of a scrap of daily bread. I was fortunate not to have lived that life, but it set us apart.

I had not heard much of Walenty's story while I was growing up, but I was fascinated by it and imagined the anguish my grandmother must have endured not knowing what had become of him during the war. When my own first son enlisted in the Air Force in 2003, America had just attacked Iraq and even though I was able to communicate with him almost weekly, each new development reported in the evening news sent me rushing to the phone, calling him to see if he was being deployed to any war zone. Not having any way to communicate with her son for months, even years, my grandmother must have been very strong to survive those long days of uncertainty.

Walenty and Natalia

By the time Walenty returned home, the family had moved to the city of Radom, which was fifty miles or so from Warsaw. He captivated all with tales of his exploits, and Janina was fond of retelling those stories.

He was among those forced to "volunteer" into the Russian Army, as the Russians propagandized, but after the Russian Revolution broke out in 1917 he escaped and joined the small Polish Army of General Józef Dowbór-Muśnicki. He was wounded during one battle and lay convalescing in a field hospital when the Bolsheviks attacked. Given a free hand to deal with any foreigners thought to be opposed to their campaign in whatever way they wished, the Bolsheviks began shooting every Polish soldier in the hospital. A Latvian Bolshevik approached Walenty as he lay immobile. The soldier directed his revolver to Walenty's head and was about to pull the trigger when the two men's eyes met.

"Let me return to my old sick mother," Walenty pleaded.

The Latvian, a man only slightly older than Walenty, stopped for a moment, withdrew the revolver, and said, "I, too, have a mother."

In the severe Russian winter, the Bolsheviks forced Walenty and a small group of Polish soldiers still in their underwear to walk eighteen miles to a distant railway station. As they were herded into a waiting cattle boxcar, the Latvian commanded Walenty to stand in the open doorway while the train began to move. Before Walenty could turn around, he felt stiff pressure from a broad hand against his back and suddenly he was flying through the cold air toward the moving frozen ground. When he landed on the icy surface, his right foot slipped and most of his weight was forced onto his other ankle. He felt a sharp pain and when he tried to stand up, his body fell into a heap. The train had gathered speed by then and Walenty could no longer see it. He was in the middle of an open field far from any sign of life. Slowly, he pulled himself along the snow-covered ground, grasping at roots and branches at the forest's edge until he reached a farmer's barn a few hours later.

In the cloudy, moonless night, he could only see a few inches in front of him. When he got inside the barn, he patted the warm hay-covered dirt floor and touched what felt like a human hand. Startled, he pulled away and listened. Only the thumping of his own heart resonated in his ears. After a few minutes, he called out, "Who's there?" No one answered, so he called out again, "Who's there?" Still there was no answer. Walenty then reached out again and patted further up the arm, which was covered with a coarse wool material that seemed to have an odd familiarity. He shook the arm gently and realized that the hand was cold and the arm stiff. He then patted the body further until he reached a pocket, which he unbuttoned. Inside, he found a small box of matches.

He lit a match and slowly moved it above his head. In the dim light, he saw bodies strewn across a narrow corridor of cattle stalls. As he brought the lit match close to the faces of nearby corpses, he saw pools of blood where eyes had been. Streams of dried blood oozed out of open mouths. From one corpse's mouth a partially detached tongue protruded and dangled on a few blood-drained tissue fibers. Next to another corpse lay a round white red-stained eyeball.

He moved a newly lit match along the length of the nearest corpse and saw familiar images—a red and white armband on an old Russian uniform, an old nicked military cross on a chest, an officer's makeshift insignia on a lapel, all temporary symbols of an army formed in haste. He then realized that these were his fellow soldiers from General Dowbór-Muśnicki's legion.

Walenty fell back and passed out.

The next morning, he found himself inside a house resting in a comfortable bed near a large stone fireplace burning with thick logs. An old Russian farmer was standing beside him. The man's wife held a bowl of hot soup ready to give to Walenty.

"You slept for two days," said the Russian. His wife handed him the bowl of soup.

"The other soldiers?" asked Walenty as he took the bowl.

"Don't worry. We'll take care of the bodies," answered the Russian.

Walenty stayed hidden in the kind Russian's secluded house for three months recovering from his wounds and waiting for the harsh winter weather to pass. By spring, he was able to leave and rejoin the organizing Polish unit.

The first time Janina recalled meeting her much older brother was when he came home from the war. However, his stay with the family was short lived. No sooner had one battle ended, then another began. In the summer of 1920, the Russians attacked Warsaw during the Polish-Bolshevik War (also known as the Polish-Soviet War), and Walenty left immediately to defend the capital. Boys of seventeen and men well into their seventies stood in Warsaw's defense. They used weapon relics of the First World War and new French-made artillery to push back this most persistent intruder. It was a monumental effort. The army and supplies were scattered and not enough military strength could be amassed in time. The triumphant defense of Warsaw was carried out by Piłsudski, while enraged citizens formed a barrier of bodies, a kind of "human wall," as those who died were quickly replaced with new bodies. On August 15, 1920, the determining battle, named "Cud nad Wisłą" (literally, "miracle on the Vistula River") owing to its occurrence on the Feast of Our Lady the Victorious (Assumption) and for its immense human sacrifice, pushed Russia back for what was hoped to be forever. Only then could Walenty finally return home to his family and stay for good.

With Poland at peace as an independent country again for the first time in over a century, there was much to celebrate. By then Janina was a precocious nine-year-old surrounded by loving parents, a heroic older brother, and a beautiful sister. Natalia was a well-liked young woman of nineteen who was studying to become a teacher. She braided her thick chestnut-colored hair into a tight rope starting high on her head, allowing it to travel along the length of her trim back. Natalia sewed Janina several dresses from remnants of colorful material left over from their more prosperous days. She even permitted Janina to rummage in her red wooden box of cherished mementos. Through her easy kindness, she endeared herself to her younger sister and to everyone around her.

Natalia developed a cough and slight fever, but she was determined to keep up with her schoolwork and continued to attend school. This went on for almost two years, and Janina began to sense her mother's growing concerns for Natalia. One day Natalia could not get out of bed. That day, Janina returned home from school early to find a large group of people gathering in the open doorway to their apartment. She saw Natalia lying quietly on a bed in the large family room near a tall window. Bright sunlight was streaming onto her face through the white lace curtains. Her eyes were closed, and Janina thought she was asleep. Natalia looked so peaceful that Janina turned to a woman near her and said, "Look, she's smiling . . . ," but before she could finish her sentence, she realized that the gathering of people meant something more serious. She caught bits of the conversations around her— "too young . . . ," "cough . . . ," "tuberculosis . . ." Anna sat weeping at Natalia's side. Jan ran up to Janina, scooped her up in his strong arms, and took her to another room.

In the days that followed, Janina would come upon her mournful father as he rested his head on the high back of a rocking chair and recited verses of Juliusz Słowacki's long lyrical poem "Ojciec Zadżumionych (Father of the lepers)":

> O! Unknown to you is this pain I bear,
> Which consumes my heart today! . . .
> Old man! Where are your children? . . .
> What am I to reply? . . . all eight . . . dead . . .
> Fire burning within their chests . . .
> And nothing is left for me but God;
> And there is my cemetery, that is my way.

Although she was pained by the sight of her beloved father grieving and the saddened face of her mother, Janina did not cry over the loss of Natalia. "I couldn't cry," she marveled at herself years later.

Late in 1922, after Walenty was awarded a handsome parcel of land in eastern Poland for his participation in the determining battle for Warsaw, the family—Jan, Anna, Walenty, and Janina—moved from Radom to Grodno into a temporary shelter that had once been servants' quarters on the former estate of Count Bisping. The newly established Polish region was the focus of a wary Polish government interested in settling only patriotic Polish citizens among the many ethnic groups. To Janina, the clean countryside, nestled within quiet virgin forests of sturdy basswoods and silver poplars, was a welcome and dramatic change from the bustle and crowds of Radom, which was more than two hundred miles away from Grodno.

An astonishing variety of wildlife exploded before her as she explored the winding Niemen River. Woodland sparrows fluttered in groups of a hundred or more, while swallows glided over farmers' fields in the gentle breezes. Sea crows and gulls, far from their native Baltic Sea, glided in the hidden valleys along the river. It was here that Janina grew to love sunsets.

By the time Janina was ready for high school, Walenty was able to afford to send her to the largest school in Grodno. She was by then a tall, slender, maturing young woman who braided her blond hair on either side of her head and then turned the braids into two large rolls. To this she added a pair of colorful ribbons neatly tied in ostentatious bows. Such eccentricity provoked comments from her teachers who thought her vain.

In 1927, when Janina was just fifteen, Walenty became ill with typhus. Although tall and strong like their father had once been, he succumbed to the disease's gut wrenching, bloody grip. In the last moments of life, when he was too weak to move from bed, Janina picked up his heavy head and held it in her arms. Sitting quietly with him, she tried to give him some water. He opened his eyes, which had been shut for hours under weighty lids, and he looked lost and dismayed.

"Janio, I will still . . . ," he began, and then he was gone.

It was one of the few times she was able to shed tears, as she surmised that he meant he would always take care of her.

Operation Marriage

The moment my sister graduated from college when I was eight years old, my mother went into high gear as a social maven, a very unusual persona from my young perspective. Suddenly, there were frequent parties at our apartment, formal Polish balls that my parents attended with Mira, and talk of suitable husbands for Mira around the dinner table. I heard the word *kulturalny* (cultured), often in reference to these young men.

"After all, he is a cultured person," my mother offered whenever a new young man was to be introduced to Mira. As a child, I always puzzled over exactly what *kulturalny* meant; my mother said it in a snobbish tone that I thought very strange coming from a woman who claimed she was proud of her family's peasant roots, though they hadn't been peasants. To some of her educated, urban Polish friends she would say teasingly, much to their chagrin, "After all, the first king of Poland was a peasant! So, we all come from peasants."

The parties were enjoyable because all the young men, potential husbands for Mira, felt it polite to dance with me, though they usually towered over me and I did not know the right steps. My father danced his favorite Viennese waltz with me, spinning me around in the small space of our dining room, with the table jammed up against one wall, until I was dizzy. Dressed in a frilly party dress that my mother had purchased for a few pennies at the local church rummage sale, I was thrilled with all the attention.

And then there were the food preparations—the endless trays of canapés of every variation that my father liked to put together with me—sliced hard-boiled eggs alternating with small, smoked sardines, sliced marinated beets, white and yellow cheeses, tiny slices of pickles, ham, salami on thin hearty pumpernickel or rye breads, and cakes of every imaginable kind that my mother made—chocolate layered cake with ganache, walnut cake with creamy coffee filling, poppy seed cake, cheesecake, and honey cake. On these occasions, there were alcoholic beverages—different wines, vodka, and cognac—which seemed especially festive to me, as my father only drank in company and my mother would almost never touch the stuff.

Everyone seemed always to have a good time. The next morning at Sunday breakfast, my mother analyzed the party—or rather gossiped about it. "What did he mean by that? What did she? Did you like that dress? It was so revealing, don't you think? Was she flirting with him or the other one? How could she like him? How about you, Mira?"

Mira was silent or at best noncommittal, shrugging her shoulders or uttering "I don't know." This was frustrating to my mother, but she continued to host parties and attend events with Mira—the old country method of chaperoned social exposure. Very modest, very cultured.

My sister was, after all, good looking; she had curly shoulder-length chestnut hair, an easy smile, an elegant figure, and she was smart on top of that. She always engaged with her friends in amusing conversation and laughter in a reserved way with her dry sense of humor that made her seem mysterious. I was too young to follow anything they talked about and didn't spend much time in their company, but I was thrilled to be included in occasional picnic outings with my "big sister."

Over time, my mother grew anxious because Mira did not settle on anyone, and the dinnertime conversations, the ones I was allowed to witness, became more serious. There had been at least three marriage proposals, all of which my sister had turned down. By that time, she was approaching her thirties. My mother was forever trying to understand why she had not accepted any of the offers she'd received.

"She had her choice, you know," my mother would say, trying to assure herself that there was really nothing wrong with Mira. I would nod in agreement. I didn't know what else to say.

And then the parties and the balls stopped.

It seemed that my mother was torn: she wanted Mira to get married but she didn't want her to marry the wrong person.

Perhaps that is why my mother rarely talked about her first marriage to Mira's father.

What she did not say about marriage began to intrigue me. Once, when I was into my teens, my mother began directing her thoughts about marriage toward me. "You can get married, of course, but you must finish school first. You never know what can happen." And, at other times, she'd say half-jokingly to my great surprise, "Don't marry a Pole!" She usually said this following some harmless squabble with my father, who, as loving and caring as he was, had staunch opinions about a woman's place.

"A woman can marry at any age," my mother began repeating to her friends and to me as my sister grew older but remained unmarried. Most of Mira's friends by this time were married and raising children. I thought about my mother's concern over Mira's lack of interest in marriage, and it dawned on me that her own experiences with marriage—first with a drunken abuser and then with a loving but domineering man—were not good examples. My mother often talked during those endless dinnertime soliloquies about other women who had been divorced or abused or left destitute by their husbands. I didn't realize how much this bothered me.

And then, of course, there was the War. What episodes had Mira witnessed between men and women in the limited privacy of those times? Was she ever abused? What did she think about love and sex? She was always reticent, especially on those topics. I asked her why she didn't choose one of her suitors, but her answers to me were just as noncommittal as to my mother's interrogations, except for the one time when she said, "I didn't want someone telling me what to do."

With my sister turning into an "old maid," my father began to oversee things for her in his usual manly manner. He was the only one who could tell her what to do; she tolerated his advice because he was level headed and logical. He helped her find her first car, which he maintained for her, and was involved in every major financial decision she made. My sister was always being taken care of, either by him or by my mother, to the point that when my parents moved to Wisconsin when I was still in high school, my sister had difficulty coping with the responsibility of managing our two-flat building in Chicago and taking care of me.

My parents and I had a standoff about dating, because they would not allow it until my senior year in high school—but what could they do about it from almost three hundred miles away? My sister became my confidante, often interceding with them on my behalf to allow me to go out. Though I had taken over most of the household responsibilities in Chicago after my parents moved away, I noticed my sister becoming more and more withdrawn. In the meantime, I raced along in my self-centered teenage life, confident and happy to have escaped the cocoon my parents had enclosed me in for so long.

My sister never did marry, though my mother corresponded with a couple of her suitors for many years, always regretting that Mira had not chosen one of them—especially the one who never married either.

Cradling Death

Walenty's death left Janina alone to provide for her aging, ailing parents. Her mother's failing health had reduced her to an old frail woman at the age of fifty. Her father's health was declining, and he was unable to work Walenty's farm. Janina thought about her brother often, recalling his heroic deeds and how he had obtained the farm that for many years had provided so well for the family. Those deeds made him famous in Grodno, so when he died, the local newspaper published a lengthy, sympathetic article about his participation in the battle for Warsaw in 1920 and his earlier exploits in Russia.

"I read of your brother's sad death," began the director of the teacher's college in Grodno. "He was a great Polish patriot," she continued, as she examined the small stuffy bedroom with its four small cots crammed next to each other in Janina's boarding house.

"What are your plans for school, Janina?" she asked.

"My father told me that he cannot afford to pay for my room and board, so I will have to leave school," answered Janina, embarrassed to admit such poverty. Mrs. Szwejkowska, who had a flair for formality, straightened up her square shoulders and said, "Well then, Miss Janina, I have good news for you! You have been granted a scholarship to attend the teacher's school with room and board to share. What do you say to that?"

Janina was stunned and hesitant. She thought she had not heard correctly, prompting the director to repeat herself. The lack of food during those last months in high school had made her so weak, and ever since it seemed that she heard things from a distance rather than as directed to her. The lingering grief of her brother's death had rekindled memories of her sister. "Words seemed to pass through my consciousness without stopping to make sense. I felt, at times, dead to the world," she would say in describing herself during those times.

Through the circumstance of her beloved brother's death, Janina's childhood dream to become somebody, an educated person, would be realized. Soon, the depression that seemed to have gripped her lifted, and she returned happily to her studies in the new seminary school.

In the two summers following Walenty's death, Janina spent her vacations with her parents on the farm. Those were lazy, pleasant days for her. Though they had little money, earning only what came from the rental of their land for rye crops, she happily cooked their meals, cleaned the house, and mended their clothes. Her parents' health continued to decline, but they managed to make the best of Janina's stay with them, hiding their growing dependence on her.

When Janina returned to school for the last year of her study, she left her parents old and weak but in good spirits. When she returned for the Christmas holidays, she entered the darkened room that served as both their kitchen and living area to find her father resting on a cot near the fireplace. She noticed that he had bleeding sores on his legs, which suggested he had been bedridden for weeks. He was surprised to see her, for she had arrived a day earlier than planned. Her mother rested in a nearby rocking chair. At that moment, Janina knew she could not leave them, and that winter she did not return to school to finish her coveted teaching degree.

Rudolf Zimmerman was twice Janina's age. He was still young looking in spite of his years of battle with the underground movement during World War I with the revered Józef Piłsudski. For his efforts during the war, the Polish government rewarded him handsomely, and Janina was impressed with his patriotic spirit. He was well-off and could offer her a house in town with servants. He seemed mature enough to take on the responsibility of a wife with two ill, elderly parents. He claimed his surname from his Austrian father, but it was through the influence of his Polish mother that he developed his unbending Polish patriotism. He was fluent in both Polish and German, but he chose to speak Polish, using German only when it was to his advantage during the years of World War I.

In 1928, just sixteen years old, Janina married Rudolf, perhaps more from dire necessity than out of great love. Nevertheless, she vowed to make him a good wife and within a year bore him a son. The baby boy brought her great joy and even enlivened her parents. However, the joy was short lived. To celebrate his birth, the proud father had taken his one-month-old son to the local hot and stuffy tavern, after which the baby promptly developed a fever.

"One moment your baby is alive and then, just like that," she snapped her fingers, "he's gone," she lamented years later.

Perhaps, that was when Janina first became distant from her husband. Shortly after the baby's death, Janina's father died. The cause of death was never determined. As she held her beloved father in her arms and stroked his still dark hair, she found herself unable to cry.

In late 1934, Janina gave birth to Mira. Afterward, she struggled with anemia that left her weaker than her ailing mother. She would rise early in the morning to explain the day's chores to the peasant servant girl and then return to bed. Twelve, even fourteen hours of sleep did not restore her, and she felt as if life was being drained from her. Her mother's health continued to decline, and when Mira was four months old, Anna was hospitalized for extreme abdominal pain. After a two-week stay, she was pronounced healthy and given years to live.

"I will help you raise Mira," she declared.

Four days later, she died peacefully in Janina's arms.

Janina was determined that Mira would be the one to survive and that together they would thrive. During the long hours between the time her husband left for work each day and when he returned late at night, usually from some local tavern, Janina was completely alone. She was too weak to busy herself with the chores of running a household, and the monotony of mere existence consumed her. Only in those few hours when she nursed, changed, and played with Mira did she find relief.

"I continued to have relations with him, you know," she would say of Rudolf guiltily. "I don't know why." She looked embarrassed at this admission. "Even after all that—after all his drunken anger, his rage, and his maltreatment of me."

In another year, another girl, Maria, was born. The baby brought Janina special joy as a symbol of life beyond the death that seemed to surround her. While Mira resembled her father with her long thin nose, tight lips, wide face and small eyes, this baby resembled Janina with her straight nose on a small face that seemed as perfectly proportioned as a painter's model. In time, Janina's strength returned, and her growing family renewed her.

On a warm summer night, five months after Maria's birth, Janina put the baby to sleep in the breezy bedroom of her house after having given her a bath. By morning, the baby had developed a cough and a high fever. In a few days, the joy that had rejuvenated Janina dissipated as she held the limp body of her baby girl, who had died from pneumonia during the night. "The death of a child is not like any other death," Janina would say. It is not like the long lingering pain of an old person struggling to hang on to life, as circulation slows and each molecule of flesh slowly succumbs, first with purple fingers and toes turning black, as the act of swallowing ceases, as speech stops and the eyes become glazed and transfixed. Janina's baby had not yet become embodied in the permanent rhythm of nature, the delicate balance of existence, where only the strongest survive. Janina looked down upon her dead baby in her arms, asleep in Heaven, as she believed.

By 1936, Janina fully regained her strength and decided to leave Rudolf. The marriage was made in desperate haste, inspired by foolish patriotism and tainted with death. The difference in their ages was too great, and Rudolf was growing increasingly reliant on alcohol. Janina resolved to survive on her own rather than embrace a tenuous state of comfort that was repeatedly shaken by her husband's drunken aggression or drunken attempts at love-making. With Mira in hand, she left Grodno, her comfortable house complete with servants, and went back to the farm, back to the family's estate, which she had inherited. There she would run a fruit farm and sell her produce in Grodno, she reasoned, and be independent and raise her child in peace. So she returned to the raw, simple farm life that was ingrained in her as a child, and there, she resolved to be finally happy.

The Farm

In the summer of 1968 I was in Chicago enjoying my time off from college, working a boring office job during the week and trying to break into modeling on the weekends. One Friday night, I stayed up past midnight preparing for an important modeling job interview the following week and was sound asleep when the phone rang at six o'clock the next morning. I heard my sister answer the phone from her room down the hall. It was my mother. A few minutes later, my sister called me to the phone.

"You and Mira have to come up here today!" shouted my mother into the phone in that all-too-familiar hysterical voice of hers that I dreaded.

"What?" I said sleepily.

"Father cut the hay yesterday and it's supposed to rain this evening! We need to get it baled and stored in the barn before it gets wet. Otherwise, it will be worthless and we can't afford to buy hay for the cows this winter. You have to come. You have to come now!"

The Vietnam War was in full swing, and many of the local young men who they might have hired had been sent away to fight, and those who had not were working their own farms.

"But . . . ," I protested.

She wouldn't let up, repeating everything all over again. Then, my father got on the phone. In a quiet, grave voice, using the diminutive endearing form of my name, he said, "Danulu, we need your help, and Mira's. Can you come?"

I could never refuse my father anything, no matter what he asked. I looked at my sister, who shrugged her shoulders. While my father continued talking, my sister interjected with a deep sigh. "I guess we'll have to go up there," she said.

"OK, OK, we're coming. Don't worry," I assured him. When I hung up the phone, my sister and I went into combat mode, flying through our new apartment gathering clothes, food, and reading materials. We filled thermos bottles with coffee and jumped into her used, large white Dodge Polara. Within an hour, we were on our way.

By noon, we had arrived. My head felt heavy from lack of sleep, though I did manage to nap between driving shifts. I was grateful there was air-conditioning in the car and that the road had been fairly empty of traffic, so we drove over the speed limit most of the way, stopping only briefly for a bathroom break and to refuel. No sooner had we emerged from the car stiff-legged than my mother ran out of the back door of the house saying hurriedly, "I have lunch for you. Father is already baling in the field."

And sure enough, I saw my father in the distance in the east field with his old, orange-colored Allis Chalmers tractor. The baler was behind it, spitting out fifty- to eighty-pound rectangular shaped bales of light green hay into neat rows about ten to twelve feet apart. He was wearing a white T-shirt and a striped engineer's cap, and I could tell from the way his body was turned that he was carefully monitoring the operation of the baler, which had a tendency to break down, as the jute string that held the bales together often got tangled up. All his farm equipment had been bought used.

I inhaled the pine-scented country air and took in the odor of freshly cut grass. It was a pleasant change from the stale air of the air-conditioned car and the stuffy, humid summer air of grimy Chicago. This time, my mother did not greet us, as she usually did, by saying "the first day you are a guest, the next you can help us out." We moved inside and had an anxious, hurried lunch of ham and cheese sandwiches and creamy cucumber salad with dill, fresh from their garden, which was all ready, so that my sister and I could get out into the field as soon as possible.

After gulping down lunch, I quickly changed clothes, tied back my long hair, pulled on heavy work gloves, grabbed a pair of bale hooks, and ran out to my father. By then, he had switched to pulling an open wagon behind the tractor. My sister and I were assigned to lifting the bales of hay, throwing them up onto the wagon, and arranging them neatly. As we worked, my father's humor returned and he even made jokes and sang to us off-key, trying to keep up our spirits in the hot, bright sun. The family dog, Tref, a golden retriever mix, ran alongside the wagon barking at the startled field mice and birds. We made run after run down the rows of baled hay. I kept a watchful eye on the sky for any sign of rain clouds, but the clouds above me were puffy white things against a sparkly blue sky.

"So, where's the rain?" I asked.

My father had stopped the tractor to rest. He wiped his forehead and squinted out toward the west. "Not today, maybe tomorrow," he said pointing as I followed his arm. "See the horsetail clouds gathering?" Far above the distant horizon where the sun was beginning to set, the clouds formed long, wispy strands across the sky, like those of a horse's tail. My father had learned to read the sky like the expert farmer he had become. We then unloaded the bales onto the barn's two-story conveyor and arranged them in the loft. In the meantime, my mother milked the cows.

The barn was only two years old, built in haste after my parents already had several cows that had to be milked in the open field, all by hand. The whole farming adventure had started backward, but now it seemed that things were running smoothly, until this sudden plea for help. We repeated the hay loading and unloading several more times by the light of the bright electric yard lantern mounted high on its own post, until the whole twenty-acre field had been cleared and the hay was safely stored in the barn. By then it was midnight, and it felt like my arms were going to fall off. I stumbled into the house, dragged myself up the stairs, and collapsed into bed without getting undressed.

The next morning my mother woke us up early again after milking the cows. The frantic effort to outpace the weather put the thought of attending church out of our minds, and I had become less inclined to attend church anyway. There was another field that needed to be hayed, but then the weather shifted northward, dissipating the immediate threat of rain. I used the time to relax and wash up, and over lunch my parents told us about one pregnant milk cow, Białka, so named because she was mostly white with only a few black spots, unlike the other cows with large blotches of black. She was about to give birth and they would need to watch her carefully to help out during the process because it looked like the calf would be large.

"Really?" I asked. "Can I be there?" I was excited about observing a live birth, something I had never experienced. Being a prospective biology teacher, I felt it was a necessary part of my education, and I admonished my parents that I would never forgive them if they didn't summon me in time. After another day of haying, I went to bed early, reminding them to let me know if the cow was going to give birth overnight. My sister decided we could stay an extra couple of days and that she would take some vacation time. I would call my supervisor at work to let her know I could not come into the office for the next few days.

The next morning around six, my mother called up to me. "If you want to see the birth, come now," she said. She sounded so matter-of-fact that I almost fell back asleep; I was still so tired from all the haying work. My arms ached, my legs felt like lead weights, my head was swirling, but then I realized what I might be missing. I dressed quickly and ran to the barn to find my father sitting on the clean cement floor, both arms around a rope that was tied to the front hooves of the calf with its head already out of the pregnant cow, who was lying on her side in her stall. The contractions came in huge waves down her side. I stopped in my tracks. My father looked up at me and yelled, "Hurry, put some straw in the trough."

As I grabbed a pile of clean straw, he maneuvered himself behind the cow, putting his feet with his black rubber boots up against the sides of her butt on either side of the vaginal opening, still holding onto the rope as the calf's body began to emerge. My eyes must have bulged, and I was rendered immobile. He yelled, "Quick, grab the calf's head. It's going to drop into the trough!" I didn't waste any time. I squatted down by his side and slid my arms under the large head of the calf. It was wet and slimy, but warm to the touch, and I tried to control my anxiety as my father pulled on the legs with each contraction. Within minutes the calf was out and ready to stand. I jumped back while my father untied the legs and maneuvered the newborn toward the mother, who immediately began licking her baby. For the remainder of my stay at my parents' farm, I amused myself by feeding the young calf a special formula from a bottle. It was not allowed to nurse directly from his mother so that there would be plenty of milk for sale, a standard milking practice.

Years later, I found myself telling this story over and over, each time feeling amazed that my parents undertook such an adventure at their ages. For my mother, the whole thing was a natural extension of her farm life in Poland. For my father too, a man of the woods, it was as if he had merely returned to a time before the War, when life had been normal. Over the years, I began to understand how important it had been for them to get back to the life they had known, to heal, to rest from the world that had so ruthlessly derailed them. I realized that they considered the farm their real home in America, their home away from their real home in Poland. It seemed that Chicago was merely another stopping place in preparation for life on the farm.

Uncertainty

Janina had no knowledge of the state of political affairs during those first few days of the war as she and Mira hid in the tiny bathroom of her friend's house. She spoke to no one. The fighting continued in the streets, sometimes just outside their window. Mira's constant questions—"Why are they fighting? Who is fighting? Will we go to jail? How long are we going to stay here?"—were beginning to unnerve Janina. She tried to comfort Mira, who complained of hunger and boredom in the confining room. Unable to appease Mira, Janina devised various schemes for their escape. To pass the time between short looks out the window to the street, Janina sang folk songs and patriotic hymns and told stories to Mira about her parents in the happier days of her early youth. She thought of her encounter with a German official from a delegation sent to Grodno earlier in the year.

"You have a German surname, Zimmerman," said the German to her when she was on one of her business trips in the city.

"Yes, what of it?" she replied defiantly.

"We are providing safe passage to Germany for all people of German descent living on foreign soil," he answered, with his head held high and his pale blue eyes sparkling beneath his thick blond hair.

"But I am not German!" she protested.

"Madame, I strongly advise you to take this opportunity . . . ," he began again.

"My dear sir, you are speaking to a patriot of Poland. This is where I will stay. Good-day," she answered.

The people of Grodno defended themselves valiantly against the Soviets, inspired as they were by the intoxicating taste of independence and a newfound freedom. Defiance was the order of the day. They refused to witness yet another political and geographical dismemberment of their country without a struggle. In the end, neither determined spirit nor feverish patriotism nor stubborn defiance could overcome the better-equipped Soviets. The Polish Reserve Army could not reach Grodno in time to save it, and the Soviets swiftly subdued the makeshift army during its fearless defense, after just three days of bitter fighting. The last of the artillery fire ceased after five days, and the Soviets took control of Grodno.

The following week, local Belarusian peasants and soldiers were encouraged to avenge the lives of Russians killed during the battle. Soviet propagandists claimed that hundreds of Russians died in the struggle, igniting a new fever of reprisal. Instigated by the Soviets, who purported to be liberators of the Belarusian people, bands of these peasants and ruthless soldiers roamed the country-side ravaging Polish villages and farms at will. Still afraid to return to her farm, Janina left with Mira to stay with another friend in the small village of Słobódka not far from Grodno. In the relative safety of a secluded country cottage, she and Mira and a group of women and children huddled in the damp cellar.

Fragmented stories from neighbors reached them suggesting a reign of terror was being unleashed. The uncontrolled shooting stopped after a few days, and an eerie quiet gripped the country-side. Janina continued to apply sulfanilamide daily to the open wound in her leg and slowly it began to heal. When she thought it was safe to venture outside, she tried to find milk for Mira. After a few quiet days, she mustered enough strength to dig for potatoes in the nearby fields.

Many groups among the different ethnic inhabitants of the lands around Grodno believed the Communist propaganda against the Poles. Upon the collapse of the city, these misinformed Soviet sympathizers greeted their new rulers with flowers and Soviet flags, expecting to be freed by them. In the next year or so, many of these people were deported to the same forced labor camps of Siberia as their Polish neighbors.

Janina and Mira hid in the cellar with an uneasy sense of security. During the following three weeks, a nagging uncertainty dominated Janina's thoughts as she anticipated the worst—that of losing Mira. She thought of the food hidden in her house, the clothes box buried in the soft soil behind the chicken coop, the farm animals she had bought with the profits of her prosperous raspberry harvest that summer. As she peeled potatoes for supper one day, tantalizing images of the newly picked apples overflowing their baskets teased her. With regret, she glanced at Mira, who was biting into a raw potato.

The tension in the cellar refuge among the women reached new heights with each tale of plundering from nearby villages and farms and each execution, sniper attack, or distant gunshot. The dozen or so women and small children hovered over a small fire in the only stove, stifled by the uncertainty of their own fate. Then one day that uncertainty came to end when they heard the commotion of men's voices outside their cellar.

"Open up! Open up!" Three Soviet soldiers yelled in Russian through the door in the cool late autumn. The women looked up the narrow stairs of the cellar as the soldiers opened the doors. They squinted at the bright light behind large masculine bodies clad in crisp new uniforms. The soldiers had followed a few of the women digging for potatoes from a nearby field to their hiding place. They now ordered the women and children to line up against the wall outside the cottage. In long penetrating glances, the soldiers began inspecting them from head to foot. Janina, barely breathing, cuddled Mira at her side and waited for the soldiers' next move. As one of them progressed down the line of frightened women and children, she could feel blood swirling in her head, and her hands and feet began to feel numb.

"Are you the wife of an officer?" snapped the soldier at her, as he pushed the tip of his revolver into her chest. Through the thin slits of his dark Mongolian eyes, he peered at her. Janina froze in her place; the unfamiliarity of such a face terrified her. She felt the hard unyielding pressure of his weapon to the left of her sternum directly over her heart. She stood paralyzed as he pushed the revolver harder into her.

Janina hardly heard his question. It seemed as if she were standing outside herself observing the scene. Mira pressed her face into the front of Janina's fine woolen skirt. The women gasped, and then a disquieting hush descended over them as they anticipated a shot.

"No, no, she's a worker, just like us," suddenly came an answer in fluent Russian from one of the peasant women.

"Then why is she dressed so well?" he pursued.

"*Vykhodnoi*, a free day, a free day from work," she said in a trembling voice.

Janina stood staring into the soldier's face, unable to defend herself. The soldier stared back at her and after a moment looked down at Mira. She was barely visible from within the folds of Janina's skirt. Terrified, she buried her face, tightened her shoulders and clenched her hands around the fabric, as if she were trying to disappear into its billowy folds. The soldier was quiet and in a few moments removed the revolver from Janina's chest.

"Ah, just a bunch of silly women," he muttered and left with the other two soldiers.

Janina hardly knew she was breathing. Quietly, she bent over to Mira and tried to release her clutching hands from her legs. The peasant woman who so boldly answered the soldier approached them and hugged them both.

"You know, Mrs., I had to say something. You had one red cheek, one white, and your lips were purple."

Following that incident, Janina decided to return to her farm, but not with Mira, whom she left in Grodno with a friend. As she walked the once peaceful country roads, airplanes thundered overhead and into the distance. Armored tanks roared across previously tranquil hills, scattering already nervous wildlife into directionless scamper. Her pace quickened and then slowed as if she were unsure how to proceed. She stared at the distant planes. With each bend in the road, she anticipated a troop of soldiers or plunderers. As she neared her house, her heart began beating so rapidly that it felt as if her chest would explode.

When she turned down the last bend in the road, she was suddenly aware of an unusual silence after so many weeks away from the quiet of the countryside. This silence was different from the peaceful, unobtrusive rummaging of field mice and birds, grazing cows, and pecking chickens. For a moment, Janina felt disoriented. There were no animal sounds, no clucking of content chickens picking out oat kernels from among small pebbles in the yard, no high-pitched bark of tiny Figa or the deeper howling of big Moja. Even the snorting of the pig and the cud chewing of the cow seemed to be missing. No one greeted her on the long tree-lined path leading to the house.

As she approached the door, the gleam of something unusual caught her eye. At that moment, a local farmer who had been made keeper of the lands by the new military power was passing by. He stopped his horse-drawn cart and called out, "Do you need a key?" He climbed down from his cart and pointed at the padlock.

"Oh, what went on here!" he exclaimed, shaking his head downward. As he removed the lock, he rambled on and on about the recent plundering.

"They didn't leave anything, but look for yourself. The lock was too late." He handed the key to Janina and hobbled back to his cart. He picked up the weathered reins in his old hands and with a flick of his well-trained wrists guided his old horse smoothly toward the road.

Janina pushed open the door and peered inside. She saw only an empty room where once there had been shelves filled with goods and several pieces of furniture. The plunderers left behind the dining table and one bed without its linens. The one remaining cooking utensil was an old dented pot that had been used to feed Figa, and only the ashes from old coals were left in the stove. Janina felt herself drifting between sadness, anger, indignation, and despair over lost gains from years of hard work and sacrifice.

"Well, Mrs. Janina, get yourself to work!" she ordered herself. She began looking for the few sacks of dried beans and other food-stuffs she had hidden in various nooks throughout the house. One sack of beans remained, but the apples, potatoes, and other fruit were gone. Outside, Janina found the two-dozen chickens wandering aimlessly in the yard behind the house. The pig was lying in the shade of a large tree and the cow was grazing contentedly in a small pasture beside the house. Only the dogs seemed to be missing. In the unusually dry summer and autumn, the well had gone dry, so she detached the two heavy wooden buckets and headed for her neighbor's deeper well.

As the beans cooked in the dog's pot, Janina looked for the rest of her belongings. Her strange moment of premonition in the earlier harried scurry for escape now proved to be life saving. She uncovered the wooden box full of clothes under the waterproof cloth. The foxtail, sheepskin jacket, coat, shoes, underwear, and Mira's coat and velvet blue dress had not been disturbed.

Life in the area settled down, as the Soviets occupied themselves with other military matters. Much of the dry food that Janina had managed to salvage quickly disappeared by delivering most of it to Mira on her weekly trips into Grodno. She did not slaughter the chickens and cow because she wanted the eggs and milk they produced. In the spring, she planned to slaughter the pig, but in the meantime, even the few table scraps for the voracious eater were scarce.

Christmas approached and Janina went to Grodno to fetch Mira. During the next few weeks, Janina and Mira subsisted on the dried beans and the few potatoes and winter vegetables they could buy from neighbors. She burned the picket fence from around the farm for heating and cooking, but as food supplies dwindled, she became more concerned about their future.

Mira walked around the cold, snow-covered grounds complaining of hunger. No plans could be made, no future determined. Christmas Day in 1939 came and went without much ceremony. Janina prayed and waited and hoped that the war would somehow bypass them in their small corner of the world.

One day Mira shouted, "Mama, Mama! Look! Figa is back." Janina kissed and hugged Figa, and then Mira ran out to frolic in the newly fallen snow with her favorite playmate.

News of the war was scattered and unreliable, as the Communists controlled radio broadcasts and the limited printed material that was made available was full of obvious Communist propaganda. Neighbors surmised, philosophized, and considered the possibilities in endless speculation about the war and their personal futures, this to reassure themselves that Poland would prevail. Janina could not believe that Poland would not be free. Many people in her region believed the same, but in their fear they fled the territory before the Soviets closed the borders to Hungary, Lithuania, and Romania. Others, afraid of being exiled to Siberia, fled to Warsaw. Alone with a small child, Janina did not want to risk such an unpredictable journey. And so she waited for their uncertainty to end.

"*Tak to było, tak to było* (That's how it was, that's how it was)," she would say of those times.

Train Travel

My most vivid memories of childhood, especially the pleasant ones with my mother, are of my days at the Wisconsin farm. In the early years, we would travel up on the train, for we only got a car when Mira finished college and began working, earning what was then good money for a woman chemist. I remember the trek with my parents to Union Station in downtown Chicago, loaded down with suitcase upon suitcase of clothing and household articles. It was the only time we ever took a taxicab. This was an expensive luxury, and my parents never used cabs on any other occasion. The luggage typically did not all fit into the trunk of the cab, huge as it was, and I would need to sit on my father's lap with things piled on the seats next to us and in the front with the driver.

We arrived at the station that was crowded with people heading to various destinations across America, for then train travel was common. A porter helped us load the luggage onto his cart, and my father dropped us off at one of the curved wooden benches that lined the huge waiting area, where the ornately tiled and painted ceiling soared at least thirty feet above. Then he took care of checking our oversized luggage into the freight car and picked up our passenger tickets. The first time we took the train, when I was seven years old, this process seemed to take an extraordinary amount of time, and I sat nervously on the bench with my mother. I worried that my father had gotten lost in the enormous station among the bustle of hundreds of people and red-capped porters hurriedly pushing large luggage carts in every direction. Had I known that my mother was an experienced train traveler, I may have been more at ease as she sat atypically calm, oblivious to all the clamor. She was going to where she wanted to be the most.

After my father finally showed up, we headed for the passenger car. "Wait here," he said once we were situated. "I'm going to check on the luggage," and then he disappeared again.

The conductor came through to check our tickets and announce immediate departure. *"Gdzie Tatuś?* (Where's Daddy?)," I asked my mother. She was comfortably settled into her seat and seemed completely devoid of any concerns. "Sit still. He'll be here shortly," she answered impatiently, and then she closed her eyes. I waited as patiently as I could, squirming in my seat, standing up and sitting down, looking out the window and toward the back of the train where I had last seen him.

The conductor came through again, saying, "Last call. We'll be on our way." People without tickets, saying good-bye to their friends, departed from the train. I was almost in tears, but just then, my father appeared as the train began slowly moving forward. He was panting and sweating but in good spirits. As soon as the train had rolled out of the station, he began digging into our bag of food, pulling out pieces of the chicken my mother had baked that morning, the peeled fresh cucumbers sliced the long way, hard-boiled eggs, tomatoes, and, of course, hearty rye bread, a virtual picnic for the six-hour train ride to the station nearest our farm.

At the small station in Babcock, Wisconsin, we were picked up by our retired neighbors in their dilapidated, forest-green 1940s Hudson with its deep seats and giant trunk for the fifteen-mile trip to the farm.

A precocious city child, I found life on the farm for the two weeks of my father's vacation completely boring. I was afraid to venture far from the house into the tall grasses of the encroaching prairie or to the nearby woods. Even a short trip through the tall grass to the hand-pumped shallow well was unnerving owing to the hundreds of large grasshoppers that jumped in my way, and I never went there alone in the beginning. There was no running water in the house, so this excursion was required several times a day.

The trip to the outdoor latrine or "outhouse," the size of a small closet, was even more terrifying, as I was afraid to sit on the old gray, splintered wooden seat. Dozens of flies buzzed around my head, and large spiders crawled above me in their webs. Who knew what other kind of insects lurked around the hole where I was supposed to sit with my bare butt. I was always afraid one of them might crawl up and bite me. My mother escorted me to the outhouse and waited outside as I fumbled with the weathered wooden door, which did not close completely in the frame, and the wooden latch that was difficult to clamp shut. "Honestly," my mother said impatiently, "who's going to see you out here?"

I often became constipated during our stay at the farm, and my mother had to feed me bowls of stewed prunes to get my system in order again. Then she made a makeshift potty in the house so that I wouldn't need to use the outhouse. It would be years before I could bring myself to venture in there alone, and only during the day, usually loaded with multiple rolls of toilet paper that I layered heavily on the seat. Before I sat down, I shoveled white lime powder in abundance over the previous deposit in the hole. The lime killed the odor and deterred the flies.

With limited luggage space, I could pack only a few toys, mostly coloring books, my favorite doll, and a few of my plastic farm animals, so I got tired of playing with those after a day. There were no real farm animals then, not even a cat to play with. The retired next-door neighbors were old, but at least they had several spooky outdoor cats, some chickens, and a dog, a stupid dalmatian that I pretended was a horse for my doll, to which the dog acquiesced. So, I used to wander over to them, a half block or so away, on occasion to help collect fresh eggs and to lunch with them in their overstuffed little house.

On the other side of us was a poor, real working farm, owned by a family with a half-dozen children, the oldest only a few months younger than I. The walk was at least two or three city blocks, and I went there only in the evenings with my mother to buy fresh milk. The three oldest children had to work the farm during the day, so only on rare occasions were they permitted to walk over to pick me up in the afternoon for a fishing expedition to the nearby river. Whatever they caught, mostly huge, slimy, ugly catfish, was dinner for them that night, much to their delight and to my amazement.

Their farm was a fascinating place for me, the city slicker girl, as they referred to me. There were at least thirty head of cattle, small brown-and-white Guernsey, stabled in a huge barn that filled my head with the sharp odor of ammonia from cow urine and the stench of rotting manure that I always seemed to find with my brand new tennis shoes. My apparent clumsiness made the children laugh. They didn't quite know what to do with me. Outside their own family, I was their first encounter with a playmate. My mother would stand around in the barn talking with the farmer and his wife while he hand milked his cows and she bounced their latest arrival, another baby boy, probably telling them one of her wartime stories, while I would run off with the three eldest children, two boys and the only girl in the family.

They were permitted to play with me for only a few minutes before having to return to their chores. I was struck by their worn shirts, ragged overalls, and lack of shoes. I had never interacted with anyone that poor—I always thought we were poor! They were all blue-eyed with almost white blond hair, even lighter than mine, and their dark tanned arms and chests made their light Germanic features pronounced. We used to run races, and I was surprised that they could outrun me with their bare feet on the gravel road. In my Chicago neighborhood, I was the fastest runner.

When we returned to our farmhouse, my mother would pour the fresh warm milk she had purchased from the farmer's wife into tall glasses and cut thick slices of the aromatic freshly baked white bread she had also bought. It was the only time during my entire childhood that my parents permitted me to eat white bread. They called the gummy, store-bought, heavily processed variety they had once tried "white sponge" because it stuck to the roof of your mouth, unlike the wholesome, grainy pumpernickel or rye bread we usually ate.

It took several days to become accustomed to the quiet of the land. To amuse myself, I would sit at the large dining room picture window watching for any car that might come by on the gravel county road several hundred feet away from our front door. Most times, only two or three cars passed by the entire day. On dry days, a car could be spotted a mile away by the upheaval of orange-colored dust that blew wide across the field, covering the wild prairie flowers with specks that the gentle rains, which came through a couple of times during our stay, could not wash off. On other days, I would lie in the colorful hammock my father had strung between two towering white pine trees gazing up at the branches with their thin soft needles against the sparkling sky. I often would easily fall asleep, much to my great surprise, the child who never liked to go to bed at home in Chicago.

Thus, over time, I became more attached to this dilapidated farm in the middle of nowhere that was our vacation home for years, the future retirement home of my parents, and their refuge from the memory of the War. Visiting throughout my young adult life, I learned to appreciate the food on my plate and found refuge from the raucous noise of the city. I became lost in thought on long isolated walks into the woods, rode borrowed horses, picked my parents' raspberries, strawberries, tomatoes, melons, cucumbers, peppers, zucchini, potatoes, and apples, read romance novels, wrote, and introduced my friends, my husband, and my son to nature, all of which allowed me to communicate with my mother in a new, meaningful way.

Part 2

_____

Russia and Siberia

The Lieutenant

In 1904, in southern Poland (then controlled by Austria during the long years of the partitions of Poland), in Rymanów, near the foothills close to the Carpathian Mountains, my father, Wawrzyniec, was born into a well-to-do family, the last of seven children. His father, Józef, had become wealthy building massive stone mansions in the town of Krosno and in neighboring communities. The family lived in one of his huge well-built houses on Kosciuszko Street in Krosno. His mother, Bronisława, was a disciplined, stubborn woman who ruled the family and their servants, sternly determined to raise her brood to be well-educated, religious, and proper Polish citizens.

With thick light blond hair and light blue eyes, Wawrzyniec was a handsome young boy. He was spoiled by his older sisters, so much as that they would argue among themselves about who would have the privilege of ironing his white, starched shirts or comb his hair or cater to any other of his needs. His one and only older brother, the firstborn, was an excellent chess player and played for hours with his youngest sibling. Wawrzyniec became as shrewd as his brother in the game and played it well into his eighties with his grandchildren.

Wawrzyniec attended a small school of ten boys; he was a good student and quickly progressed to the head of the class. In those days, students were required to memorize long poems, excerpts from historical texts, and long passages of Polish literature. The teaching of such subjects was permitted in this part of Poland occupied by the Austrians, who were tolerant of Polish culture, unlike in the regions occupied by the Russians and the Germans after the partitions of Poland. He could recite these poems long into his old age, entertaining his audience with their subtle humor and playful rhythms.

As a young boy, he loved to play with his hunting dog, Lump, who was so well behaved that when Wawrzyniec's mother sent the dog to the butcher for meat to carry in a special bag under his neck, the dog returned home without once invading the package. It was a story he loved to tell. He loved dogs, and he instilled a compassion and love for animals in others. As a teenager, he became interested in photography, an interest that ended up lasting well into old age. Better cameras and new techniques were being introduced, and photography was increasingly seen as an art. He developed his photos in a dark corner of his room that was on the third level of the house and created many albums, one of which was preserved for many years by his older sister, Flora, long after the war ended. The photos in that album were of his dog and his high school sweetheart, as well as scenes from around the small town—the central square, the church where he served as an altar boy, the church bell tower, the museum with its artifacts from the early days of the development of lamps (Ignacy Łukasiewicz, who had invented the oil lamp, hailed from the region), and of course, his favorite nearby mountains, the Bieszczady, where he used to hike for hours with his friends.

During World War I, Wawrzyniec ran away from home to fight the Germans after he witnessed a German bomber attack an innocent farmer crossing a field with his horse. He was about thirteen years old when he joined a band of hastily formed resistance fighters. As soon as he left home with only his hunting rifle, he was cut off by a German ambush. He hid in nearby woods for over three weeks while his mother prayed for his safe return. The ordeal became an important lesson, and when the war ended, Wawrzyniec organized the region's Boy Scout troops, becoming the head of the town's large organization. In the wake of World War I, scouting became an important part of every child's education; it provided a practical way to teach survival skills and to instill strong moral character and loyalty to God and country, an ideology Polish people staunchly embraced in their newfound freedom.

After the war, Wawrzyniec continued his studies, graduating from Szkoła Główna Gospodarstwa Wiejskiego w Warszawie, while his father's construction business flourished in the newly independent Poland. It was a luxury to be able to attend a university, and by 1930 he had completed his education with the equivalent of a master's degree in forestry. He had married and was living in a small community near Warsaw with his new wife, Maria, who was pregnant with their first child. His father became gravely ill at this time, and so Wawrzyniec made the long journey by train to Krosno to be with his dying father and then turned around to go back to Warsaw to be with his wife during her prolonged labor. The little girl, Lucyna (or Luta), was born healthy, but in the meantime, Wawrzyniec's father died. On rare occasions, he recalled this episode and conveyed his grief in an unusual display of regret, for he was not one to dwell on the past.

Wawrzyniec loved the woods and longed to work there in some capacity so that he could ride his beloved horse, hunt ducks, pheasants, and geese, and most importantly escape the bustle and noise of city life. A short time later, he was granted a position as caretaker of Count Łubieński's large estate in Ruchna, about sixty miles east of Warsaw. There, he was in charge of the vast lands. He had to make sure that the count and his party had plenty of game to hunt and that the groundskeepers maintained the forests and guarded the lands from any poachers. He used to pay the peasants one *złoty* for each cat tail that they brought him, for feral cats were overpopulating the woods and attacking desirable game. By then, another daughter, Krystyna, had been born. His wife soon became pregnant again, but the baby boy was lost in a miscarriage. It was a loss he mourned for rest of his life, for the baby was the only son ever born to him.

In the days leading up to the outbreak of World War II, most of Western Europe seemed to ignore the threatening presence of Germany at Poland's doorstep. In compliance with the wishes of Lord Chamberlain of Britain, Poland had refrained from mobilizing its army even though everyone was well aware of the incidents of German aggression at its western border for months before the Germans invaded on September 1, 1939. Acquiescing to British and French pressure, Poland's scattered reserve forces and meager weaponry waited idly. It turned out to be a futile attempt to appease

Hitler and the German government. The explosive political atmosphere that had prevailed in Europe since the end of World War I suddenly grew uncontrollable.

On August 31, 1939, one day before the long-anticipated attack by Hitler on Poland, cavalry reserve officer Wawrzyniec Solecki received his mobilization orders. With mobilization, he became a second lieutenant whose task was to defend the borders of eastern Poland near Białystok, not far from Grodno. Merciless air bombardments by the Germans, however, forced the cavalry unit to move its operation northward toward Wołkowysk. When Soviet Russia invaded Poland on September 17, 1939, Lieutenant Solecki and his unit were sent east to block the way.

"We were to defend transportation routes, the main target of the Soviets," he explained. "Our unit could not reach Grodno in time to help the civilians trying to fight off the attack. Instead, my unit retreated into the densely wooded Augustów Forest to defend the bridges across the Augustów Canal. When we arrived, Soviet tanks were already guarding the canal. Its defense on horseback was impossible, so we retreated into the safety of the forest."

Though he was an excellent horseman, his horse was uncooperative. "Our training was incomplete and I rode a poorly broken horse who circled nervously, unresponsive to my commands. The commanding officer had given a signal that the tanks were ahead and we heard the sound of a few shots. My horse bolted for the woods. I could not control this half-wild animal. Finally, I managed to escape to a small clearing in the woods, where I fell off of him."

The soldiers' food supplies were dwindling, so to maneuver more freely through the woods they released most of the horses and escaped on foot, heading toward the Lithuanian border. Another battle erupted as the Soviet tanks continued across the border into Poland. Their only defense against these massive iron machines was hand grenades. Lieutenant Solecki ran through machine gun fire across a road into an open field near a river and jumped into the cold water. He was a strong swimmer, but as he struggled across, he felt himself being pulled down into the murky mass. He looked back and saw two of his soldiers holding on to his long coat, which had spread out on top of the water. He yelled,

"Let go!" but they held on. He yelled again, but they clung on. Then, he yelled, "I'll kill you if you don't let go!" They must have been in a panic, but they released their grip and he was able to pull himself on to the steep bank of the river. Then, he pulled the two soldiers up behind him.

After they had crossed the Marycha River, they stopped and rested in a nearby village in Lithuania for several days. However, their freedom was short lived. Lithuanian soldiers were required by the Soviets to intern all Polish soldiers, and on September 23, 1939, they escorted them to the resort area of Birstonas along the winding Niemen River. At the internment, Lieutenant Solecki held his father's Austrian-made revolver from World War I for a long time before surrendering it. He caressed the large white ornately carved handle and thought about the day his father had given it to him when he was just sixteen, saying, "You are now a man. Take good care of this and yourself." He never saw the revolver again.

For the first time in almost two weeks, he was able to remove his clothes and bathe. After life in the resort town settled down, the Polish soldiers were free of restraints, so many of them escaped. Slowly, news of their fate reached those soldiers that had stayed. "Many escapees found only the solace of a Soviet bullet, while others crossed the Bug River straight into German hands," he recalled. By November, the weather had grown so cold that the resort area became intolerable. Along with two thousand other interned Polish officers and soldiers, Lieutenant Solecki was sent to the nearby city of Kalvarija, to a former mental hospital that had been converted into temporary shelter. For Christmas that year, the Lithuanian-Polish community provided the interned soldiers with traditional holiday food.

"We stared at the delicacies of beet soup, pierogi, cakes, and tea, and no one wanted to eat," he lamented. "After two months away from home, Christmas was only a grim reminder of our plight and separation from our families. We celebrated by singing carols like 'Hush Little Jesus' and 'God Is Born' in tearful harmony. The room filled with the grieving sobs of grown men."

It was a memory Lieutenant Solecki buried deep within his soul. It resurfaced only at Christmas each year.

The Impact

At Christmastime when I was growing up, my father made the holiday seem like a large family affair, though there were only four of us in America. He waited until the morning of Christmas Eve to bring in the huge tree, which I had been anticipating for weeks. He wedged it carefully into a wooden stand he had made at S&C Electric Company's factory, where he worked as a saw man, building transport crates for huge electric transformers.

I always admired my father for taking such a job given his high level of education. He was committed to supporting our family and his relatives in Poland, whatever it took. I thought he was humbled by the experience, though he was naturally a humble person. With his poor English, advanced age, and difficulties getting his school diplomas from Communist Poland recognized in the United States, he was lucky to find any good-paying job. After he was granted American citizenship, seven years after we arrived in the United States, he received an offer to work for the U.S. Forestry Service in Oregon. By then, he was well into his fifties and had bought the farm in Wisconsin, so he and my mother decided to stay in Chicago until his retirement.

The tip of the tree just barely touched the nine-foot ceiling in our living room. I remember the year when I had turned ten and stood in awe staring up at the giant tree. "We'll start dressing it with your favorite angel, and then the star," my father announced in his usual booming voice. After my father strung the candle-shaped bubble lights and the big colorful bulb lights, we hung a few store-bought thin, glass blown ornaments and several hand-made ones. There were yards of colored paper strips looped into a garland that my sister and I made and little dwarfs my mother had made from colorful yarn wrapped around wire shaped into minia-ture bodies. My father attached his favorite shiny blue and green glass birds with matching tails made of real feathers. The finishing touch was silvery foil icicles that broke easily if pulled too hard, so usually my father was the one to hang those all over the tree. It was comical to see him carefully pulling apart the delicate icicles with his big hands and wide fingers, but he seemed to be happily lost in the task.

My favorite task was to arrange the small figures of baby Jesus, Mother Mary, Joseph, the three kings, several shepherds, and various barn animals in the small manger that my father had built. It was complete with a small light bulb ingeniously concealed under the roof that made the inside of the manger glow as if that eternal star of Bethlehem was indeed shining in. Seasonal music played on the radio's classical music station as we worked on the tree. Colorful hard candy lay in glass bowls and tempted me, but I had to wait for Christmas Eve dinner. My mother had prepared baked and fried fish, boiled potatoes, and pierogi with fillings of cabbage and sauerkraut, mushrooms, and my favorite, potato and cheese. These were popular where she grew up in eastern Poland, and she made dozens of them, as my father could easily consume at least a dozen by himself. She also made Belarusian beet soup, a creamy fresh vegetable soup garnished with dill and sour cream that was different from the sour, clear beet soup that Polish families normally served at the holidays. She even made gefilte fish, much to my father's amazement. "Jewish fish on Christmas Eve?" he questioned. My mother laughed and dismissed his remark, saying, "I got the recipe from our good Jewish neighbor."

Once the tree was dressed and the meal was ready, we retreated to get dressed in our formal Sunday best and then gathered at the festive table to share *opłatek*, the host that we had received from relatives in Poland a few weeks before. Thinking about my father's relatives sharing the same wishes of good health and happiness helped keep our connection with Poland alive. Everyone went around the table sharing the host and kissing each other on the cheek in a tradition that was intended to mend any family squabbles and to start the New Year afresh.

After the sumptuous meal, we unwrapped the presents and sat around the brightly lit tree and sang Christmas carols in Polish.

My mother and sister carried the tunes in perfect harmony, while my father and I, both of us tone deaf, sat together butchering the songs, all to my mother's and sister's amusement.

"Mother once had a beautiful voice," my sister assured me.

"Yes, I did," my mother chimed in. "It was the climate. That Siberian climate—dry air filled with the sap of hundreds of old pine trees."

I too wanted to be able to sing beautifully. I wanted to know what it was like in that mysterious land called Siberia, of which they so often spoke. And then, there was that secret, knowing exchange of glances between my mother and sister as they smiled to themselves. I felt as if my father and I were part of a different family, especially when my mother looked over at us and said, "Eh, you, Daddy's little daughter." Then she and Mira both laughed that small quiet chuckle elicited by things that only they found amusing.

Later in the evening, my father, mother, and sister fell into contemplation staring at the tree, and things became strangely quiet. I thought I noticed a tear or two roll down my father's face. Though I hadn't realized it then, every year he remembered that lonely and sorrowful Christmas in prison during the war. It was strange to see this normally cheerful and composed man so sad.

Then, the four of us played Dominos late into the night. It was a relief that at least for this one family gathering, the war stories temporarily ceased.

The Arrest

"Open the door!" shouted the Soviet NKVD secret police officer from outside Janina's farmhouse. She sat up in bed and stared at the door, while Mira rubbed her eyes and began to slide out of bed. Then, a loud pounding of something metal against the wooden door startled Janina and she jumped out of bed.

"Don't move! Mira!" she whispered and pulled her back onto the bed. Janina stepped slowly to the window and peered out. She saw three young soldiers standing motionless, bayonets glistening in the faint moonlight. They looked like giants in the shadows of their lanterns.

"Your weapons!" the officer shouted in Russian. Janina opened the door slowly and a cold wind rushed into the house. She had no weapons to surrender. It was four o'clock in the morning on a bitterly cold day on the tenth of February 1940. She was not surprised by the intrusion. Her few remaining neighbors had been warning her of this for weeks. It was to be the first massive deportation.

"In the eerie silence, I realized that I had had this premonition," she said of the incident years later. "I stood in the doorway, half-dressed with a cold wind pressing my nightgown against my body and Mira clinging to my arm. It was a peculiar sense of relief. I knew our fate then. That long unnerving wait was over. These young soldiers were in control of my life."

Although Janina sensed the purpose of this early morning intrusion, she acted indignant.

"What are you going to do with us?" she demanded, hoping to dissuade them from their mission. The soldiers remained standing outside in silence.

"Are you going to shoot us?" she challenged them.

As she looked out into the darkness, Janina could not see the soldiers clearly from behind the point of bright light from their lanterns, but she knew from their shadows that they were pointing their rifles at her. Then the officer walked up and jabbed the tip of his bayonet into her chest.

"We won't waste ammunition on you," he said, laughing. "You'll die from starvation where you're going anyway!"

Janina pleaded, "Why are you here? You've taken Poland from us. Your government is here. What can I, a woman alone, do about it? I am neutral in politics. I know nothing. I am only trying to raise my child!"

As she pleaded, she began to gasp for air. The soldiers stared at her without saying anything.

"What am I being arrested for?" she finally demanded.

"For crimes against the state," said the officer with deep intonations, as if trying to make his young voice seem more menacing.

"What crimes?" she persisted.

"We have witnesses," he yelled.

"But, I've had no trial, no judge. Where are the witnesses? How can you . . . ?" she continued as he abruptly waved his hand in front of her face.

"The trial has already taken place. You've been sentenced to ten years of hard labor. Get your belongings! You have one hour to pack!" he retorted. With that, he turned on his heels and left with the other soldiers.

Janina stood on her doorstep, trying to comprehend the sentence that the young officer had announced with apparent delight. He stared back at her as he mounted his horse.

"As I watched those soldiers leave, I knew I had no choice. First they robbed us of our life's possessions, and then they came to arrest us," she lamented many times.

"I was twenty-seven-years old and still quite beautiful, as I was told, in spite of years of hardship. I wore my long blond hair neatly braided and wound around my head and it framed my deep-set blue eyes, my straight nose, high cheekbones and narrow lips." She always pointed out how straight her nose was, how Romanesque, how royal! "I come from peasants," she would say proudly, as if the memory of her arrest could be alleviated by the recollection of her heritage. In that time and place, it seemed that such beauty had been wasted.

Janina gathered as many of their sparse belongings as she could carry. She tucked Figa under her coat. An hour later, a straw basket under her arm, she picked up her suitcase with one hand and held Mira's with the other and walked outside through the snow to the waiting wagon. A peasant driver sat ready to take them to the train station.

As the wagon carried them away from the farm, Janina watched the snow-covered apple trees blend into the distant white horizon until they became a blur. She thought of the few sacks of buckwheat, beans, and potatoes still hidden in the cellar, the livestock left behind. In the last few weeks, she and Mira had survived mainly on potatoes and salt, conserving as much of their other food as possible for the future.

"We didn't even taste one chicken," she later mourned. "They laid only a few eggs. The cow gave miniscule amounts of milk but I kept feeding it what little I could."

"How stupid!" she said abruptly as the jostling of the wagon in the bitter cold shook her. Mira looked at her, surprised. "How could I think they would leave us alone?"

Figa suddenly jumped from her arms, leaping from within the snuggled warmth of her coat.

"Figa, Figa," she called, but the dog's instinct for survival must have been stronger than her long, loving attachment to Janina, who watched helplessly as Figa disappeared into the snow and into the darkness of early morning.

"What does she know that I do not?" Janina asked herself.

The trip to the railway station was short. With the rising sun, the icy horizon emerged in the distance. The old black steam locomotive stood waiting for its reluctant passengers, spewing out white vapor in short bursts. The engine snorted like a race horse at the starting gate, and its billowing white fog engulfed the train's engineers in a cloud that seemed to levitate them. For a brief moment, Janina thought of trying to escape in the commotion of the transfer to the train, but there beside her was Mira clinging to her hand. With the suitcase and basket in her other hand, escape seemed impossible. They boarded the train under the watchful guard of armed soldiers. Hundreds of deportees scrambled onto the boxcars, and once inside, they jostled for spaces on the few crudely installed rough wooden benches as the doors rolled shut.

People settled into place and guarded their few possessions by tucking their baggage under their feet. Small children sat on suitcases. Janina recognized some of her neighbors, but few people spoke to each other. The train departed the station and sped on for several hours through the cold, snowy landscape. As it slowed briefly near the Polish border, all who could reach the high small square windows in the boxcar peered out through the wires covering the openings. Embedded in the frozen ground Janina saw a white and red Polish flag drooping under wet icy snow, but a slight breeze brought it back to life, as if there were still hope for freedom.

People choked back tears. Shouts and laments echoed through the cramped boxcars: "Ojczyzno, moja Ojczyzna (Country, my country)." And then, almost as if by command, people broke into a chorus of "Boże Coś Polskę (God thou hast Poland, or God save Poland)," Poland's defining religious hymn. Their singing rose above the rattle and drone of the train's metal wheels against the tracks:

> God, Who held Poland for so many ages
> In Your protection, glory, and great power,
> Who gave Your wisdom to Her bards and sages
> And gave Your own shield as Her rightful dower,
> Before Your altars, we in supplication
> Kneeling, implore You, free our land and nation.

The singing soon died out and only the occasional wail of the locomotive's whistle broke the silence and the children's cries. Mira joined in the sobbing as she cuddled at Janina's side. The farther they rode away from Poland, the heavier the mood became among the deportees.

The boxcar was so confining that even small children could not stretch out. Thirty-eight people with their baggage were crammed in the drafty, malodorous space. A small hole in the middle of the floor, with a thin sheet strung around it in a futile attempt at privacy, served as the toilet. However, this was not the most humiliating. Along with everyone on the train, Janina and Mira became the unwilling hosts to lice left over from previous occupants, which they referred to as "loyal Soviet citizens." Both day and night, these tenacious pests crawled over every inch of available skin and scalp, digging in for their blood-sucking nourishment with stings that caused the affected area to itch interminably. Each day, Janina brushed Mira's long blond hair, trying to rid her of these repugnant parasites. Mira turned her fear and disgust into a game by trying to catch the dark critters. She was most successful nabbing the ones that crawled at the base of her head. It was a hopeless, never-ending chore. The sudden abundant human food supply caused the number of the insects to swell to massive proportions. Streams of them marched in columns up the wooden walls of the boxcar.

The train stopped every few hours for water and fuel for the steam engine. If their guard for the day was a humane sort of soldier, they received water to drink. If not, one person was allowed out to gather snow to melt for drinking water. They were fed every three or four days, an unidentifiable watery soup with some coarse rye bread. There was a small stove near the makeshift latrine, but not enough firewood was provided. The deportees burned the benches, making the already cramped quarters even more stifling. Those who stood in rotation with others against the walls nearly froze as cold air seeped through numerous cracks and pressed against their backs.

"Mama, I'm still hungry," Mira cried along with the other five- and six-year-old children.

"Quiet, soon we'll get food. Just a while longer . . ." Janina whispered, but she sensed conditions would be no better ahead.

At one point, the train stopped outside a railway station near the city of Ufa at the foot of the Ural Mountains. Knowing that no one would try to escape from this desolate place in the middle of a cold winter, the Soviet soldiers permitted some of the deportees to walk along the tracks that led through the nearby mountain railroad tunnel. Leaving Mira in the warmth of the boxcar, Janina decided to take a short walk to the tunnel. Stepping onto wide-spaced railroad ties, she breathed in the cold mountain air.

"The view from the tracks swept me into a kind of trance. I devoured the beauty of this seemingly peaceful city nestled in the mountains that towered over us," she recalled. It was a stolen moment, uncomfortably enticing. Knowing that she was an unwilling guest in this land, she tried to resist enjoying its alluring beauty, but nonetheless it was a welcome relief from the stuffy overcrowded boxcar.

Janina walked down the tracks ahead of the train into the tunnel. Her head heavy, she watched her feet maneuvering the slippery railroad ties. Her eyes adjusted to the dimness in the tunnel as she came upon a strangely lit area of rock wall that seemed smoother than other parts of the walls. Carvings of letters and numbers drew her closer. In 1830 and 1863, there were bloody uprisings in Poland against the Russians. Under the headings of these dates, she read the names of the revolutionaries who had lost those battles and who were sentenced to work in Siberia. Their slave labor, which ultimately killed them, built the tunnel.

"I read each name out loud as if to embed it into my mind forever," she said. "My heart felt as if it was being pressed, and a terrible sadness overcame me. They died for us, a failed quest for our freedom, and look where we ended up anyway!"

While still in the tunnel, Janina was startled by the sudden clang of the train's bell. She quickly returned and boarded the train. As they passed the carvings, she held back tears, closing her eyes in a moment of silent prayer for those forgotten heroes.

The next stop was outside the larger city of Chelyabinsk on the other side of the Ural Mountains in Siberia. The deportees were allowed to depart the train again for a short break around the railway station. She again left Mira behind in the warmth and relative safety of the boxcar. She wanted to use the opportunity to buy some food and clothing, but in the tightly controlled Communist system, there were no private stores for such basic items, especially not for foreigners. Soon she came upon a special "Communist Party" store where rich Russian women, elegantly dressed in sable coats with matching sable hats and muffs, casually entered through nondescript gray doors. Janina slipped in, unnoticed by the guards at the door. The ostentation of the interior of the store contrasted sharply with the poverty she saw along the way in Russian villages. It overflowed with racks of men's fine woolen suits, luxurious cotton underwear, and rows of similarly alluring goods. Janina passed by each aisle, gently gliding her fingertips along the finery, until a guard noticed her and shooed her out.

"I had neither the correct identification papers for permission to purchase those goods, nor the large sums of money in the proper currency," she said. "I returned to the train empty handed and waited for its departure."

After five weeks, the seemingly endless train ride came to an abrupt end. The soldiers commanded Janina and Mira, along with mostly other women and children passengers to gather their belongings and leave the train. As she threw down a louse that she had just plucked from Mira's hair, Janina muttered, "Thank God we're leaving these living prison walls!"

Soldiers stood monitoring and motioned the deportees to a waiting area in the middle of a field deep with newly fallen snow, which in some areas had been trampled hard as ice and in others was so soft that it engulfed its lightest intruder. Janina's boxcar was near the end of the train, and by the time she gathered her things and wrapped Mira in her coat and blanket, she was almost the last to reach the group of frightened people. The cold cut into her face, as the early morning sun had not yet warmed the air. Everyone stood dancing from one foot to the other in a futile attempt to try to stay warm. After a few hours, the prisoners started fires from the small amounts of wood provided by the farmers, and more of the barely edible soup and coarse rye bread was distributed by the soldiers. Having received very little food during the journey, people devoured the soup and bread.

By two o'clock in the afternoon, as the short day shrank into sudden night, a parade of horse-drawn sleds appeared, some of which were more spacious than others. People scrambled aboard the larger, more comfortable sleds while Janina struggled in the deep snow carrying her suitcase, bundle, and basket. She and

Mira rushed toward the last remaining sled. It was small and narrow, large enough for only one person with some baggage, and it was driven by an old Russian man in a tattered sheepskin vest. As he maneuvered his tired old horse up to the long line of waiting sleds, he pleaded in Russian, "Hurry, hurry! If we fall behind the others, we'll lose our way in the darkness." He helped Janina pack Mira and their baggage onto the sled. In their haste, Janina had just enough time to wrap Mira in a large blanket and to tie a puffy feather pillow around her. She tied the suitcase and basket behind her just as the driver struck his reluctant horse with his whip. "*Wjo* (Onward)," he commanded the horse as Janina ran behind the sled.

The other sleds were already far ahead, as the vastness of the Siberian iceland seemed to be closing in around them. The driver whipped his horse to quicken its pace. The tracks in the snow made by the wider sleds caused his narrow sled to teeter. Janina adjusted it constantly as she ran along its side. She struggled to stay in the packed tracks, but most of the time her feet sank several inches with each step. She could keep up with the sled only by holding onto it, and at times it dragged her along. The distance between them and the larger sleds was increasing, as the small sled continued turning onto its side. In his haste, the old man did not notice the predicament, and at one point the sled turned completely upside down, landing Mira and the pillow against the snow on the ground.

"Stop, stop! My child will be killed!" screamed Janina, but the old man could not hear her. Finally, she rushed up to him and pulled his shoulder so forcefully that he almost fell off the seat. He stopped only long enough for Janina to straighten the sled, so she could not check on Mira. As he drove his horse even faster, she struggled to run alongside the sled.

The sled ride continued for what seemed to Janina like at least twelve hours, past midnight, through thick forests where the sound of wolves' howls echoed in the distance. Penetrating coldness held all living things still. There were few signs of homes or farms along the way, and Janina understood the old man's concern to keep up with the others.

"By then, I was convinced Mira could not have survived in that icy, snow-covered bundle. Despite my best efforts, the sled still dragged upside down along the hard ground for a large part of the journey. The old man would not stop long enough for me to check on Mira," she recalled many a time.

In the early morning, they reached an abandoned brick building in the middle of a desolate forest. Janina untied her precious bundle, releasing Mira from the crust of icy snow. She popped out warm and sleepy.

"Mama, now will you feed me?" she asked.

Janina laughed a nervous laugh with a sigh of relief and bowed her head, lightly touching Mira's forehead. Her hot, steamy breath condensed into a fog as she hugged Mira. Then she looked around at the glazed, cold faces of her neighbors. They sat immobile on the larger sleds. Though exhausted, unlike her companions, she had stayed warm from all the running.

People pushed their way into the large building. A stove burned wood in the middle of the room. The Russians fed them their watery version of vegetable soup and *kipyatok* (plain hot water). It was their first food in almost a day; Janina blew on the hot soup as she slowly fed it to Mira.

In one corner of the room, a young Soviet soldier, a Russian, sat eating the same brew. Janina turned to him asking in Russian, "Where are the factories we are to work in?" The soldier laughed, almost spitting out his soup. "Factories? We'll give you factories! You'll see what work you'll have!" he sneered. Puzzled, Janina finished her soup and joined the others to rest. At noon, they boarded their sleds for the final short journey to the camp that was to become their prison.

Family Secrets

While I was growing up in the 1950s and 1960s, politics and religion were recurring topics of conversation in our family, but there were some things that were not discussed. My mother's divorce from my sister's father and my own father's divorce from his first wife were well-kept secrets until I was almost a teenager. For a long time, I thought my sister must have been adopted because she had a different last name and because she was fifteen years older than I.

My parents tried to protect me from the social stigma of divorce in the close-knit Polish Catholic community in Chicago, but I always sensed there was something I was not being told. They had not wanted to live in the culturally segregated Polish neighborhood, with the old Polonia, near downtown Chicago, where Polish immigrants had settled beginning in the late nineteenth and early twentieth centuries. Theirs was a tightly knit community where poor former peasants labored day and night in factories and managed to build elaborate churches similar to the old ones they had left behind in Poland. Polish priests, particularly Reverend Vincent Barzynski in the late 1890s, were good at persuading them to donate vast sums of money and their labor for these efforts, but the churches provided a connection with Poland and the families they had left behind in search of freedom and economic prosperity.

My mother had a profound distrust of priests in general, and more stories from her life in Poland emerged around that favorite topic. There was the priest who condoned a peasant farmer for beating his wife, and then the priest who would not permit a poor sickly peasant woman, who already had half a dozen children, to obtain an illegal abortion. I was surprised to hear this from my mother, and her attitude had a much greater impact on me than my otherwise very Catholic upbringing. My mother's encounter with the ruby-ringed and ermine-robed bishop was one of her favorite stories. The bishop visited the countryside demanding that his hand be kissed and that poor peasants donate the last of their money to the church. She did on occasion recall how a poor priest had helped someone. In spite of her dislike of priests, she was religious and believed she could pray and be close to God, and especially to the Virgin Mary, without having to listen to priests' sermons. "Hypocrites," she liked to call them. It seemed to me that my mother was ahead of her time by standing up for the well-being of women, incited by the harsh realities of her women friends and neighbors.

I was acutely aware of my mother's attitude toward priests and the church as I was growing up. I would quiz my father why my mother rarely attended church on Sundays with us. Though he was talkative, it was one matter on which he had little to say. I did not know it at the time, but his divorce and civil marriage to my mother were not recognized by the church, and that weighed heavily on him. Because of it, he was not permitted to receive Holy Communion during Mass, the church ritual considered the holiest of holies by Catholics. He considered himself unworthy, a burden he felt for the rest of his life, he told me years later. My father had been an altar boy and a fervent churchgoer in Poland. For a long time, his avoidance of Holy Communion was a great mystery to me, for his kindness and generosity made me think of him as a saint.

Though I was baptized in the church and later confirmed, I always had a sense of being different. At the age of eighteen, I decided to leave the church. Years later, when my first child was born, I became a Unitarian Universalist, joining a community of liberal religious thinkers with various levels of belief in a higher power, God included. Ironically, a tradition of religious tolerance in Poland permitted a founding Unitarian community to thrive for about a hundred years in Raków, not far from Kraków, before it was completely suppressed. That same religious tolerance welcomed Jews, who readily settled there, and by the start of World War II they made up about 10 percent of the population of country.

My father very much regretted my decision to join a new religion. He often tried to convince me to return to the church, sending numerous writings and prayers ranging from Native American chants to articles criticizing other religions, my new one included. Being Polish and being Catholic were one and the same to him, and to the rest of the Polish community. It was all about tradition. To some extent, though I continued to see the world through "Catholic" eyes, I felt I had abandoned not only my religion but my heritage and I was never quite at ease with that.

My mother did not mind my self-imposed excommunication from the church. She only wanted me to believe in God and to pray. "Do you believe in God?" she would ask at obscure moments, the last from her nursing home bed, only a few weeks before she died. "Sure," I said. "I believe." It was not entirely true, but I had not ruled out belief in God as a possibility. I considered myself an agnostic, but trying to explain that to my mother seemed like a futile endeavor and it made no sense as she lay on her deathbed.

The politics surrounding Poland before, during, and after World War II were discussed at our dinner gatherings as often as the stories of my parents' and sister's ordeals were recounted. During Polish school and Polish Girl Scout troop meetings, I learned that freedom in the newly independent Poland between the World Wars was slow to be recognized and that after the war, under Soviet-style Communism, Poland became a dramatically different country. I struggled to understand all the nuances of these differing political perspectives. Impassioned Polish patriotism was never completely eradicated by those conquerors (Germany and Russia) or later by world powers (Britain, the Soviet Union, and the United States) who were using Poland as a chess piece in an endless pursuit of world peace. My father used to say that the "battle over resources" caused this turmoil, as if it were all inevitable.

My mother taught me about Piłsudski, the man who by some was considered a maverick, unbecoming of genteel society and politics, whom she unquestioningly adored. His soldiers were famous for their drunken rowdiness and their unrelenting quest to free Poland by any means during World War I. Poles needed a leader strong enough to unite them and the lands of the three partitions and to navigate the political waters of a world ready to pounce on the weak. He preached for treating all the various ethnic groups equally, particularly Jews, in the new Poland. His methods were not always appreciated by everyone, but he was viewed as a hero by many. My mother always kept his photograph hung beneath a cross and a picture of Matka Boska (Mary, Mother of God) next to her bed, as his anticlericalism mixed with a cult-like reverence of the Virgin Mary appealed to her rebellious nature.

I grew up absorbing my mother's patriotic fervor and even to this day, hearing the Polish or American national anthems brings tears to my eyes. The Polish anthem, "Jeszcze Polska nie Zginęła" ("Poland Has Not Yet Perished"), was a favorite of mine and that of my Polish friends. We stood proudly in our Polish Scout uniforms before the dual raising of the Polish and American flags during our summer camping trips to Michigan or Wisconsin. We belted out those lyrics as if we too had endured the oppression. Its marching rhythm and rousing words inspired a proud camaraderie among us. My mother often stood solemnly at the singing of that national anthem. She stood equally enthralled at the singing of America's national anthem and taught me that America was her new beloved country, that she never had it so well, that it was a miracle to be in America, and that I should be forever grateful, but I always sensed in her a longing for the Poland that was no more.

Though my parents always dreamed of returning to Poland after the war, they never did. During the Cold War years, my father was afraid to return, fearing reprisals for his involvement in uncovering and discharging Communist infiltrators from the Polish Army during the war. A number of his officer friends who had returned to Communist Poland immediately after the war ended up in Soviet gulags or labor camps, never to be heard from again.

At the time of the outbreak of the war, my mother had not fully realized the depth of Communist oppression, but as she endured the labor camps and spoke to Russian peasants after her escape, she learned the true meaning of Soviet Communism—the false promises, the unequal distribution of wealth, the squelching of freedom. It seemed to me as I sat listening to the long discussions my parents had with friends and neighbors that the topic of Communism could never be exhausted. What they relayed was a forewarning, an attempt to convince those around them who had no idea about Communism and who could scarcely believe what my parents were telling them, that Communism was reprehensible. I learned about the murders of thousands of Polish officers and intellectuals at the Katyń Forest massacres in 1940 by the Russians, long before most of the West learned of the international conspiracy of silence to cover up the atrocities. In the end, after the fall of Soviet Communism in 1989–90, we learned that twenty-two thousand Polish officers and intellectuals from several camps had been murdered by the Soviets, a massacre that is collectively known as the "Katyń Massacres." Having survived one of those camps, Kozelsk, my father warned, "America needs to be strong to fight off the Communists."

"Communists are liars and deceivers," my mother chimed in. They believed that wherever in the world Soviet-style Communism existed, it should be destroyed. In a quieter moment she would reflect on her outrage and say that she never had anything against the Russian people. It was only the Soviet Communists that she hated. "The Russian people helped me many times," she added.

"I have no one to return to," my mother stated firmly again and again as if hoping it were not true. "America is *my* country now," she would say in such a way that I never believed she did not long for the land of her parents. And then, of course, another story of the War emerged and the subject of visiting Poland was momentarily dropped.

Soviet Labor Camp

The Soviet officer announced in Russian, "You are free workers," as Janina helped Mira off the sled. Janina looked at him suspiciously.

"You will be paid. You will have shelter and food, and be able to buy clothing. You are not prisoners," reassured another guard. He seemed to be smirking.

"Free, but nowhere to go," muttered Janina under her breath.

The caravan of tired, hungry old men, women, and children approached the camp gates of Baza Mikulińska. They were somewhere in the barren forests of Siberia, beyond any visible signs of civilization. The camp was tucked away in a dense virgin forest. Its fortress walls were the distant howls of hungry wolves and the invisible sword of bitter cold.

Her head heavy from lack of sleep and her feet stinging from the cold of the long journey, Janina stared at the distant dark barracks lying low in the deep snow. As she approached them, the outline of a white figure appeared in stark contrast to the surrounding grayness. The clean, brilliantly white, and intricately crafted sheepskin coat of the NKVD camp commander seemed to explode against the dreariness of the prison campgrounds behind him. As she passed him, she looked into his slanted eyes, barely visible from beneath his matching white sheepskin hat. He reminded her of the Mongol who had almost shot her at the cottage near Grodno. Trying to assess his character, she sensed his importance in determining her fate in her new home.

Is he a human being or not? she wondered.

The Communists organized their labor according to the prisoners' backgrounds in Poland. Those who came from cities were assigned lighter, easier work on the farm collectives. Those who had been honed by the hardships of country life were assigned to hard labor. When these reserves of human workers were depleted, no one was spared the endless tasks of building the massive Soviet projects, so that intellectuals worked beside peasants and were treated with equal harshness.

"From where do you come?" barked the Soviet guard in Russian as Janina stopped in front of her newly assigned barrack.

She muttered, "From Grodno."

"Where is your husband?" he asked as he glanced at Mira.

"He is here in the camp, but not with me," replied Janina, growing nervous with this line of questioning. The guard checked his list attached to an old tattered board. He examined her tall sturdy body, scribbled something, and handed her a ten-pound axe from the wagon beside him.

"To the forest, tomorrow. Be ready at six in the morning. And don't be late, or you'll be docked a third of your salary," he announced in a loud voice as if to warn the others as well.

Janina was among the few women assigned to do hard labor, which consisted of chopping down and sawing huge birch trees in the centuries-old virgin forests. Each day she carried the heavy axe four miles to and four miles back from the timber operation site. Many of the other women in the camp had husbands or older sons who could satisfy the workforce quota. Without her husband to work for her, Janina was left to pursue the meager salary alone and there was little she could do to bribe the men in charge, as she had few belongings left.

The most difficult thing was leaving Mira alone in the camp. "Stay close to the other children, Mira," she warned. "I'll be back at the end of the day," she said trying to sound reassuring. There was no real school, only a makeshift gathering of mothers who were permitted to stay behind and who gave the children lessons mostly from memory, as there were few books.

For the first time in many months, Janina was separated from her neighbors, who had also been deported. She longed for the security of familiar surroundings. As she walked the long route to the timber site, she remembered with deep sadness her brother's vigilance toward her, and she mourned the loss of Poland's tenuous freedom. For perhaps the first time in her life, she paid little attention to her natural surroundings, hardly noticing the towering beauty of the trees around her. Large steamy clouds emerged from her mouth and nostrils as she tried to catch her breath. Suddenly, she spat onto the snow as she thought about that lost freedom, relieved that her parents would not be witnessing this new siege and her captivity. Then she stopped to rest on a nearby fallen log.

"I would often sit like that, trying to appreciate the beauty around me, resting before I had to continue the hard work, but it was difficult to admire any of that knowing I was a slave," she recalled.

Janina's job was to chop off the felled trees' huge branches, which were the thickness of her waist. As hard as she pounded, she often barely got past the bark of the fresh hard wood with the dull axe. Once the long heavy branch was cut off, she dragged it through deep snow to the cleaning site where the smaller branches were removed and destroyed in immense fires that burned all day. The warmth from these fresh wood fires was one benefit of this difficult work, but their sparks shot high into the air, settling upon the workers' woolen scarves and clothing, burning holes in the material.

Four hundred people were detained at this camp, housed tightly in large one-room barracks, ninety or so in each. Not only did the deportees have to cook for themselves but several families had to share a single wood-burning stove with only two cooking burners. Most of the time all they could make was a bland gruel of barley. The wait to use the stove tested the patience of even the most charitable and considerate people. Wails from small children and screams from infants filled the stuffy barracks, and mothers grew desperate to feed their undernourished broods. Squabbles broke out over the precious burners, but intervention from the assigned barrack supervisor resulted in resigned compliance. Usually a non-Pole was assigned to this coveted role, a Belarusian or Ukrainian who lived with his charges as a pampered spy of the Soviet commanders. More often than not the supervisor settled disputes according to his whims, favoring those who could afford to buy his sympathy with food or clothes.

"Move your pot over," shrieked the supervisor at Janina. "Yours is too large," he nagged. Janina could not argue. One word from him to the commandant could send her deeper into Siberia to endure harder labor and even more demoralizing conditions. Her most dreadful concern was that of losing Mira to the Soviet orphanage system. Janina was prepared to endure the most humiliating circumstances if only to assure their continued survival together.

Life in the barrack was stifling. Flimsy wooden walls separated families into small compartments, but nothing could stop the lice and bedbugs from freely crawling over their unsuspecting hosts. The barrack lice were more persistent than their boxcar counterparts that could be washed out of clothing and hair. Bedbugs clung to walls and penetrated beds, mattresses, and clothing. They marched over every item and every person, stopping for nourishment in the already depleted resources of human flesh. Exhausted from the daily hunt for these creatures, Janina once took the blanket from her bed and shook it over a huge bowl of hot water like a madwoman. Within minutes the entire bowl filled with the squirming bodies of these repulsive parasites. Afraid to say anything to the camp authorities, the families endured these assaults on their bodies, killing the parasites as they could. It was a constant chore and enough to drive one to insanity.

In the darkness of night, a larger form of scavenger prowled the camps. As Janina tried to fall asleep after every draining day of work, she heard the flicking scratch of toenails as rats scampered their way across the naked wooden beams of exposed roof rafters above her. In the faint starlight radiating through tiny windows, she saw the sleek dark bodies of these skillful invaders. In the few minutes it took for her to fall asleep, she amused herself with the reappearing shadows of their stealthy movements. After a while, their nocturnal rummaging no longer repelled her, and she grew to anticipate their lulling noises in the night.

One night, as she returned late from work, Janina dropped like a dead weight onto the bed next to Mira, who had fallen asleep hours earlier. They shared a single narrow bed, and to gain more space, they slept diagonally so that their feet lay next to each other's faces. Janina adjusted the remaining woolen blanket over

Mira, trying to roll her closer to the wall, and then she fell back onto the lumpy straw mattress in a dead heap.

"How she ever could sleep with me next to her, with the involuntary jerking of my tired legs into her head, I will never know. I must have kicked her in my sleep, but she never complained," Janina said years later.

In those few semiconscious seconds before sleep liberated her, Janina was watching the ritual dance of the rats on the wooden beams in the silvery light of the full moon. As she closed her eyes, a warm scratchy lump suddenly thumped onto her chest and began squirming for escape. In her stupor, Janina casually lifted the rat by its back and tossed it to the floor. As the noise of the rat's scampering faded, sleep engulfed her.

Majorettes and Identity

When it came down to what my children would be doing on Saturdays, I thought of my own Saturdays growing up, spent entirely at Polish school and Polish Girl Scout meetings. It was more of a social time than an educational one, and it was a relief to be with friends of whom my parents approved. My parents required this weekly ritual as a means to preserve the culture of our heritage, while at home they would not permit me to speak English so that I learned Polish better; they insisted that I keep a circle of Polish friends, whose families also maintained the same commitment to Polish culture and identity and who likewise had poor opinions of teenage American culture. For all of us growing up in America, it was difficult not to be influenced by American culture, and most of us did not want to be isolated from it.

In my American public high school, there were various groups of teens, from cigarette-smoking "greasers" bound mostly for the trades who largely ended up in Vietnam, to the preppy college-bound who wore penny loafers and mostly ended up avoiding Vietnam. I so longed to belong to that American culture. In my sophomore year, without seeking my father's approval, I decided to try out for the Majorettes, the exclusive group of baton twirling, beautiful, popular girls who wore short white swirly skirts and white uniform jackets trimmed with royal blue piping and blue decorations, a costume not unlike the ice-skating outfit my mother had sewn for me. They performed at all the football games and at some school assemblies. A few times I managed to sneak away with my non-Polish friends to football games on Friday nights, and I found myself completely enchanted with the Majorettes' military precision in marching, legs bouncing with ballet-style grace, clad in white cowboy boots, white cowboy hats, with their baton twirling—that wonderful twirling, all in rhythm to the drum beat—and with the raucous good cheer of this totally American sport. My heart would pound in my chest; I wanted so much to be there with them.

When I made it to the finals, much to my surprise, I was uncomfortably ecstatic. I had to tell my father the bad news that if I made the cut, I would need to miss Polish school and scouts on Saturdays, scout camp in the summer, and even our summer Wisconsin vacation at the remote farm where my parents kept me hostage. On top of it, I would need sixty dollars for the uniform, a ridiculously huge sum of money for me on my poor weekly allowance of a dollar fifty. I would also need to stay in Chicago during spring break instead of going on our spring trip to the farm so that I could practice during the critical last sessions before the final trials. No, no, and no, said my father. Dejected, I went with my family to the farm and practiced as much as I could in the gravel driveway, alone, without critical guidance from the group.

At the finals, I panicked. The head Majorette liked me and told me I had a very good chance of getting in. I panicked some more. If I got accepted I'd have to decline, so what was the point? My father made it perfectly clear that he would not allow me to participate in something he did not understand, nor care to understand. He wouldn't allow me to miss Saturday school and scouts or particularly the summer scout camp and wouldn't give me the money needed for the uniform. As they called my name to the final tryout, my father's words were still in my head. I walked into the middle of the huge gym floor with several dozens of students watching. I was so nervous I could feel blood rushing to my ears. I was paired with one of my classmates who was as tall as I and had blond hair like mine and was about equal in ability.

I made her look good. She was picked to join the group. I was not.

I slunk away, dismayed that I had performed so poorly. It was a regret I carried within my secret self for the remainder of high school. Nerves had gotten to me, and I understood the importance of practice, practice, practice. Yet, I was somehow relieved that I would not need to face my father with the bad news that I had made the squad.

Prison without Bars

The days began to blend into each other: there was the same monotonous work, the same bitter cold, the same hunger pains. Janina grew increasingly concerned for Mira. Miles away from the barrack in the forest, she moved clumsily in the deep snow as she lifted the heavy axe, bending forcefully from her waist to add momentum to her weak stroke. Her worn-down gloves revealed patches of reddened skin. As she chopped off small branches, the friction of her hands against the wooden handle of the axe warmed her nearly frozen fingers. Snow swirled above her head and a deep snowy cocoon of tangled fallen branches protected her from the piercing cold wind. Janina sensed that her body was growing weaker.

A white hare hopped across the delicate crust of three-foot-deep snow, and a dislodged field mouse ran to safety through the tunnels created by the workers invading this virgin land. For most of the day, Janina and the others worked unsupervised. To pass the time and distract themselves from the drudgery of the repeated chopping, dragging, chopping, Janina and her work team sang Polish folk songs and interjected a patriotic hymn for inspiration, much to the chagrin of their watchful Soviet guards who came to check on them a few times during the day. The clean snow offered a soothing coolness, and with trembling hands Janina scooped up the soft powder into her mouth. Just then, she heard a bird's shortened song, and she looked into the tall tree branches, hoping to identify the lone creature, just as her father had taught her to do during his tales of life in the woods.

Janina's thick *valenki* (woolen boots) kept her feet warm for most of the day. They were made from compressed heavy wool that remained dry, but as the sun faded early in the winter afternoon her feet began to stiffen with the cold. She walked in exaggerated movements in a futile attempt to restore circulation, while her steamy breath chilled into ice drops that settled onto her jacket. Her tightly fitting sheepskin jacket hung over her pants and she prayed that the heavy wool would last the winter.

Throughout the day, to everyone's great relief, water could be heated on the immense fires burning the smaller twigs and branches. Janina carried an empty metal can and filled it with clean snow. She threw in several scraps of burned bread crust to create the illusion of real tea. During the half-hour midday break, she sat on a log and consumed the imitation brew and a small ration of rye bread that she brought from camp. These were a few stolen moments during the day to reminisce about better times, and her thoughts drew her away from her gnawing hunger and the biting cold and from her constant concern for Mira.

Janina and Mira's stay at the camp lasted only two months. One day, without warning, they were told to prepare for departure to another labor camp near the city of Perm (Molotov). Janina found the new camp, Baza Czarnuszka, equally unhygienic, overcrowded with Poles and Belarusians occupying cramped barracks. The weather was warmer, and so the onslaught of vermin was more horrendous. Janina was given the same job, and before long, their lives settled into an all too familiar monotony.

During the long day while Janina was away at work, Mira tried to obtain the rationed bread by standing in long lines. At the end of the day, she would report her ordeals to Janina, who listened sadly, thinking of her own experiences at the same age waiting in food lines during World War I. As one of the youngest children in the camp, Mira could not compete with the older, larger children and women. She often returned to their stuffy compartment without that day's ration. Janina understood the difficulty facing Mira but insisted that she get as much of the needed nourishment as possible, prodding her to outmaneuver the maddening crowds.

One day, Mira stood in line again and after several hours found herself almost at the front of the tall counter in the shop. An immense woman stood behind her, and Mira felt the woman's elbow pressing against her head. The woman did not notice Mira below her and looked only high above at the shelves of quickly vanishing bread. Behind the woman stood another, smaller woman who was being pushed and behind that woman was another, all being pressed against one another in a never-ending, squashing queue. As Mira neared the counter, the crowd grew restless because it appeared that the day's allotment of bread would be exhausted.

Slowly, she felt bodies pushing her out of balance into the rough edge of the wooden counter, and with one great shove of human mass, her head became locked between the counter and the huge woman behind her. Unable to move, Mira began screaming, "Help, I can't move. I can't move," but no one seemed to hear her in the commotion. The pressure of human bodies increased, and she felt the sharpness of the wood against her temple growing more intense. She cried again, pushing weakly against the woman, but there was no response. The smaller woman finally saw Mira and quickly shoved the large woman aside. She reached for the counter with both arms on either side of Mira's head and locked her elbows to block the crowd from her.

"Stop!" she screeched. "There's a small child here. Stop! You are going to crush her head!" Mira jumped out of the line, crying from the pain at her temple. The woman gently rubbed the spot and gave her a ration of bread. Mira returned to the barracks, happy that at least this time, she was able to obtain that day's only food.

"*Ludzie, ludziska* (Humans, human-animals)," she would later say scornfully when she recalled the incident.

At five years of age, Mira was often beckoned by play more than by the pursuit of food in the harsh waiting lines. Time seemed to pass slowly as she waited for Janina to return from work, and it was difficult to take everything seriously. Even on unsuccessful days in the bread lines, her creative mind constructed amusements for herself and the older children in the barracks. Ticks and bedbugs could be tormented into running races, empty wooden spools of thread served as imaginary race cars, and mischief could be had in the piles of ragged clothes strewn throughout the barrack. Ignoring hunger pains in her perpetually underfilled belly, she endured hours of aimless existence.

Janina grew increasingly fearful that Mira's malnourished state would lead to more serious illness. When Mira developed a visible case of jaundice, Janina sold whatever clothes, and especially undergarments, she dared. With the small amount of money, she bought an old nanny goat, which she discovered was too wild to be easily milked. The malnourished goat provided only about half a glass of milk each day. For that luxury, Mira had to chase the feisty animal throughout the entire camp.

One time, she caught up to the ornery goat, but it would not be placated with the small handful of tasteless old straw that Mira offered. Then Mira grabbed the rope around the goat's neck and tied her to a tree. She positioned a small metal cup under the goat's udder, yanked on one of the teats like Janina had showed her and to her delight a few streams of milk landed in the cup, but several more missed. Leaning her head against the goat's side like Mira had seen Janina do, she yanked some more. Startled, the goat kicked Mira and the pot fell over as Mira tried to dodge the flailing sharp hooves. Precious drops of milk trickled onto the dry earth. "Stand still," Mira yelled, but the goat ignored Mira, whose small size posed no threat to the goat's long, curved horns. Eventually, between Janina's and Mira's milking attempts, the small supplement proved worthwhile. Together with some occasional gruel, as well as Janina's own sacrifices of bread, Mira's jaundice disappeared.

Janina learned that there were a few remaining Ukrainians among the Polish laborers from the previous wave of conscripted workers. She found out that in the Ukraine, the Bolsheviks took over privately owned lands and divided them into farm collectives. Those Ukrainian farmers who did not agree to give up ownership were forcibly transferred hundreds of miles away to work in the Siberian forests. Their salary was meager and little food was provided by the Soviets. They sold their warm pants and other clothing to the Polish laborers only for cash. During these exchanges, many Poles learned of the real conditions of these citizens of the new Soviet Russia that was purported to be a workers' haven.

On one of her treks back to camp from work on a deserted dark route through the thick forest, Janina met a sympathetic Ukrainian man who fearlessly told her about his early ordeals in the camp.

"I came here in 1934 with twelve hundred of my countrymen from the Ukraine. We slept under barren skies. There were no barracks like you have."

Janina squirmed and shifted her position on her tired feet, looking around to see if anyone was watching them. The Ukrainian seemed unconcerned about possible eavesdroppers and spoke freely in a loud voice. "It was winter, cold as this year's. We got two slices of bread a day. We dug deep holes in the ground to get away from the cold and covered the holes with leaves and bark from birch trees. Those *ziemianki* saved the few of us who could get enough food," he said, his voice fading as he recalled those pitiful times.

Pausing, the Ukrainian smiled, looked around and moved closer to Janina. In a whisper, staring wide-eyed, he resumed his gruesome tale. "Cannibalism, Madame. One man ate all six of his children," he nodded.

Janina felt as if her eyes must be popping from her head, and she took a short, uncomfortable step away from him. Now speaking more to himself than to her, he continued, "After six years, there were only eight of us left!" His intense gaze never left Janina's eyes. He waited for a response from her, but she was too stupefied to answer.

Finally, he relaxed his stare. "Yes," he said, pointing in the direction of the camp. "Those barracks were all built with our blood and sacrifice. You are fortunate to have a roof over your head!"

Janina stood in silence, reflecting on the man's words, as he scrutinized her. "Well, dear lady, may God keep you and yours in good health," he said and walked away with a brief wave of his hand.

Janina never met the man again on her daily treks to and from work. That night, her return trip to camp was hastened by thoughts of the thousands who came before her to this inhuman land. The weight of the axe upon her shoulder and the distant howl of wolves were small discomforts compared to these ghastly images of death that seem to engulf her.

It was through these Ukrainian sources that Janina obtained greatly needed thread from garments that she unraveled. Sewing needles were also a scarce commodity. While warm clothing was a necessity, the Soviets did not provide even their own people with the materials to make life tolerable. After saving a few rubles on her sixty-ruble monthly salary and obtaining with difficulty the necessary permission to buy winter clothing, Janina embarked on a much-anticipated trip to the camp's only store. Much to her amazement, she found only six-hundred-ruble evening dresses for sale, an absurdity that defied comprehension. She left the store laughing in despair.

There was no possibility of arguing against the illogic of the Soviet Communist system. Although Janina worked from seven o'clock in the morning to five o'clock in the afternoon and some-times eight o'clock at night, she was permitted to buy only one and a half pounds of rationed bread each day for herself and for Mira. One pound of bread cost one ruble, leaving her with almost nothing for other necessities such as undergarments and warm clothes. A meal at the camp-operated kitchen—consisting of a tasteless gruel, fish soup, and one spoonful of watery stew—cost six rubles. Soap was in such short supply that Janina was compelled to make her own using ashes from the stove. One time she used too concentrated of a mixture to wash her few remaining under-garments, and the worn cloth disintegrated from the harsh chemicals. When she complained about these conditions, she was told, "You are not a good worker. That is why you make so little."

While the salary was meager, the long wait in line for food was more demoralizing. Mira waited in line in place of Janina one day for over four hours when she heard sugar was available, but by the time Janina arrived, there was no sugar left.

"We only have this hard candy. Do you want it or not?" asked the storekeeper sharply when Janina reached the counter. She hesitated over buying the poor substitute.

"Yes, all right. How much?" she asked in Russian.

"Three rubles."

Janina took the bag of candy and gave a piece to Mira, saying firmly, "Now don't eat these all up at once."

Mira smacked her lips as the candy, which was coated with layers of syrupy sugar and had some indistinguishable flavor, rolled around her tongue. She was delighted by this special treat.

When Janina left for work the next day, Mira devised a plan to make the candy last longer. "If I only lick each piece once and put it back, it will last longer!" she reasoned.

A few days later, Janina reached into the bag and found a sticky mass. "Mira, what's this?" she asked with a reprimanding tone.

"But, Mama, I didn't eat them all!"

Janina could only laugh.

The Longing

In the first year of my father's retirement, when my parents moved away to the farm in Wisconsin, I began my college studies at the University of Illinois at the new campus near downtown Chicago. It was a long commute from the apartment I shared with my sister on the north side along the lake, bordering the northern suburb of Evanston, so I used the time to read and catch up on correspondence. One chilly autumn morning I gathered my mail and tucked it into my briefcase, so that on my return trip home that evening I could read a new letter from my Aunt Monika, my father's youngest sister in Poland. I looked forward to these letters from Poland, which in those days could take as long as a month to reach me. At least by then the Communist censors in Poland did not open every piece of correspondence, which would have delayed things even further. Usually, there was a letter from my grandmother tucked inside.

Settling into a seat on the train, I first examined the intricate artwork of the Polish stamps that I saved for my collection, and then I gently opened the tissue-thin envelope, its red and blue border emblazoned with "par avion." My Polish was not bad, but reading my aunt's stylized handwriting was sometimes difficult, so it usually took me about two or three passes at a paragraph to fully understand the meaning. This time, however, I understood the words right away. "*Babcia zmarła* (Grandma has died)." I had to read it again to make sure there was no mistake in my understanding. I put the letter in my lap and looked around. The train was crowded with people returning home from a long day of work in downtown offices. All the seats were taken, and the aisle was jammed with people hanging onto overhead handrails. The person next to me was busy reading a book. Everyone seemed to be caught up in their own thoughts. The train's wheels droned along the rails, the rhythmic rocking of the car lulling many tired passengers to sleep.

I wanted to cry. I thought I should cry. I was too embarrassed to cry in such a public place. I was eighteen years old and I had never met my grandmother. How could that have happened? All my Polish friends had at one time or another visited their families in Poland. Why hadn't my parents sent me? I wanted to turn the clock back and begin again. This next time, I imagined, I would go to Poland during the summer between high school and college like my friends had done. This next time, I would not have to work during the summer to save up for college tuition. This next time, I too would have adventure stories to tell like my friends. They came back from their trips as if landing on a cloud, their eyes shining from all the love that had been bestowed upon them by grateful relatives, who so appreciated a visit from someone from that great country they all revered, America!

I kept thinking there was some horrible mistake. I had not ever experienced the death of anyone close to me. But then, was I really close to my grandmother? I grew up thinking I was from all the stories my father told me about all the antics he had perpetrated, much to his mother's frustration and amusement. I heard about the strong character she had to have to raise such a brood. The lessons of life he taught me seemed to all come directly from her. In her physical absence, he had created a sense in me that she and my aunts and cousins were really at my side all the time; that our small family of four in America was much larger, as if we could just hop on a bus and meet in an hour.

As I sat holding the letter, I realized that though I had grown up corresponding with my grandmother, aunts and cousins, I had never met them. I vowed that no matter what, I would visit my family in Poland before another one of them passed away, and I would not allow politics or lack of money stop me.

It would be eight years before I saved up enough money on a teacher's salary to take that first trip to Poland. I withdrew the last dollar from our savings account and boarded a plane to London with my husband. I had some vague notion that I might try to follow the path my mother had taken from her birthplace near Warsaw to that far eastern portion of what was no longer Poland but now Belarus, which included the city of Grodno. From London we traveled by rail, visiting my birthplace in Coventry and then heading slowly through France, Switzerland, and Austria. The whole time I was consumed with the thought that I was about to finally visit Poland, the land I had grown up being taught to love, and meet the family I missed so much.

It was 1976, and throughout our European trip we kept receiving news that there was civil unrest in Poland. In Vienna, on the day before our scheduled train ride through Communist Czechoslovakia into Kraków, I was reading an English version of *Time* magazine showing street riots and armed Communist soldiers in various cities in Poland. After almost a year of planning for the trip, I was on the very eve of meeting my family for the first time, and so I could not bring myself to turn back. I thought about all the stories I had heard from my parents of how Communists treated people. I thought about my mother's ordeals in Siberia, about my father's incarceration and near murder in Russia during the war. I thought about the visa application I had to file with the (Communist) Polish embassy in London for permission to enter Poland. The application had asked for the names of all my relatives, about my father. I froze. Could what happened to my parents happen to me as well? It was a concern that seemed to develop a life of its own, and I deliberated for a day before buying those train tickets to Kraków.

On the train, I couldn't sleep and was awake most of the night. The trip took about three times longer than scheduled, as the train inexplicably stopped several times in small towns throughout Communist Czechoslovakia. With each stop, Communist Czech soldiers with submachine guns passed through our first-class compartment demanding passports and visas. One of them, a pudgy man in his forties, leered at me with a drunken smirk, focusing on my blond hair, cropped neatly at my chin, and then he slowly moved his eyes down my body to my legs, which were covered halfway by my denim skirt. I squirmed in my seat and looked over at my husband, who was sound asleep. The soldier spoke to me in Czech and I could understand him, as Polish is similar. He wanted to know why we were going to Poland. I explained in Polish that I was a teacher in America on my first trip to Poland. He grinned at me with glazed-over eyes, and so to divert his attention, I volunteered in as cheerful, naïve voice as I could muster that I was traveling with my husband. He looked at my snoozing husband and reluctantly handed back our documents. After another brief glance at me, he left the compartment. I sighed, but my stomach was in knots and there was no way I was going to fall asleep.

Finally, at about nine o'clock in the morning, we rolled into the train station in Kraków. I had managed in the end to get in a few naps, but I was still very sleepy and craved a good strong cup of coffee, like those I had learned to enjoy in Vienna. I didn't know exactly what my cousins looked like and I wasn't even sure they had received my telegram that we would be arriving on the morning train, which by then was much delayed. Then I saw them. Darek looked exactly like my father, a strong Paul Bunyan type with wide shoulders, a sparkling charismatic smile, blond hair, and eyeglasses similar in design to my father's. Kindness seemed to ooze from him. With her blond hair neatly coiffed and her demure manner, Marysia reminded me of Mira. Both were about the same age, around forty, unmarried, modest, and soft-spoken.

After hugs, tears, and gifts of flowers from them, we gathered our luggage, and I asked if we could get a cup of coffee before proceeding to the family home where more relatives were waiting. Rather hesitantly, Marysia said, "I'll see if they have any," and went off to the kiosk inside the train station. My mouth already tasted the coffee, the medicine I needed to wake up and be able to savor every moment with my family.

"There's no coffee," she said when she returned after a few minutes.

"No coffee?" I asked puzzled and somewhat perturbed. My husband and I looked at each other while Darek explained that there were severe food shortages in Poland and imported goods, coffee in particular, were in short supply. People were rioting because of the shortages.

"Would tea be all right?" Marysia asked hopefully.

The absence of coffee was a small thing, but it was the first of many times during my visit that I was made aware that Poles at the time lacked basic necessities. My aunt prepared a sumptuous first meal for us, which included meat. Four family members sat across from us at the dining room table, encouraging my husband and me to eat but not eating themselves.

"Aren't you eating with us?" I asked.

"Oh, no, we already ate," said my aunt.

I received the same response at several more meals until I finally realized that they did not have enough food for all of us. I later learned that they were having far more simple meals, usually without any meat. They had used up their share of rations in order to feed us.

Even though our family had regularly sent clothing and food packages to Poland for as long as I could remember, I was aware that people in other parts of the world were less fortunate than me. I myself had never experienced a lack of food, had never known hunger, had never been humbled by something so basic and out of my control. I was later to learn that the Communist government deliberately withheld food as a way to control the people during those politically charged times.

I tried to visit my mother's birthplace near Radom, but I was stopped by the entrenched bureaucracy of the Communists who, unbeknownst to me, were trying to subdue violent food strikes taking place there. The unrest eventually spread throughout Poland, leading to Solidarność, the Solidarity movement that years later toppled the Communist government. During my visit, I felt constantly watched and nervous about having to leave my passport at the hotel in Warsaw or having to walk along streets where soldiers marched in groups of three with submachine guns strapped to their backs. I was then suspiciously "interviewed" by a man posing as a taxi driver regarding my father's whereabouts, as he ushered me to sit next to him in the front of the cab, leaving my husband to sit alone in the back seat. I knew the man had to have been connected to the Communists, as he was much too content for those turbulent times and, with his round belly and heavy jowls, clearly much too well fed. He was unusually curious about my family to have just been engaging in polite conversation. He wanted to know if my father was still alive, where he was living, if he was ever going to return to Poland. I laughed in his face, saying, "My father will never return—Poland has changed too much. It's not the same country that he left in 1939." The man nodded in acknowledgment.

That first trip to Poland was short but significant. I could feel Communist oppression like that which my parents described from their wartime ordeals. I could feel the indignation and frustration of the people as I stood in long lines for train tickets or food and was jostled by people pushing forward full-bodied against me, trying not to lose their place after hours of waiting. Since I spoke fluent Polish and dressed modestly, they thought I was one of them and showed little respect for my body space. Everyone was visibly demoralized by the constant struggle to obtain basic goods.

When I returned from that trip, I began to reflect on my life, comparing it to the life I might have lived had I been born and raised in this new Poland and pondering what life might have been like if the War had never happened. I began to realize for the first time that had it not been for that war I never would have been born. So who was I? I grew up thinking that I was Polish, but Poles in Poland viewed me as American, with my accent and distinctly American ways, and Americans viewed me as an immigrant, with my Polish name and customs. I began to feel like a person without a country! Though I was more confused than ever, the longing for knowing Poland and my family there was temporarily quieted.

Undeserved Beauty

By June 1940, the Soviet Union had forcibly annexed Lithuania, and by July, the status of the interned Polish soldiers had been changed to prisoners of war. Lieutenant Solecki and the others were moved by freight train to an old Russian monastery in Kozelsk. Sixty men were crammed into boxcars with small boarded-up windows. For two days, they rode squashed together, sleeping on narrow wooden bunks crudely constructed in haste. When they arrived at their destination, they poured out from the boxcars in sweaty masses, gasping for fresh air and begging for water.

Surrounded by barbed wire, the ancient monastery stood on a wooded hilltop. It had been transformed into a detention center for the purported enemies of Soviet Communism and now served as a prisoner-of-war camp. Within its old, thick brick walls, three or four levels of cots made from rough-sawn boards were stacked upon each other, two-feet wide and five-feet long. Rickety ladder steps led to the narrow top bunks, which could barely support even an average-sized man. These often broke, and the men tumbled down on top of one other.

There were bedbugs everywhere, penetrating everything. At night, these parasites dropped onto the prisoners' faces, into the open mouths of those unfortunate to suffer from a cold and into the ears of those who slept on their sides because they were not able to shift position on the narrow cots. "A bedbug lodged itself in my ear and could only be removed with several washings," Lieutenant Solecki complained. The conditions at the camp were horrendous. The prisoners were given little food or protection from the harsh weather.

"On a wooden board at the latrine were mysterious engravings in Polish from former prisoners. They read, '150 sent to an unknown place today,' '200 sent,' 'the last 150 sent,' '15 May 1940.'

We wondered what it all had meant," he said. Many years later, it was verified that the officers had been taken from the camp to the Katyń Forest and executed by the Soviets. Lieutenant Solecki had narrowly escaped the same fate when he arrived shortly after the majority of the killings had occurred and he was assigned to hard labor elsewhere.

In 1943, Polish investigators concluded that thousands of missing Polish officers had been murdered by the Russian Communists in the Katyń Forest and then buried in a mass grave. Although it was the Germans who first found the graves, for decades the Soviets accused the Germans of the massacre. In the early 1990s, with the fall Communism in the Soviet Union, it was confirmed, along with Russian admission, that the Soviets had indeed committed the crime.

One Polish officer in Kozelsk spoke fluent Russian and liked to engage a Russian peasant man who washed their latrine. The man commented, "Yes, comrades, there were 'gentlemen' here before the Communists took over, and we were poor. Now, there are no more gentlemen, but we are still poor! I eat only bread for breakfast, and my life is no better than before."

By the first day of June 1940, Janina had gathered seven hundred bundles of fresh twigs to feed her goat. She hid the precious supply in the small loft above her barrack compartment and warned Mira not to allow the other children to play there. One day, however, despite Mira's efforts to keep the older children from invading the space, they proceeded to explore the inviting loft.

"Mama, I watched the children climb the ladder, and I didn't know what to do. When one of them was almost in the loft, I yelled, 'Don't go there—there's a ghost up there!'" Mira laughed.

"But one of the boys looked down at me and kept going up the ladder, so another girl said, 'Let's pray to scare the ghost away.'" Mira and the other children gathered into a circle and she pretended to be frightened. Distracted with thinking how to keep the children from the loft, she repeated the prayer one or two words behind the others. The children stopped praying and listened, and when they resumed, Mira fell behind once again.

"The ghost!" screamed a girl. "He's coming after us," added Mira, as they scattered out of the barrack. They never tried to climb up into the loft again and Mira enjoyed proudly telling the story often.

Springtime brought great relief to the deportees in the labor camp. Heavy tattered coats and boots were no longer needed. Extended daylight meant that more work was required, but it also allowed time to secure other food. Bright greenery burst out from among the drab grayish-brown masses of decaying vegetation exposed by melting snow. Mira ran with the other children into the tall grasses of the small meadows interspersed throughout the forest to pick sorrel grass, which made a tasty sour soup. Leeks were poking out from the ground and the air was filled with the newness of life awakening from a long cold winter.

Janina searched for ways to supplement their meager food rations. For a little more than half a ruble, she could buy a packet of poor quality smoking tobacco, called *maxopka* in Russian, which she later exchanged for potatoes. Even at low prices, the tobacco was a rationed good and like everything else, the workers needed permission to purchase it. For one packet, she could buy a brimming bucket of potatoes from a distant farming village. The same twenty-five-pound quantity cost twenty-five rubles at the heavily controlled collective farm, or the equivalent of about a two-week's salary.

One night after work, when she had collected enough tobacco for three buckets of potatoes, Janina set out on the thirteen-mile trip to one of the villages. Darkness came quickly as she stepped over moist branches and damp soil along the forest path. She began her long journey back to the camp late at night with the valuable load of potatoes packed into one large burlap sack. Heaving the sixty or seventy pounds onto her back, she balanced it by carrying it bent over at the waist. The sack seemed heavier with each step along the worn trail, so she dragged it along the uneven surface, stopping often to rest. The journey home would take several hours longer than the four-hour walk to the village.

Near the halfway point in the thick forest stood an abandoned grain mill where Janina stopped for a rest. It was a quiet moonlit night, so she laid down her cargo and sat next to it. She closed her eyes and listened to the sounds of the forest. A soft breeze swayed the tops of tall thin pines that grew so closely together that they created a thick wall. The wavelike rustling of pine needles against each other in the breeze sounded like melodic whispers of a distant choir. An owl hooted its warnings, while crickets chirped and mud frogs bellowed their throaty calls from a nearby riverbed, all forming a strange mating symphony. A distant bird, startled in the night, perhaps losing its hold on a perch and confused by the brightness of the full moon, began an abbreviated song in anticipation of morning. The peacefulness of the forest reminded Janina of similar trips near her farm on weekly excursions into Grodno or to a nearby resort town during the raspberry harvest in order to sell her crop.

Janina closed her eyes trying to recollect those happier times. She began to dream about Mira playing with the dogs among the large yellow dahlias, red and white roses in the front garden, and the tall poplar trees along the road. Figa would jump around Mira, especially when Mira snuck her cheese blintzes from her dinner. Life had seemed endlessly peaceful back then.

Janina could have easily gone to sleep in the lulling quiet of the warm, still night after her long day's work, but suddenly a thumping sound from the direction of the nearby bridge startled her into a sitting position. The brightness of the moon was obscured by shadows of something large and treelike, only ten feet in front of her. She looked up at two enormous moose, whose antlers extended like giant parasols at least five feet across, supported by massive shoulders. They stomped their heavy hooves against the wooden planks of the bridge, grunting loudly and butting each other, during this peak mating season. In the distraction of their territorial dispute, they had not sensed her presence, and she sat frozen and awed by their beauty, enjoying the fierce display, strangely unafraid. When the weaker moose finally ran off, Janina gathered her sack of potatoes and walked swiftly away down the path to the camp.

Janina returned at the resonating sound of the morning gong at nine o'clock, twelve hours after having left the village. She dragged the sack of potatoes under her bed and sat down upon the hardened straw mattress. It was Sunday; she was not working during the day, as that week her shift was at night. Mira was anxiously waiting for her to cook the potato treats. Janina smiled at Mira, gently stroking her hair, happy that she could provide something more nourishing for her thin child. After a quick wash in some cool water, Janina sat down beside Mira on the bed and peeled several large potatoes that had shriveled somewhat from the harvest the previous autumn. The anticipation of the meal and the peeling were just enough to keep Janina from falling asleep. Her elation spurred her on to sing a favorite song.

> When will I return your way,
> Where the pines, oaks, and maples grow,
> Where the white birch scatters its leaves upon your stream?
> Listen to the blustery tempest after the sunset,
> Which flies like the leaves of the autumn wind,
> And within the fragrance of meadows, orchards, and fields,
> Runs my mysterious, hidden pain.

The weather of the spring season enhanced Janina's singing voice. She could not remember the last time she sang so well, and many requests for her singing followed during the following short weeks of summer.

The work in the forest ended temporarily, and Janina was transferred to a different site where the night shift work was to dig a tunnel to the Kama River through a rocky mountain. In the dimly lit piles of rock, she pounded away with her axe and spade, loading small wagons full of rock that were then rolled along narrow tracks. The workers were paid for each load, but a full load was determined by the fickleness of the Belarusian or Russian gang leaders. If Janina was fortunate, the wagons only had to be filled to the top in order to pass inspection. If she was not so lucky, the wagons had to be filled in rounded heaps above the sides, which meant that the rocks would fall out as the wagons bumped along the uneven tracks.

Thousands of small black flies descended on the women's bare skin, entering easily under their loose skirts. They gnawed at the soft flesh of the women's thighs and genitals. Janina did not have a pair of pants, and so she danced in place to escape the brutal pincers of the flies as she chipped away at the solid rock. The short summer seemed to heighten the aggressiveness of all creatures that came alive. Mosquitoes were equally obnoxious. In seconds, they covered her arms and face in voracious layers. She swatted wildly at them to no avail.

As summer continued, the twigs to feed the goat dwindled and Janina used the opportunity of her nightly work excursions to sneak up to the commandant's camp and steal hay from the well-stocked shed. She hid the bundles in the loft as before and implored Mira to keep the other children away while she slept during the day.

On one warm evening, Janina crept away from the shed with an armload of hay. In the heavy night air, she heard a man's cough, and in the faint moonlight she saw an NKVD officer looking her way. Stopping in anticipation of his approach, she wavered in her decision to drop the hay and run or hope for a pardon, as this was her first encounter with the young man. Slowly, he turned away as if to light a cigarette and waited for her to escape. Janina was baffled by the incident and concluded that even among such ruthless captors, compassion was still alive.

On the other hand, the Belarusian Nikolay Zorko, supervisor of Janina's barrack, was another kind of human being. He maligned his Polish charges at every turn. Belarusians tried to win the favor of the Communist leaders with their ability to make the workers conform to strict regulations. He particularly enjoyed harassing Janina, who demonstrated her rejection of Communist ideology by stubbornly refusing to refrain from singing Polish patriotic songs.

One day, as she passed his compartment on the way from the well, he deliberately stood in her way and then tugged at her shoulder, which caused her to spill some water from her bucket.

"Look what you did," he said. "Wipe this up or I'll report you to the camp commandant." Janina looked at him with a blank stare and continued to her compartment. She knew she could be severely punished if she didn't do as he said, but to avoid his sneering glance, she returned with her much-used rag to wipe up the spill only after he had gone.

Zorko relished in initiating political discussions with the few Belarusian families that were at the camp about their views of the inadequacy of the Polish government. Speaking loudly in full view of the Polish workers, he taunted them, inciting them to betray their patriotic spirit and to join in what could prove to be an incriminating discussion around the stove, along with the other families. Janina, along with most of the Poles knew the purpose of this ritual, but she staunchly displayed her patriotism, commenting, "Long live Poland" and then bursting into song: "As long as in our hearts there is one drop of Polish blood . . . the Polish people will prevail."

"In Russian! In Russian!" Zorko chastised her as he pretended not to understand her Polish.

By attempting to indoctrinate the masses of Polish workers, especially the children, these Belarusians sought to impress the Communists who were in a position to promote them to better conditions. Ironically, as volunteers, they complained about their conditions in the camp.

"Why aren't you satisfied?" Janina asked, toying with Zorko. "After all, you are in *your* own country now!" She spoke with a twinkle in her eye, emphasizing the word, "your," knowing well that Zorko was also displaced from his homeland. Then she teased, "I am happy here. Why aren't you?"

Zorko stared at her with piercing eyes and, without saying another word, rose from his chair and returned to his compartment.

The following day, Zorko's wife spoke to a friend of Janina's, telling her that her husband planned to report Janina for stealing hay, something he may have discovered while snooping around her compartment. The friend rushed to Janina's compartment.

"My dear, you must try to get away. You will be arrested for certain. Here are ten rubles to help you on your journey."

She spoke anxiously as she tried to make Janina take the money. Janina stared at the money in the woman's hand and, closing her fingers around it, said, "I could not escape. Where would I go, so far away from my own people? And what of my daughter? I could not leave her here to be sent to one of those Soviet orphanages, never to see her again. Thank you from my heart. You are too kind, but I cannot take your last money. You have four children of your own to feed."

Unbeknownst to Janina, the Soviets knew what to think about ingratiating stooges like Zorko. They were more interested in reaching the work quota. She waited fearfully, ready to be summoned about the incident. After several days, she assumed the matter had passed and returned to her patriotic songs, ignoring any threat of further reprisals on Zorko's part.

The incident, however, did not go unnoticed. Five weeks later, Mira came screaming to Janina on the road as she returned from work. Tears streamed down her pale cheeks and through hysterical sobs, she blurted out a few words at a time.

"Mama . . . they're going to arrest you! They found . . . the hay . . . the hay in the loft!" she gasped.

Janina dropped the heavy axe and knelt down to hug Mira. "Don't cry. They won't arrest me," she said trying to sound reassuring.

"No," protested Mira. "Four of them, two . . . two NKVD officers and the camp commandant with the prosecutor are there now!"

Mira had stolen small amounts of hay herself and was worried that the soldiers had come to arrest Janina because of that. Janina took Mira by the hand and led her back to the barrack. As she approached their compartment, she realized that it was too late to attempt to hide her "crime." The men were still examining the compartment when she got there. The small pile of hay was fully visible.

"Do you see any hay?" asked the commandant of the NKVD officer.

"No, it must be in another place," he replied. With an abrupt turn on his heel, he left with the other three men, completely ignoring Janina's presence.

Janina did not know what to make of their pretending not to see the hay, and so the following nights were sleepless for her. One night, so not to awaken Mira, she lay as still as possible on the narrow cot, sometimes imagining being dead. In this forced immobility, all sensation departed from her legs and arms, breathing became laborious, and she suffered from a headache. Her thoughts bounced between visions of gulag prisons for herself and the Communist-indoctrinating orphanages Mira would surely endure. She moved her now stiffened body to the side, hoping to erase the memory, but her fantasy became more real with each recurring thought, as if she were possessed by it. In the dim morning hours, her sleep-deprived body finally succumbed, just in time to rise for the day's work.

After several days of worry, Janina stopped wondering why she had not been summoned for her hay stealing. "I can't think anymore," she moaned. That night, turning over on her side on the cot, she said, "Let the world fall apart" and covered her head with the worn woolen blanket.

Janina came to understand her value as a capable worker in the Communist system. While the Belarusians were concerned with petty grievances, the commanding Communists were trying to maintain rigid production schedules with every able-bodied person. Maximum work for minimum investment in food and shelter was their goal, and small infractions of the rules did not warrant arrest and loss of valuable labor. Janina sensed she and Mira would be safe, at least for a while.

Homeland

In 1992, I returned to Poland, after the fall of Communism in 1989, and finally traveled to my mother's birthplace. I followed the path that she described from the tiny village of Kaszewo, where she was born, to Radom, where she had moved at the start of World War I. I tried to imagine her life along the way. I didn't find the house that her father had built, but there were plenty of other similar ones. I brought along my young son of ten. I tried to instill in him the patriotism that I had learned and the appreciation of Poland's newly found freedom from Communism. I was as excited as I had been on that first trip with my husband.

My cousin had grown more gray hairs but was still as kind and generous as I remembered him. He guided us throughout our trip, first to the coal mines where he had worked as a mining engineer, then to the church in Warsaw where a popular young activist priest, Jerzy Popiełuszko, was buried. He had been murdered in 1984 by agents of the security services (Communists as far as our family was concerned) during the Solidarity strikes in the early 1980s. The struggle of extreme food shortages, the interrogations, and the humiliation my cousin had to endure for his work with the Solidarity movement to topple the Communist-led regime of the Polish People's Republic (PRL), as Poland became known after World War II, had not dampened his deep devotion to God and country.

Believing that my father would finally feel safe from any Communists' reprisals against him from the war years and that he would want to return to Poland, I had asked him to accompany me on that trip, but he declined. "Maybe, someday. Maybe when Mother is well," he said hopefully. I sensed that my father was avoiding the difficult task of a trip to Poland. After all my parents' pronouncements of their desire to see Poland again, I had always thought that given the chance my father at least would visit Poland, but he was just as reluctant to go in 1992 as he had been when I had proposed he accompany me on my first trip.

It had been sixteen years, and I was shocked by all the changes brought on by a renewed sense of freedom that I witnessed. No longer did I feel the need to look over my shoulder. There were plenty of goods everywhere. The shopkeepers were friendly and eager to help, not like in 1976 when people trudged uninspired and hopeless through their difficult daily lives under the watchful eye of Communist Party neighbors and officials. This time there was a sense of prosperity, and it felt much like America and Western Europe. I was delighted by all the activity.

After I returned and told my father how things were in Poland, I realized that such a journey would have been emotionally devastating for him, especially at his age. He was eighty-eight years old by then. I showed him new photographs of his boyhood haunts, and he was astounded by how much they had changed. I told him how different Poland was now than it was in 1976, with its Coca Cola advertisements everywhere and the McDonald's built into an old cavernous cellar in Kraków. He only nodded. I sensed his sadness, but I understood that he was not eager to embark on a trip there any longer.

Fleeting Summer Breezes
and Conspiracies

Janina's newfound sense of security as a valuable worker in the Soviet Communist system was soon shaken by further interrogations by the NKVD. One day, she was summoned to a formal hearing in a village far from the camp.

The NKVD officer in charge approached her. "Are you a spiritual person?" he inquired in an unusually soft voice as if he wanted to befriend her. She stared at him, tired and bewildered by the question. After a moment, she shrugged her shoulders and said slowly, "Yes, I am!"

He narrowed his eyes, looked into her face and suddenly barked, "Are you the pope's priest?"

"No!" Janina replied.

"But, you read prayers on Sunday evenings to the rest of your people in the barrack," he continued angrily.

Janina stood still without answering while three other NKVD soldiers glared at her. Tired after her full day's work and the four-mile trek to the interrogation site, the pettiness of these personal questions angered her. Children went hungry and workers collapsed daily from the bitter cold and exhaustion, and so she had no patience for these soldiers with their contrived seriousness, for these small-minded men probing into the trivialities of people's lives.

Let them do what they want with me, she thought. She leaned over, almost falling. Her body was ready to crumble from its load of tired muscles and jangled nerves. Random thoughts unrelated to the precariousness of her immediate situation began to fill her mind. Danger seemed distant. Ready to be condemned for the slightest offense, Janina closed her eyes, oblivious to her plight. If only they would let me get some sleep, some food, she thought, staring blankly at the officer. Anything can happen now. Mira? Where is she? My child. My poor child. . . . She leaned over to the other side trying to balance her body. What are they waiting for? Why don't they do with me what they summoned me for? Oh, I don't care anymore. With that last thought, she startled herself, unsure if she had actually spoken those words or only thought them.

"Do you believe in God?" she heard in the muted distance of her consciousness. The NKVD officer had raised his voice, but to Janina the sound was buried in the numbing silence of her mind.

"Do you believe in God?" he repeated loudly.

She deliberately widened her eyes, took a deep slow breath, and looked at him. Then angrily, she snapped, "Yes, I believe in God and you can cut me up into little pieces, but I will not betray God!"

Stunned, the officer backed off and quickly said, "No one is going to cut you up." His poor attempt to sound reassuring made him sound hypocritical, and she challenged him with her glare. Following a short pause, he continued, "All right, all right. What about this other woman? Is she the chaplain?"

"No, we all take turns leading prayers. There is no priest among us," snapped Janina.

Standing up from his desk, the officer looked down at his documents and began shuffling around. Janina followed his movements in the dimly lit barrack office. Their eyes eventually riveted on each other as if competing for sincerity. Janina stared at him without blinking as she heard the distant midnight gong of the camp bell. She had now been interrogated for four hours.

"You can go," he said as he averted his eyes. Janina sighed under her breath.

Although exhausted from the ordeal, she fumed the entire way back to camp. "How dare they question me so about my beliefs! Those scoundrels, those atheists!" she shouted, not caring who might hear her. Her anger seemed to propel her to new levels of energy, and before she realized it, she had reached the camp.

Mira had been patiently waiting for Janina to return, but sleep overtook her and she lay curled up on the cot in her clothes. When

Janina returned, Mira jumped into her arms and began sobbing. They sat that way for several minutes until Janina managed to loosen Mira's tight hold around her waist. "Let's go to sleep," she said. Mira nodded and fell back onto the cot.

Following the interrogation incident, Janina became more cautious about her actions and what she said to people, but everyone's mood seemed to lighten as the warmth of that first summer took hold. Summers were short and hot in the remote Russian forests shadowed by the Ural Mountains. During the two summer months, all greenery seemed to blossom overnight. Oats, potatoes, and vegetables planted in the surrounding collective farms grew and matured within days. As an experienced farmer, Janina was awestruck by such rapid development, which she observed during her daily trek to work at the edge of the Kama River. They had finished the work of loading the rocks for the tunnel and now were assigned new work.

Immense volumes of water overflowed the Kama, which resembled a sea more than a river. Janina stood at the bank looking for the distant opposite shore but could not see it. Trees that had been felled during winter and cut into huge logs were now being moved to the river's edge. These massive sixteen- to twenty-foot logs were attached with large chains to horses that pulled them to the water. Women walked alongside the workhorses and guided them with long leads over terrain that was bumpy from bushes and rocks. Though the work was not physically difficult, it was dangerous. The long logs slid from side to side in unpredictable, sweeping arcs as they moved over the wet soil. The women often fell and barely had time to regain their balance before a new log would come sliding toward them. One day, a friend of Janina's was hit by a log and killed instantly. The official death notice the woman's husband received described the cause of death as heart attack.

On a bright cool day, Janina stood waist high in the fast-moving waters of the river, pushing the huge logs with a long iron hooked rod and trying to stay out of the logs' way. The water that day was unusually fast flowing and the logs seemed to find their own unpredictable path. Her rubber waders were full of holes and quickly filled with freezing water. The rippling of the water was so loud that it was impossible to hear voices. Tensions rose among the workers as they struggled to keep the logs moving and away from themselves. Although only men were supposed to be assigned to this work, the Soviets often disobeyed their own rules in the face of expediency, and the workers had no recourse.

The river water never completely warmed as summer continued, and Janina developed a bladder infection from being constantly immersed in it. The infection was so bad that she could not control her bladder or keep her undergarments clean for even an hour. She sought medical attention at the hospital in the small town nearby because the pain was so severe, but the woman doctor there did not give her any medicine and sent her back to work the next day. Eventually, the infection subsided, but not before she spent many hours coping with debilitating pain and discomfort, and the condition returned with her immersion in the slightest cool water.

By the end of summer, Janina became so demoralized by her continually bothersome infection, the freezing water, and the dangerous work at the river that she began to feel as if she were losing her mind. To escape this misery, she succumbed to an oblivious, captive state of mind, resigned to her plight. "I felt brainwashed," she would say of herself in later years.

It was only during brief discussions with a young Russian Communist woman of about nineteen who had been assigned to work with her that Janina awoke from her stupor. She had little patience for the political ranting of this idealistic young woman who tried to engage her in debate every day.

"Warsaw is a Russian city, you know," the young woman said proudly one day in Russian as she pushed a log. This was the final breaking point for Janina, and she reared up her head, not caring whether or not a log knocked her over. Through clenched teeth she shrieked at the impudent youth, "*Warszawa* is the capital of Poland and it has been that way for centuries and before that it was Kraków!" Janina deliberately responded in Polish. Her voice trailed off as she exhaled the last of a long breath.

The young woman stopped her work. Gasping for a breath, Janina continued her tirade in Russian. "What pig's garbage did they teach you in your schools?" Infuriated, the woman picked up her long, sharp, iron rod and swung it at Janina, aiming for her head. The rod missed Janina's head when she ducked. "How dare you lie to me!" shouted the woman, astounded that Janina would question her knowledge. The intensity of the woman's swing and the weight of the heavy rod threw her off balance, and she fell over into the water.

Janina became suddenly quiet. She wanted to laugh but stopped herself and examined the young face whose innocence was lost in anger. She stood motionless; she could not believe that so young a person would attempt to kill her over a few words. The woman had been so indoctrinated that she never questioned her Communist authorities. Janina shook her head, unable to think of anything more to say as the woman glared back at her and emerged from the river completely soaked. Confident that she had made an impression, Janina walked away.

Soon afterward, the work at the river was completed. With the rapidly approaching cold of autumn, the workers reluctantly prepared to return to the timber operations. Janina saved enough money from her meager salary and the sale of her few remaining possessions to buy a new pair of much needed woolen boots. The Communist officials claimed that they were "giving" these necessary items to the workers for fifty-seven rubles, the equivalent of about one month's salary, and Janina was given permission to purchase one pair.

On a cold morning wearing her new boots, Janina set out for work without her jacket when she noticed some approaching dark clouds. Without adequate protection, she was certain to become soaked, courting illness she could not afford, so she risked being late for work and returned to the barrack for her jacket. When she arrived at her work destination, the work gang leader shouted, "Fifteen minutes late, Zimmerman," and noted her tardiness in his papers.

In the meantime, Janina's supply of saleable goods was dwindling, and acquiring extra food was becoming more difficult as winter set in once again. A nearby farmer was giving one bucket for every twenty buckets of potatoes dug out from his field. That night, Janina set out to the farm after work, telling Mira not to worry if she did not return soon. She dug potatoes until midnight. Moving the packed dirt off the mounds of potato plants was backbreaking work. Every night she earned several buckets of potatoes, of which she brought back two buckets. Together with her friend she would eat one entire bucket while digging, without cooking the delicacy. At the end of three weeks, the farmer loaned her a horse and wagon to pull her share of the crop to camp, which she hid under her cot. Only when the last of the potatoes was safely hidden did she notice her exhaustion. Every night she had walked nine miles to the farm, returning in time to catch only three or four hours of sleep before the next work day. Having had no time to change her clothes, she noticed their stiffness from dirt and sweat as she took them off for the first time in three weeks.

Following her success with the potatoes, Janina set out to acquire a little meat or fat to add some flavor to their meals. The bilberry season was just beginning, and so after she left work, she went off to pick the wild berries in the forest so that she could sell them in a distant village. In two days, she picked enough berries to fill two large buckets, which she hung from wires attached to a wooden branch laid across her shoulders. The walk through the dense birch, oak, and pine forest was lonely and tiring, but she carried the precious crop all night. At the outskirts of the village, she laid down for a short rest and waited for the market to open. With the money from the sale, Janina bought some smoked pork fat. That evening, she decided to prepare potatoes with it, much to Mira's delight. Janina stirred the large pot with a stained, battered wooden spoon and brought the hot liquid to her lips for a taste. The only light in the dark barrack was her makeshift lamp of a tall bottle of naphtha in which she hung a cotton string. As she began to sip the hot liquid, she noticed an unrecognizable long, thick, white shape floating in the spoon. It was the larva of some insect. Startled, Janina threw the spoon back into the pot. As she brought the lamp over the pot, she saw at least a dozen of these creatures floating on the surface of greasy soup. Janina swallowed hard, feeling cheated and saddened for Mira who was anticipating a good meal. She resisted making a contorted face and half-jokingly said, "Oh well, they are protein too!" as she served the sumptuous concoction, which they both ate.

Janina had nearly forgotten about the tardiness incident. She had watched the gang leader make his notation that day but had dismissed it. As the first snowfalls gathered in thick layers on the freezing ground, Janina received a summons for her "crime" of tardiness. As the day of the trial approached, she prepared herself for the two-day journey to court. She obtained a release from work and arranged to stay at the collective farm of a Russian woman she had met while digging potatoes.

Winter wrapped the Russian forest and plains in an icy blanket once again. Several layers of hardened snow already covered most of the bushes and other landmarks along the road to the court. The main road looked like another barren stretch of meadow between engulfing dense forests. Except for the thin dark telephone wires dangling from wide-set posts, there was no other sign of civilization. As she walked, Janina never let her gaze stray for too long from those precious landmarks. Against the whiteness of the falling snow, the swaying dark lines were becoming obscured, and she feared she would lose her way, freeze to death, or be devoured by wolves. The only sound was the hard-packed snow that crunched under her weight. New snow obscured any tracks left by previous travelers, and she did not see or hear any form of life at all the first day of her journey. It was only the tenuous security of the wires that comforted her and kept her on course.

As night approached, distant howls of wolves broke the deafening silence in the snow-insulated land. Janina spotted one pinpoint of light from a collective farm, and she quickened her pace in rhythm to the wolves' songs. The farmhouse appeared deserted, but a solitary light shone from a room deep within its wooden walls. After she knocked loudly several times, the door finally opened slowly, and a tall old man with a gray beard and long disheveled gray hair stood in the doorway. Background light glowed around his head, and he looked like one of the saints with flowing robes whose picture Janina had kept in her Bible as a child. With a thin arm, he motioned the way into his house. Without speaking, he pointed to a small cot. Janina entered cautiously, inspecting the room.

"Where is the mistress of the house?" she asked in Russian.

The old man pretended not to hear her and returned to his place before a small elaborately decorated altar where several burning oil lamps surrounded an icon of the Blessed Virgin. He stood before it, bowing from the waist several times and folding his palms together. He appeared to be deep in prayer. After several minutes, he glanced at Janina without turning his body. Then he reached for a large unpeeled potato lying in a wooden bowl on the floor and handed it to her. The potato was cooked and most likely intended for pig feed, but having had no food since leaving the camp at dawn, Janina devoured it. The man returned to his bowing and praying, and in a few minutes, he reached for another potato. Again without speaking, he gave it to Janina. She took it gratefully and ate quickly, stuffing her cheeks like a chipmunk.

When the old man finished his prayers, he sat down next to Janina on the cot and stared at her. After a while, he asked, "Would you like to stay here and keep house for me?"

Janina was taken aback.

"I make good money repairing woolen boots," he continued in Russian.

Janina smiled and said, "I am not free to do as I wish with myself. I am what your people call a *neblagonadezhna*, a person unworthy of trust, and I am on my way to court. Who knows what awaits me there. The NKVD would never allow me to stay here, but thank you for the offer," she answered in her best Russian.

In a few moments, a woman entered the room carrying a large pot of soup whose aromatic broth filled the small room. She set the heavy pot on the wooden table and began scooping out thick noodles and potatoes flecked with small pieces of meat. Then she cut ample slices from a large loaf of rye bread and invited Janina to begin eating. Politely, Janina ate pretending to be ravenous in order to hide the man's earlier secret gift of potatoes. For the first time in months, Janina felt completely full and grateful for the kindness of these Russians. She soon fell into peaceful sleep on a hay-filled mattress that had been laid out for her on the floor of the cramped house.

In the morning, she awoke to the delicious aroma of fresh warm tea and toasted rye bread. Refreshed and supplied with directions to the court, she continued her journey along the same road with the isolated telephone lines. Only the blinding mono-chromatic whiteness of fresh snow greeted Janina the second day. Near her final destination, she found the collective farm where she would spend the night before her trial the next morning. The two meals at the first farm were a blessing, for the dedicated Communist Party people at the second farm did not even offer her any hot water to drink.

The next day, as she made her way to the court, Janina tried to predict her likely punishment. The most obvious one would be a loss of salary. She wondered how she would be able to feed herself and Mira on her already low income. She approached the magistrate in the barren room of the makeshift court chambers.

"Are you a *peresedlanka* (transferred person)?" asked the woman judge.

Janina thought for a moment and reluctantly answered simply "yes," leaving it at that out of fear of angering the judge with any added comments. A transferred person had no rights and the judge could do anything with her as she pleased. Quickly and as politely as possible, Janina described the circumstances of the tardiness incident as the judge listened with obvious disinterest. Without another word, the judge ordered a 25 percent reduction in Janina's salary for the following three months. Janina watched the judge write the order down in her documents, but the thought of protesting did not enter her tired mind.

Terms of Endearment

My father and I were sitting alone at the dining room table one summer day at the farm a few years after he and my mother had retired there. I was somewhere in my twenties and on a summer break from my teaching job. My mother was in Chicago visiting my sister. I was thrilled that for once I had my father all to myself. We sat in unusual silence after our lunch of whole buckwheat kasha and buttermilk, a favorite of my father's that I had prepared for him. It was a hot day, and a floor fan whirred by the open door to the front porch blowing in warm air from the garden. I tried to ignore how clammy I felt; I wished I could jump into the secluded pond in the back field, but the thought of leeches and snakes dampened my desire, so I just sat still trying not to sweat. I was thinking about how comfortably different it felt being there without my mother.

Whenever my mother was around, the family conversation mostly revolved around what she wanted to talk about—the gossipy antics of a neighbor or friend, with her usual criticisms, sometimes things they'd done years earlier, or something she thought we should be doing, or the war years, whether the First World War or the Second. Sometimes I was confused by which war she was talking about. My father never liked the gossip and usually told her that it was not polite to say unflattering things about others or that it really was none of her business. Most times, she would stop gossiping after he said that, but without a suitable substitute the conversation would then end in an uncomfortable silence. At that point, my father would get up from the dining room table, gather his empty plate, and cheerfully say, "OK, I need to get back." Get back to work in the barn or the field or the garden, that is. He did that a lot, much to my disappointment.

My father and I continued to sit together in silence. I wanted to share so much with him—my plans for the upcoming school year as I prepared my biology lessons for my students, vacation plans to go camping in northern Wisconsin with my husband, the ongoing struggles of relatives in Communist Poland, and his favorite topic—his ever-expanding vegetable garden and the antics of his favorite milking cow. He was such a good conversationalist and always had amusing things to say. He understood me and asked me poignant questions that I enjoyed answering as I lost myself in the creative moment, free to speak my mind, for I knew he would never say anything critical of me.

This time, however, he seemed particularly quiet and sad.

"I don't know what to do about Mother," he began.

I braced myself, not knowing what to think. It was unusual for him to admit that anything could be amiss with my mother. It seemed that my parents had adjusted to each other's peculiar ways and tolerated each other by then.

"We had this awful argument," he continued.

Now I was starting to worry, thinking he would be telling me that he wanted to divorce my mother. I don't recall the subject of their argument, only that my mother had gotten so drunk that she ended up falling over into a pile of hay in the barn when she followed him there after the argument. Afterward, she had fallen asleep in the hay until dawn. It sounded comical, though I didn't laugh. I could not imagine my mother ever being drunk.

On rare occasions, usually celebratory, I had seen my mother sip sweet homemade honey liquor or some watered-down brandy. She always criticized those who drank and especially their neighbors, an older couple who managed to squander away several inherited farm estates through their daily trips to local taverns. They had sold the farm to my parents in the hopes that my parents would default on the payments so that they could again reap the benefits from another sale. At least that's how my parents interpreted their neighbor's proposal to "not worry about the payments," but my parents paid off the loan in just five years. In a short time, the man died and the wife became destitute.

My mother's attitude toward alcohol was one of extreme aversion. Alcohol was a major reason for her early separation from Mira's father. The effects of Mira's father's alcoholism played a role in our lives more significant than I would ever have imagined it would—it was the cause of my mother's staunch intolerance of those who drank ("stupid drunks" she called them)—so it was surprising that she could justify taking a drink or two herself. Despite what my sister knew about her father, she would often try to defend him and would refer to him using terms of endearment. My father, by contrast, only drank alcohol in company, never alone. I came to appreciate the differences in our experiences with such different fathers, and I felt sad for Mira.

My father and I continued to sit in silence that made me uncomfortable following his surprising story about my mother. "Strange woman," he added as he stared at the floor and as I tried to think of something encouraging to say. I realized then that his escape was his work on the farm that left him tired and exhausted with little time to consider the past or his new life with my mother, who seemed to be completely enthralled with country life. And then, just as he had done so often, he got up suddenly from his chair, said thank you (for the meal) and headed to the garden.

The Human Commodity Market

That second winter in the camp, Mira stood by a small window in their barrack and watched a torrent of wet snow falling on the frozen land. Icy flakes pounded down and covered the dark ground with layer upon layer of crystalline whiteness. It would soon be one year since they had been imprisoned. Mira watched the melting snow run along the wavy glass of the window. It had been a long year, that year of 1940. Her sixth birthday had passed without Janina barely even noticing. St. Nicholas Day had also passed without any gifts.

"I never had anything to give her," Janina lamented years later.

Mira threw on her coat and ran outside to play in the snow with some of the older children as Janina prepared for work. It would be another lonely day.

"I got used to it," she would say. "That's how it had to be. Mother had to go to work."

Far away from the camp at the job site, Janina gasped in awe at the beauty of the forest as mountains of snow piled gently upon the landscape, creating a deceptively soft appearance on the needles of towering pines. She marveled at nature, both enticing and deadly, trying to reconcile such beauty with the land that imprisoned her. Janina was growing weaker and tired more easily. Time passed slowly in the monotony of the hard work, and life had stabilized into a peculiar norm of lowered expectations and an unrelenting, frustrating contest for food and clothing. It was easier just not to think at all.

As if by command, the sky cleared and the snow stopped falling. The earth's new white blanket glistened in the sun's fleeting rays with a teasing radiance. This small turn of nature brought great joy to Janina as she bent over some branches of a newly fallen birch tree. With its century's old virgin trees, the forest lay before her in a tangled web of rubble. Tree trunks were so large that hundreds of years might have passed before their hard wood would begin to decompose. These immense fallen logs lay on top of larger ones intertwined with smaller branches and dried leaves. The entanglement provided a cave-like refuge for wildlife from the gripping frost of winter, while the remaining gaps in the forest floor invited new life to flourish. Creatures of different sizes scurried about trying to escape the constant plunge of saws, axes, and tractors, and Janina delighted in seeing such life disturbed from its winter hibernation.

Standing in the rubble of some huge branches of other fallen trees, Janina watched two men saw a four-foot-wide tree trunk. The unfortunate old birch's monumental life was about to come to an end. She closed her eyes; sheer exhaustion engulfed her, and the muscles of her neck and shoulders loosened their hold. She fell into a trance as images of days long gone in her native farm woods flashed through her mind. She was startled when she felt herself lose balance as she leaned against her axe, but she kept her eyes closed and listened to the workers talking and moving around the tangled branches. Their words sounded muted, as if spoken in a distant chamber, unintelligible in her meditative state. In the distance, she heard a loud creaking sound, but she resisted the temptation to open her tired eyes. A hushed silence prevailed and curiosity overcame her. Forcing her eyes open, she stared ahead and watched the last of the saw men stepping away from their massive conquest. The tree stood teetering slightly as a gentle breeze came up several hundred feet above. Janina stood still, awed by its immense size as it swayed and tilted in her direction. She stood staring up at the tree moving closer and closer to her, watching the crown falling from the crystal clear sky.

"Move! Get out of there!" someone screamed.

"The tree! See the tree!"

Janina now saw her precarious position, but she could not move. Her legs were paralyzed, unfeeling stumps like those of the massacred trees around her.

The shouting continued, but she stood firmly. At the last moment, without thinking, Janina jumped into a cave-like indentation of two other naturally fallen trees. The sound of breaking tree branches startled her as the crown of the huge birch came crashing down around her. The tree bounced several times on its own springy branches and settled into a tangled mass of wood.

She was trapped underneath, but felt oddly safe within the haven. The silence was broken only by the throaty call of a song-bird that seemed to be asking, "Is everything safe now after all your noisy rumbling in my forest?"

"Janina, Janina!" her fellow workers called. "Zimmerman, Zimmerman!" shouted the gang leader angrily. From within her hiding place, Janina could hear voices and cracking sounds as they ran saws across the large branches in an effort to free her. In a few minutes, the last branch was lifted, and Janina emerged untouched, saved by the massive tree trunks that formed a temporary shelter. She stepped onto a large branch and dusted pine needles off the sleeves of her sheepskin jacket, some of which had knifed their way into the seams. She looked at the dumbfounded crowd gathering around her expecting to see a corpse and smiled at the gang leader who was angrily shouting, "What are you doing? Did you not see the tree, hear the warnings? What do you think we are doing here? You stupid woman! You could have been killed! I am not going to prison because of you!"

Janina began laughing hysterically. The irony of the situation dawned upon her. The loss of her life would be a loss to the Soviets of a capable worker and the gang leader would be punished for it.

"What do you mean?" she said, laughing.

"You, you . . . If you want to kill yourself, do it somewhere else, but not in my work gang!" he stuttered, pointing a finger into her face.

Janina laughed out loud again with her mouth gaping wide open, her eyes crazed, jeering at him and defying his nervous warning.

"Ha, ha, ha!" she continued as she picked up her axe and with exaggerated swings began chopping off thick branches of the tree that had almost killed her. The gang leader said nothing more and, looking over his shoulder at her, moved quickly away.

Janina often spoke of this incident, expressing surprise at herself even years later over how defeated she had become during her imprisonment. "I was unable to think, as if I'd been brainwashed," she repeated. Abuses of power and the absence of all fairness had by then left her completely resigned. The daily grind of work and the struggle for food had sapped her strength and will for anything beyond basic survival. In the early days, Janina would have protested, argued, fought. Now, she was happy to be allowed to return to camp, to the tenuous safety of her cot, but it was Mira who reminded her that she must muster the strength to go on.

The gang leader watched Janina suspiciously for the next few days, but she did not allow his hounding stares to bother her. It seemed there was little more the Soviets could do to her. She had survived nearly one year of forced hard labor, overwhelming concern for her child, incessant hunger, and squalid living conditions.

On another clear day in the wind-protected undergrowth of the massive forest, Janina again stared into the blue sky, taking a moment's rest from the exhausting chopping and dragging of the heavy branches. The gang leader caught her inattention to the sawing activity nearby and immediately shouted at her, "Are you trying to do it again, Zimmerman?" Janina looked at him, amazed that anyone would think she was suicidal. She shook her head and returned to her work. He walked away, turning his head often to check on her movements. Janina continued working, smiling to herself.

The incident did not pass unnoticed. Convinced that Janina was trying to kill herself under his command, the gang leader reported her to the commandant. In a few days, as she prepared for bed in the oppressive winter darkness, a young Russian woman came to speak to her. Janina looked at the woman's worn, dirty clothes reeking from benzene, grease, and oils and was perplexed by her presence in the barrack. In an unrecognizable Russian dialect that Janina could barely understand, she said, "Report for work at the tractor garage tomorrow." Then she dropped some heavy, dirty, oil-soaked overalls next to Janina's cot and left. The stench from the coarsely woven cloth quickly filled the small compartment, so Janina rolled up the overalls and stuffed them under her bed.

Alarmed by her apparent suicide attempt, the Communists decided to put Janina to work in the tractor garage for a higher salary of 120 rubles a month rather than to lose a young worker. She was ecstatic with the doubling of her salary. "And, I can also make an additional 60 rubles for bringing ten barrels of water to the garage every night," she reported to Mira.

The work alternated between day and night shifts, each a week long. It was physically harder work than in the forest, requiring particular care so that the tractors functioned properly. The young Russian woman showed Janina where to grease the massive machines, how to fill their immense fuel tanks and change their oil, and how to pour the volumes of water needed to run the one huge steam-powered tractor. There were eleven tractors under the care of two mechanics, and Janina followed their instructions carefully. In her filthy overalls, she lay on her back under the ominous machines, unscrewing large worn bolts to drain the used oil. The oil usually sprayed into her face and ran down her arms to her elbows before she could move away. It was impossible to work in gloves and her hands remained covered with cold oil or grease throughout most of the freezing night.

In March 1941, temperatures plummeted as the sun and moon shone together near sunrise, a condition called *yutrenki* by the local people. Days were only four hours long, and the temperature held its freezing grip at below-zero levels. Janina developed a sharp pain in her side from the constant exposure to the cold ground, but neither her frostbitten hands nor her pain prompted her to seek help for fear of losing the high-paying job. She often escaped the vise-like cold by standing near a large fire burning in the garage that kept the water hot for the steam-powered tractor. An old Russian woman was engaged to keep this eternal flame alive. In her fearless old age, she liked to complain about the Communists. "They have nothing but lice," she said scornfully. "That gang leader who sent you here," she continued, "he likes to talk about wealth and abundance of life these days, but for dinner he eats only dry bread and a raw potato! He said to me the other day, 'Look how much better your life is now! There is freedom. No more czars. No more rich people ruling the rest of us poor. We are

all the same.' I told him we were all the same, all right. All poor!"
she chuckled.

By late spring, Janina was sent to work on the tractors left in the
forest during the night. One time, she met some Russian tractor
drivers returning from their day's work.

"Who goes there?" they shouted suspiciously.

"*Zapravshchitsa* (the maintenance woman)," Janina assured
them.

"Oh, *Pania* (the grand lady)," one Russian spoke, bowing
deeply, concocting a gentrified form of the Polish proper address
of "Pani." Janina ignored their scorn, knowing that it was simple
jealousy of her higher salary, but she was concerned that being
alone at night in the forest might provoke a sexual attack. When
they went along their way, she concluded that her grimy and
smelly appearance must have deterred them and that they were
too drunk, as drinking was common.

Janina continued her work in the forest as the intense cold
gave way to the warmth of early summer. Now, instead of hurrying
from work across the frozen ground, Janina stopped along the
forest path in the early morning hours to pick newly ripened
berries. While the sun's first rays peeked through slender openings
of the thick treetops, she gathered the dark fruit into a glass jar,
thinking how happy Mira would be with the delicacy for breakfast.
During these walks Janina often rested for a few minutes under
young soaring pines and birches. Competing for light in the occasional gap left by an older fallen tree, their thin branches stretched
toward these narrow openings in the forest's crown. The young
trees formed a stark contrast to the older, darker pines competing
for light.

One time, she lay on a soft mantle of moss, leaves, and pine
needles, watching the branches sway against the blue-gray sky
peeking through the thickness of the treetops. She closed her eyes,
lying peacefully for several minutes. The warming earth enveloped
her with a cool morning mist and the strong pine scent cleared her
muddled mind. In the silence, she felt the thumping of her heart
resonating in her ears. Suddenly, a rustling of leaves startled her. A

few feet above her stood a mother deer and her two newborn fawns. Unaware of her presence, they proceeded to graze on the new sprigs of grass and succulent young twigs of the birch in the clearing. Janina lay breathless as she observed the deer, admiring their grace and gentleness, their delicately sculpted heads and large brown eyes. The mother moved one small step after another and then stopped into statuesque stillness. Her two fawns followed her lead. For a brief moment, Janina met her watchful gaze and their eyes locked. At almost the same instant, the deer jumped to the side, spun around, and leaped into the thicker underbrush, the lighter-colored underside of their tails flashing like beacons in the grayness of the morning hour. Janina lay back down for a few more moments of peace, wishing that Mira could be as free to roam as those deer.

The work led Janina to different parts of the forest every week, as the tractors rammed their way through the wilderness, hauling out massive trees. On a few occasions, she was so far away from camp that she had to spend the night in a temporary barrack for all the workers, men and women together. There, she would drop onto the nearest available cot and sleep for hours. The cots were arranged in rows throughout the one-room barrack. Wool blankets covered the cots but were filthy and had a stench of human sweat from overworked bodies. Janina was usually so tired she ignored the odor, which had an odd familiarity.

As she fell into deep sleep one time, strangely erotic odors induced sensations she had long forgotten. She woke up and noticed young Russian women and men embracing under the filthy woolen blankets. The blankets bounced rapidly upon the backs of the men groaning with each thrust into the compliant women beneath, pulsating bodies creating a rhythmic creaking of the old wooden cots. Then, one by one, giggles accompanied by muted words and sighs of satisfaction emerged from an unmistakable climax. Janina shuddered and pulled the blanket over her head.

A Less than Normal Childhood

As my mother recounted her stories of those times in the camp, I could hear the panic in her voice, and I wondered what effect that had had on my sister. The arrest, the trip to camp, and camp life were only the beginning of many frightening events in my sister's life and the end of anything that could have been considered a normal childhood.

Many years later, in the early 1960s in the middle of the Cold War, long after those ordeals, Mira took Russian language classes.

"I knew how to speak Russian, but I never learned to read or write it. At one point, the teacher asked me in her thick Russian accent about my time in Russia. 'So, how did you like Russia?' she asked me in front of the whole class as if I had been there on vacation. I was stunned. All I said in my best Russian was that I was very young when I was there. I paused and then I added, 'I was freezing. I was starving. I was petrified.' She never asked me anything more about it."

By the end of the first year in the camp, people were selfishly focused on the basics of life. Once gracious, civilized human beings, they were reduced to acting on animal instincts—acquiring food, shelter, and clothing. The finer things in life had become inconsequential—presents and frilly clothes, genteel music and inspiring artwork, polite company, and the air of sophistication were relics from a life in Poland few imagined they would ever experience again.

My mother's lifelong preoccupation with obtaining the basic necessities of life led her to focus on that rather than on relationships, or so it seemed to me as I was growing up. Such intensity explained why celebrating birthdays, anniversaries, and holidays meant so little to her. She did not know how to accept a present or how to give one. "No one ever gave me presents," she said of her childhood. "I could never give Mira anything," she would lament.

The War intruded on me everywhere: it interfered with the food I ate, the clothes I wore, the friends I wanted to have and insinuated itself into shopping expeditions, vacations, social gatherings. But most painfully, it encroached on the relationship I had with my mother.

"Ey, you, American," said my mother, pointing at me with her fork, which she bounced lightly between her thumb and her index finger. She and I were having lunch together at the farm one summer when I was fifteen. She chomped with her mouth open as she ate a baked potato and chuckled to herself. I tried not to pay attention to her. I was annoyed by her manners and her lost expression that didn't seem to include me in her thoughts.

So, is she going to say something more to me or not? I thought. And, what does she mean by calling me "American"?

I cringed and waited for criticism of something I did, something I wore or ate, or her feeble attempt to engage me in a conversation I didn't want to have. She ate the potato slowly and thoughtfully, savoring each morsel, grinning between bites, pointing at me with her fork.

"I remember," she interjected between bites and waves of her fork, "in Siberia, when I came back to the barrack with that load of potatoes I had dug and Mira was so hungry, I gave her a raw potato to eat." She laughed a small joyless chuckle. To her Siberia and Russia were one and the same.

"With the peel and all?" I asked.

"Why not? They're just as nutritious raw as cooked. The peel has most of the vitamins and minerals," she responded.

"And you didn't get sick?"

"No, never. Try one sometime."

"No, thanks," I said and rolled my eyes.

I was annoyed once again. I didn't want to be constantly reminded of the War, but my curiosity was nevertheless aroused. Later, I took a small bite of a peeled raw potato when my mother wasn't watching. It was chalky, grainy and flavorless, but I thought about how it must have tasted to Mira. She probably didn't care. I thought about my father's mantra that life is a "battle for survival" and his often repeated adage that "What you have to eat today, save for tomorrow; what you have to do tomorrow, do today." I could imagine that, on the edge of existence, a lowly raw potato must have seemed like a precious treat.

I could also imagine that any scrap of cloth must have seemed a treasure, and slowly I began to understand the frugality with which I grew up, my parents' preoccupation with accumulating provisions for the future in case of war, their caution with strangers.

In the winter when I first started elementary school, my mother insisted that I wear a pair of her heavy warm wool knit thermal undergarments that were way too big for me and an awful faded light pink color. We were not permitted to wear pants in my Catholic school in the 1950s but only skirts or dresses and later a school uniform. The bulky undergarments were not only too large for me but very itchy. As we walked together to school, I would stop often to roll them up so that they could not be seen from underneath my uniform. I wondered why my mother made me wear her undergarments and why she did not buy smaller ones for me.

"Hurry up!" my mother insisted, as she pulled me along the street. "You'll be late," she repeated in that panicked tone of hers that made my heart flutter and caused me to breathe hard as I struggled along trying to keep up with her. By the time I reached my classroom, the pants were hanging well below my uniform's hemline. I could feel my face turning red as I looked around to see if anyone noticed. All I could manage to do before the class bell rang was to run to the girls' bathroom and remove the offensive pants. As the final bell rang, I scurried to find a good hiding place for them in the locker I shared with another girl.

One time I was caught with them. "What's that?" asked my locker partner as I quickly rolled them up into a ball. I barely understood her since I was not yet that familiar with English.

"My mother makes me wear them," I answered slowly. She walked away and I saw her giggle to another girl as she whispered something into her ear.

I protested to my mother the next day, but she insisted on my donning the offensive pants. I threw a temper tantrum. "No, no, I won't wear them!" I yelled.

"Yes, you will or I'll tell your father!" she said. I didn't want my father to be angry with me so I pulled on the pants and cried all the way to school.

Most times, I forgot to bring the pants home, which angered my mother even more. My mother seemed totally unconcerned about my embarrassment, and I was equally upset by her insensitivity. It was that way with a lot of things. She seemed to have this uncaring attitude about what anyone might think of me, acting as if my physical well being was more important than the opinions of others. I am sure she must have felt that I should have been more appreciative of the things I was being given. After all, Mira never had these things.

There was a sense of urgency in everything my mother did. She was never one to deliberate much over the important things in life. There were only the regrets—her lost youth and beauty, her interrupted education, the carefree childhood Mira never had.

"I was beautiful once. Your father thought so," she assured us on more than one occasion. "Don't you agree?" she would ask in order to solicit a compliment from me or my sister. Even as a ten- or eleven-year old deep into my tomboy ways, I learned to be leery around my mother and to not answer her when she asked such unanswerable questions. It seemed that she was always trying to recapture her youth, her good looks, and her health, trying to turn back the clock to a time before the War.

I later learned that in a fit of jealousy my mother dyed her hair black to try to imitate the hairdo of an Italian-Polish aristocrat my father almost married in Italy right after the war. After my mother died and I was organizing the numerous photographs my father had taken of her, I realized that she had really been a beautiful woman in her youth and, to my surprise, a natural blond. Then I saw a face I had never known as a child. It was a face without the wrinkles of age and the grimace of pain. It was the face my sister had known. It was the emaciated face my father had pitied when he first encountered her and Mira in the desolation of the Soviet Union. It was the face of the woman he met again and married in England after the war, when I became their lovechild.

"I saved my complexion in Siberia by applying cream from that goat's milk," she said. She did have youthful looking skin long into old age. I always wondered how she got the cream or managed to spare it rather than eat it.

Thus, my mother's regrets ranged from the seemingly frivolous to the seriously disturbing. I learned to be cautious around my mother's outbursts about what she called her "maltreatment," brought on, I suppose, by her daily pain of reliving those war events. As a child, having little understanding of the turmoil that seemed to consume her, I did not share my sister's sympathy toward our mother. My sister's perspective of her was one of a savior. Mine was one of a tormented woman who was stuck in the past.

As a teenager, I often caught my mother staring at me for long moments with this curious half smile on her face.

"What?" I'd say, irritated by this intrusion into my privacy. As she continued to gaze at me, she'd say, "Nothing. It's nothing."

"What?" I'd repeat, frustrated by her secret thought that somehow didn't seem to involve me.

"Oh, it's something . . ." she'd say as her voice trailed off and she averted her gaze down into her clasped hands. I just *knew* she was thinking of something that happened during the War. Perhaps she was reckoning with the past, asking herself the "What if . . ." of life. What if there had been no war? What if she and my father had not met? What if my father had married that Italian-Polish aristocrat he met in Italy after the war? What if he had moved to South America to start that forestry business he dreamed of? What if I had not been conceived? It took me a long time to come to terms with my mother's consuming regrets and incessant revisiting of the past. I had to convince myself to move forward, to live in the moment, prepare for the future, a lesson that I learned well from my father, who preferred to think ahead, who was always positive, always hopeful, in contrast to my mother's attempts to lure me into the regrettable past.

My mother had an uncanny ability to reach the heart of a soul with one brief conversation. She was a quick judge of character. She could look a person straight in the eye and ask the most intimate questions, much to my surprise. Sometimes, she did not even need to ask any questions. Her target's eyes revealed everything to her. By sharing an incident from her life of sorrow, which she was able to weave into any topic of conversation, she managed to become intimate with almost any stranger, especially if those strangers were women, and particularly women who had been abused in some way by a man.

One time during my early childhood, I walked in on a conversation my mother was having with a friend who had just given birth. The woman seemed very sad, and my mother, probing in her typical way into what ailed a person, said something to the woman that has haunted me ever since: "*She* had bruises all over except where the baby extended from her pregnant body." I never learned who she was referring to, but I was afraid she had been talking about herself.

On another occasion, a first visit to our neighbors in Wisconsin, a poor farming family, my mother started a conversation with the farmer's wife.

"Oh, yes, I was poor at one time. In Siberia, you know . . ."

"Really, you were there?" asked the farmer's wife as she rocked her baby, the sixth in their brood. I had noticed how astonished she looked.

"Yes, and let me tell you . . . ," my mother would continue in a self-pitying voice, as I ran off to play with the older farm children after they finished their milking chores. Later I heard my mother saying to the woman, "You know, you should talk to a doctor so you don't have more children," much to the woman's embarrassment when she noticed my presence.

That penetrating intimacy of my mother unnerved me, especially as a teenager. In comparison to what she and Mira had endured, my privileged American life was mundane indeed. So anything I disclosed to her became magnified, and she questioned me in what seemed like a feeble attempt to get closer to me. More often than not, she made my story more serious, more important than it really was, but she always managed to get to the heart of what ailed me and more often than not, I ended up crying. At other times, when I would have welcomed a confidante, she was too embroiled with her own demons to pay much attention to any life crises I thought I was having.

I cannot to this day even recall what we talked about that so upset me. In the end, I stopped telling my mother anything important, though she pleaded with me in Polish. "Tell me something, *moja córa* (my daughter)," she would say. I would think about it for a moment trying to identify something from my personal life that could not be misinterpreted in her mind, something I could explain well enough in Polish, for by the time I reached young adulthood, my innermost thoughts were formed in English and translation became difficult, if not impossible. I tried to tell her something she would want to hear, like that I was happy, that I really did believe in God, that I still prayed.

My mother was an expert at finding perfect strangers to help her, and she never showed any reluctance to demand such help, much to my embarrassment as I was growing up. I wished that I had understood then how she had acquired that boldness. There was no sugar coating, no diplomacy about her, only this resolute sense of urgency. She was direct and to the point. Looking back on her life, having experienced my share of sadness, I understand it now. She was a mother with a young child, whom she was going to save, unlike the other two she could not. In the end, it was the child, my sister, who saved her, who saved them both.

The Polish Army, Tatishchevo, Russia, November 1941

Below: Scenes from Polish Army camp from Wawrzyniec's album, Tatishchevo, 1941

Татищево З.S.S.R. 1941

Pluton gońców Szwadronu N.P.

Przejazd transportów z płn. głęb. na połudn. ZSSR.

2-ch - Tatiszczewo - Krasnyj Ułan

p. Sądzą... w 1/z pinstolu

Widok mostu w Tatiszczewie

Kazach

otkrycie na stacji km. radzieckiem

Zabitym ... obst. oraz szwadr. pluton instrument. z orkiestrą Szwadr. łączn.

Pluton gońców plutonowy

Mira and Janina after leaving the Soviet Union and the labor camps, Tehran, 1943

Mira in Tehran, circa 1943

Lieutenant Wawrzyniec Solecki, Egypt, 1945

Lieutenant Wawrzyniec Solecki working as an adjutant, Egypt, 1945

Janina and Mira, India, 1946

Mira in Polish folk costume, India, circa 1946

Lieutenant Wawrzyniec Solecki with Lord, his police dog, Italy, 1945–46

Wawrzyniec and Janina with Danuta, Coventry, England, circa 1951

Janina and Wawrzyniec, Chicago, circa 1953

Janina with Danuta, Chicago, circa 1953

Janina Zimmerman Solecka, Chicago, circa 1953

Mira with Danuta on day of Mira's college graduation, May 1958

Janina and Wawrzyniec with Danuta and Mira, Wisconsin farm, 1960

Danuta and Janina with friend Małgosia after marching in the Polish Constitution Day parade, in Polish Girl Scout uniforms, Chicago, May 1965

Part 3

Choices and Destiny

Amnesty

In spring 1941, a group of Soviet officers arrived at the prisoner-of-war camp in Kozelsk to examine the prisoners and determine their physical fitness for hard labor. As a large, husky man, Lieutenant Solecki was among those chosen. Some of the prisoners had already been sent north to the Kola Peninsula, a lonely, flat-topped mountain in the desolate tundra where the men were ordered to build a small military airport. Lieutenant Solecki was assigned to work there because, despite months of imprisonment during which the food rations were meager and he was exposed to disease, he was well enough. In June, he joined the others for transport to Murmansk at the Kola Peninsula, but on the way his train was abruptly stopped at the station in Gryazovets. Without explanation, the prisoners were ordered out of the train, given a poor supply of materials, and told to build barracks in the nearby fields. The resulting structures were only three-sided and too flimsy to block out the cold winds of this northern region. The men slept on narrow three-tiered bunks covered with only a wool blanket, if they were fortunate to have one, or they used their tattered army coats for warmth. They waited there for weeks not knowing what was happening in the world or the reason for their aborted journey up north.

At about the same time, Janina returned to work in the timber operations near her labor camp.

"I felt totally numb by then and unable to think clearly," she would recall years later. "I remember singing. My favorite was our patriotic hymn, 'Jeszcze Polska nie Zginęła.'"

> Poland has not perished yet
> So long as we still live.
> That which alien force has seized
> We at sabre point shall retrieve.

Those words gave her hope while constant prayer gave her the strength to endure. She had proven to herself that the challenges of camp life could not diminish her resolve to live in freedom once again. Like a nervous doe never closing her eyes to rest while a predator is near, Janina kept a watchful eye on her captors, sensing their strange unease as summer progressed.

"You are free workers," the Soviets insisted, but Janina and her fellow countrymen knew they had become the spoils of war and that freedom was as elusive as the fleeting summer breezes.

Unbeknownst to the rest of the world, the Germans and the Soviets had divvied up Poland even before the war began, so sure of victory were these long-time aggressors of Poland. The secret additional protocol to the Ribbentrop-Molotov Pact of 1939, not made known until 1989 when the Soviets admitted to it, called for an easy slicing up of Poland into yet another partition. Unaware of these political intrigues or the state of the war, Janina and thousands of other prisoners saw Poland's sad fate in their frost-bitten hands, malnourished faces, and their children's cries from hunger and illness.

The political pact that had bound them into such bitter slavery was about to be broken. Germany violated her own agreement with the Soviet Union and on June 22, 1941, attacked Russia. In response, the Soviets prepared to force this persistent aggressor out, in part with the blood of her foreign prisoners. On July 30, 1941, as Janina prepared for work in the forest, the Soviets signed an agreement with the Polish Government-in-Exile in Great Britain annulling the Soviet-German treaties of 1939 by under-taking, as the agreement stated, "the formation of a Polish Army on the territory of the USSR, . . . and granting amnesty to all Polish citizens deprived of their freedom either as prisoners-of-war or on other adequate grounds." At that point, General Władysław Anders was released from the Lubyanka prison in Moscow and given orders by the Polish Government-in-Exile to form this new Polish Army with the soldiers remaining in Soviet prisoner-of-war camps and with men from the labor camps. He began visiting the various camps, including the one where Lieutenant Solecki was being held.

Unbeknown to Janina, the impact of those events in London were about to bring an end to her imprisonment. In the warm sun, she thought only of the berries she might still find for Mira on her way home that evening. The eight-week-long summer, which had put everyone in a more relaxed mood, including the vigilant Soviet guards, drifted into its final phase. With the fleeting fragrances of summer's vegetation giving way to the crisper scent of fall, forest creatures scurried about to gather up the last seeds and nuts for the long winter's hibernation.

As the Soviets prepared for war against Germany, Janina's work day began to stretch into twelve-hour shifts. News of amnesty finally reached the camp workers, but demoralized and weakened from months of hard labor, broken promises of better work conditions, and the lack of food, the prisoners listened dispassionately as a fellow prisoner related the good news.

Slowly the realization that they were able to leave the Soviet Union seeped into their dulled consciousness. With trepidation, people debated the best course of action. Women could register as army nurses while men might volunteer as soldiers in the newly forming army, which was located in the Soviet Union hundreds of miles away. Without a husband to take responsibility for her, Janina's only hope for leaving the labor camp was to volunteer as a nurse. In this capacity, she could join the Polish Army, which she expected would offer relative safety and provide adequate food. She was the only woman from the camp who was willing to brave such a trip alone. With a small child in tow, it would be a dangerous journey, but she was determined to leave. It was better than staying in that place and risking Mira being taken into an orphanage for "Sovietization," she reasoned. To help her carry through with her decision, Janina sold all of her worldly possessions. Her bucket, cooking pot, and goat were scarce, precious commodities and giving them up committed her to departure.

"Mrs. Janina, did you get permission to leave from the commandant?" asked a barrack neighbor. As Janina wrapped up the last of her belongings, she paused and looked over at the woman, attempting to assess her intent, and answered, "Why do you ask?"

The woman said, "I heard that another woman was denied permission to leave."

Janina grew uneasy. "But why? We've been granted amnesty!"

The woman shrugged her shoulders and replied, "They say the Polish Army is overwhelmed with the number of civilians trying to join them, that they have too many women from all over the Soviet Union, that they don't need any more nurses." Later, it was learned that the Polish Army did accept all who requested help and that the Soviets were merely trying to deter people from leaving the labor camps by spreading such rumors. They did not want to lose valuable workers and were slow to respond to requests for permission to leave the camp.

Janina stuffed the last of her few remaining clothes, a few family photographs, and old documents into a small suitcase. Mira stood watching with her eyes wide open, on the verge of tears. She said nothing and grabbed the small basket and bundle Janina handed to her as she nudged her out the door.

To avoid being denied permission to leave the camp, Janina decided not to check in with the commandant. She walked straight to the wagon that a few days earlier she had secretly arranged for transport. She took the path farthest away from the commandant's barrack, warning Mira to be quiet as they walked. At the camp gate, the wagon was already full with about half a dozen men. Janina's basket with a few blankets and other bedding was already on it. The driver motioned with his arm and called out to her in a low voice, "We must leave now!"

She quickly climbed aboard and with Mira nestled in her arms, they watched the distant barracks disappear from sight. As the only woman on board, Janina looked at the anxious faces of the men sitting silently in front of her, their eyes transfixed on the forest clearing that had been their involuntary home for so many months.

"It seemed to me that we all had developed a strange sense of attachment to that hostile place. After all, though camp life was difficult, we knew what to expect. It wasn't much, but we did have that one loaf of bread a day. We had shelter. Where we were headed was unknown. None of us knew anyone who had traveled through those strange lands before, but I knew I had to leave. I knew I had to find freedom, to return to Poland someday, to save Mira."

Soon the Volga River stretched before them, as wide as a lake and flowing with wavy crests, bouncing small tree branches along its edges. A huge steamboat waited at the dock for people to climb aboard. In order to travel, Janina needed official documents that she could obtain only at the NKVD post located in the small town. For this, she first needed a photograph of herself. Having left the camp without official permission, she fretted about obtaining the documents that would allow her to join the Polish Army camped far away near the city of Saratov. She looked around the dock. A crowd of people had already gathered for the next passage onto the boat, and Janina reluctantly decided to leave Mira while she tried to pursue the documents.

"Mira, guard the baggage and get in line as soon as it forms," she instructed her. She felt torn about leaving Mira alone, but it would have been too difficult to maneuver through the crowds with her and the baggage, and it was already late in the day. Mira sat down obediently on the suitcase as she watched her mother disappear into the crowd.

People began boarding the boat and the dock soon became deserted. The paddle boat departed and a smaller boat took its place. Blood-red curtains hung in its large entrance and flapped softly in the gentle breeze. A large man dressed in a dark uniform coat stood next to the boat holding the reins of a horse harnessed to a small elegant carriage. Mira noticed the man staring at her.

"Mother was gone for almost half the day, but to me it seemed much longer. Everything was so strange. All those Russian soldiers—I was afraid they had arrested Mother. That man—he was one of them, and I thought he might be there to arrest me as well. I began to cry, a stream of tears soaking the front of my coat. By late afternoon, I had shed all the tears that seemed possible. I was thirsty, and my wails must have sounded terrible for people stared at me from all around as they gathered on the dock for the next transport out. No one came up to me," Mira recalled years later.

It would have been common to leave a young child alone during such times. After almost two years in the camps, most children Mira's age or younger had already died or had been sent to Soviet orphanages after their parents died. People leaving the camps were psychologically numb to one degree or another. Seeing a small child wailing alone was not unusual. Unless they knew the child, in their desperation they would most likely ignore the situation. For Janina, leaving Mira alone was a guilt she felt for the rest of her life. "I had to leave her alone. I didn't know what else to do," she would say years later.

"*Ludzie, ludziska* (Humans, human-animals)," Mira would chime in again, and they would both shake their heads in agreement as they stared out with vacant expressions.

When Janina finally returned to the dock, she found Mira shaking, her face drained of any color. She hugged her and handed her a large doll with two long braids of blond hair and dressed in peasant folk clothing.

"Look. Look what I bought for you. She looks just like you," Janina said as she tried to comfort Mira. Then she gave her a large slice of bread smothered with butter, but Mira was too upset to eat, so she held up some pieces of paper. "I have the documents. We can go on the next boat."

By then, hundreds of people had gathered on the small crowded dock. Janina and Mira guarded their belongings as the space between them and the next group of families filled with bundles and suitcases. As more people moved closer to the entrance of the boat, occasional jostling disrupted the otherwise quiet, restrained atmosphere. These deportees, now refugees, were on the same, desperate mission—to leave the Soviet Union as quickly as possible.

Workers on the old steam-powered paddle boat dropped the flimsy restraining ropes across the gangplank and slowly allowed people to enter the once luxurious boat, a pre-Revolutionary czarist vessel. Remnants of velour curtains hung in shreds across private compartments. Richly carved handrails still revealed their intricate designs, though most had been worn away by the thousands of peasant hands that had rubbed them. The crowd carried them forward, while sailors struggled to check each person's ticket.

"Ah, Mrs. Janina, I see you are able to leave this 'blessed' land," said a man with a familiar-sounding voice from behind her. It was one of the family men who had lived in her barrack at the camp.

"Oh! Sir, I didn't recognize you," Janina said to the tall, emaciated man, whose long thinning hair was disheveled along a receding hairline. He was leading his four small children up the plank onto the boat.

"I'm sorry about your wife," she added. The man's wife had spared herself so much food while saving it for their children that she died from starvation and exhaustion shortly before amnesty was declared.

The children held onto each other, struggling with small bundles as they moved up the steep gangplank, some ten or more feet above the water's surface. Suddenly, the movement of people on the open plank stopped as sailors made room for the crowds who had already entered the boat, confusing the passengers and blocking the entrance to the boat for several minutes. The boat bobbed up and down in the cold waters of the Volga as Janina, Mira, the widower, his children, and several other people waited on the gangplank, balancing from side to side in order to stay on it, holding onto the flimsy rope that served as a handrail.

"What's going on there?" someone shouted from deep within the crowd still waiting to step onto the gangplank.

"Move up! Move up!"

The crowd pushed forward, each person slammed full-body against the next one in front. People on the gangplank continued to push into one another. Only baggage separated them, but even these small barriers disappeared as the crowd shoved forward. With each slight motion of the boat, the crowd grew restless, and a collective moan came as the loosely anchored gangplank shifted a little further away from the dock under the weight of all the bodies. The widower's children held onto each other as a new wave of human motion thrust most of the people forward. The boat rocked and the gangplank slipped away some more from the dock.

In that moment, a shrill scream like that of a sea bird startled everyone and diverted their attention to the splash that followed.

"Help! Help her!" shouted the widower.

Janina turned to see him frantically screaming at the sailors.

"Throw her a rope, a life preserver! For God's sake, do something, do something now!" His voice cracked on the verge of hysteria and was unrecognizable as a man's voice. He motioned with his arms waving and pointing down toward the water, trying to get the sailors' attention.

"My God," yelled Janina as she looked down into the murky water and saw the man's six-year-old daughter flailing her arms and gasping for air as her head bobbed up and out of the churning water.

Unable to move forward or backward along the narrow gangplank full of people, her father knelt down and watched helplessly. Then he stood up as if ready to jump into the water after her, but two of his other children held onto his coat and he pulled back, choking on dry sobs.

"Help her, please! Oh God!" he cried weakly.

The sailors were now shouting at him. "Keep moving, no stopping."

The line of people in front of him on the gangplank had already moved forward onto the boat, and he was blocking the way for the others. Then, the girl's body disappeared under the boat.

Those who witnessed the incident watched for her to surface, but as one moment passed into the next, no sign of her appeared. Janina pushed Mira's head into her side trying to keep her from watching, but Mira stubbornly resisted and peered over the side of the boat trying to catch a glimpse of the girl. The girl's two brothers and sister cried as their father pulled them off the gangplank onto the boat. Once he was able to leave them with another woman, he returned to look for his daughter. After watching for several more minutes, shouting to anyone who would listen, he sat down on the plank and put his head into his hands.

The girl must have bumped her head against the large paddle and then got caught in it, as her body was lost in the swell of water under the boat. With a pained, lost expression on his contorted face, the father returned to his other three children, who stood crying on the boat. As the boat moved slowly forward through the water, people watched for the girl's body. Occasionally, they caught a glimpse of what appeared like a part of her in the murky waters. For days, people talked about the incident as they watched the girl's body appear and reappear in the water. The sadness among the passengers was so overwhelming that Janina had only to look into anyone's eyes and tears would begin to run down their faces.

"What is the life of one more Polish child to the Soviets when they have already let hundreds die?" was the frequent refrain repeated among the passengers.

"The Soviets behaved as if a rag doll had been dropped into the water. It was of no consequence to them," Janina would say of the incident years later. After witnessing so many similar ordeals in the camps, she had begun to expect such callousness from her former captors. Exhausted from her own struggles, she choked back tears and clung to Mira, never releasing the grip on her arm, fearful that a similar fate might befall her.

In the churning waters in front of the flat side of the boat, the pale, bruised, and stiffened body of the girl reappeared, bobbing like a frozen log, unceremoniously pushed forward by the boat. Had it not been for this constant reminder, the incident might have been forgotten, accepted as another casualty of this inhuman land. The captain made no attempt to extricate the corpse or even to avoid it while navigating the boat. In hushed conversations, people spoke of the hideous nature of the situation, and parents tried to keep their children from viewing the body. At the end of three days, the boat's movement pushed the body to the edge of the boat and dislodged it, and it flowed freely away to its open grave down the wide flowing Volga.

The Fittest Survive

The transport of Polish refugees ended at the bustling city of Saratov after three weeks of slow travel over more than one thousand miles. Having subsisted during that time mainly on dried food rations, people poured off the boat in search of fresh food. At the railway station, Janina entered elegant toilets, opulent remains of the czarist era, to find a young woman standing with her legs set wide apart for balance, madly rubbing her back against the corner of a wooden door, her dress flapping between her knees. Janina and another woman watched with dismay while the young woman moved up and down and around the door with her shoulders, meticulously reaching each square inch of her small back oblivious to anyone's presence.

"What?" she said in Russian when she noticed the women staring at her. Janina turned to her companion and said, "Lice, no doubt." The woman stopped her fanatic activity and in broken Polish and half Russian chastised them.

"Scratch, scratch, all right! In five weeks' time, back and forth on train, no bath, you'll see, you'll see! Ha!" She gave them a look of disdain and returned to rubbing her back against the door.

It did not even take that long for Janina and the group of refugees to be subjected to the same agony. Although they had been given new underwear, there were body lice everywhere, and the chore of ridding themselves of the blood-sucking creatures began anew.

"What is it with this country? Do they only know how to breed these creatures?" asked a man.

Another retorted, "They are all comrades!" The men broke out in laughter as they scratched themselves.

In the meantime, after General Anders visited the prisoner-of-war camp, Lieutenant Solecki and the other soldiers began the long trek back south to become part of the new Polish Army on

Russian soil. Supported by provisions from Britain, Russia had acquiesced to this formation under pressure from the British and the Polish Government-in-Exile.

"We marched together to another distant railway station happily singing. Rain mixed with snow poured on our heads, but the weather could not dampen our spirits. We sang for hours as we marched through villages and meadows, fields and forests. It was strange that no one caught a cold or fell ill. All we had on our minds was that this was the way to our beloved, lost homeland," he recalled.

They arrived at a train station and boarded the simple boxcars. The long train journey to Tatishchevo near Saratov was interrupted by endless stops at small train stations. At each, hundreds of Polish civilians ran to the army train with outstretched hands begging for help.

"We had so little to offer them. We gave them a third of our food rations. They were mostly emaciated women and older children. By then, there were few small children left."

The Polish Army camp at Tatishchevo along the Volga River teemed with activity in preparation for the continuing war with Germany. Thousands of Polish soldiers, recently released from confinement as prisoners of war, along with civilians from labor camps, gathered in the open fields. There was an obvious absence of officers, but no one knew why. No one knew then that many of them, along with educated professionals, had been murdered in the Katyń Massacres.

The camp was an old Russian summer training post. Soviet officers and soldiers housed themselves in several small barracks and new tents, while the Polish officers and soldiers had to sleep in leaky old tents. The Soviets allowed them to use the nearby fields for their camp and to cut down massive trees in an allotted section of a forest several miles away. This new Polish Army would be fighting Hitler on the Russian front. It was later determined that the Soviets were afraid of arming the Poles on their soil for fear of reprisals. After all, the mass deportations and murders had been an attempt by the Soviets to eliminate the educated Poles, the intelligentsia, so that Poland would never again exist.

It was the beginning of November, and the bitter cold of a Russian winter was setting in quickly. Janina and Mira stayed in a leaky tent and watched the Polish men happily join forces for the work. Janina wondered where they found the strength. Their jubilant singing created an atmosphere of warmth and camaraderie. Shoulder to shoulder they marched from the army camp to the forest carrying back heavy logs from early dawn to late into the night. Under the direction of skillful carpenters, the few officers worked next to foot soldiers with zeal and no apparent sign of fatigue. Having worn out their boots in coal mines and forests or digging out canals during their imprisonment, the men tied rags around their feet. Dressed in tattered uniforms, these scrawny, weakened soldiers poured incredible energy into their mission. The Soviet officers shook their heads in disbelief and declared that they'd never finish before the first snow fell.

The Polish soldiers proved them wrong. As cold rain turned to snow, in only four weeks, the camp, complete with a hospital and kitchen, was finished and ready to house the thousands of soldiers and civilians. It was rumored that General Anders himself would be coming soon to assess the situation.

Among the hundreds of women who had applied for work as nurses, only forty young women were chosen. Because of her responsibility for a young child, Janina was denied permission to join them and she and Mira, along with other displaced women, were temporarily sheltered in a small wooden house near the Polish Army. Due to their unofficial status, the army could not afford to feed these hundreds of civilians, so soldiers volunteered money and their rations for them.

In her relentless search for food, Janina set out alone one day for a nearby village with some of the donated money to look for milk for Mira. As she approached rows of simple white houses, she noticed that there were no people outside, no children's laughter, no animal sounds. She looked through a window of the first small house and saw dirty plates on a table and chairs that had been pushed back and turned over as if its inhabitants had left in a hurry. In the next house, she saw a similar scene. Convinced that the village had been abandoned, she turned to walk back to the camp when suddenly she was surrounded by a pack of large herding dogs. Through the gaps of their open mouths, she saw sharp yellow teeth and heard a slow menacing growl emerge from the largest lead dog. She looked around for a way to escape but the dogs blocked the only way out. She braced herself against the wall of the house and watched. The dogs began leaping at her feet, the pitch of their howls and barks rising. One grabbed her calf and held on. As the pressure of his teeth tightened through her woolen boots, she stood motionless with only her eyes moving.

"The largest of the pack, a wolf-like mongrel, leaped up onto my chest with his large paws pressing against my shoulders, his worn teeth snapping at my face," she described. "He was so close I could smell his hot breath, but I stood like a stone statue."

She kept her breathing to a shallow motion in her chest. She focused her eyes straight ahead, avoiding his. Suddenly, the dog retreated but kept his vigil, pacing around her. The other dog kept his grip on her calf. She moved only her eyes.

"Trying to calm myself, I had the odd idea to count them. There were fourteen dogs of various sizes and breeds."

The standoff continued for several more minutes when suddenly and almost in unison, the dogs turned and ran off. "I stood stiff as a corpse for several minutes unsure of whether to move or not. I think they must have been repelled by some strange odor from my body." When she returned to the camp, she learned that the village had been occupied by Volga German peasants, descendants of German immigrants from the eighteenth century. When Hitler's forces approached the Volga River, the Soviets carted the German villagers away to labor camps.

Over the next few days, Janina tried to establish some sense of normalcy for Mira amid the uncertainty of their unofficial status. Under Janina's direction, Mira learned to read some Polish, and as the youngest member of the group of displaced civilians, she was selected to recite a poem that someone managed to piece together from memory for General Anders. The general finally arrived to review the work that had been done to assemble the scattered Polish soldiers who would eventually form the Polish Second

Corps. In recognition of his honored status as commander, the women prepared a tribute to welcome him.

"Oh, I'm glad to have saved this velvet dress for you," said Janina, admiring Mira as she stood ready to recite the poem. Mira looked down at herself in the dark blue sheen of the dress and ran her fingers over the cool smoothness. She pressed her thin fingers into the material and let the short, straight fibers, somehow un-crushed even though the dress had been stored for months, dig under her fingernails. Janina had combed her hair into two short braids and then rolled them up on either side of her head.

"You look like a doll!" Janina declared. Then she escorted Mira to the front of the barrack where a group of civilians had gathered to meet the general. After some brief introductory remarks by a group member, Mira curtsied and began reciting. "My country with whispering forests, when the sun shines in the azure blue sky, you are covered with sparkling tears." Her small but steady voice was confident. She had rehearsed the poem for days with Janina.

Mira continued. "In a faraway land, among strangers, lonely, I brood over you and miss you." Her voice grew louder. She stared ahead, unseeing, as if to concentrate on her lines and the fluctuations of her voice the way Janina had taught her. "Each morning when the day begins to awaken, I long to see you before I go to my grave, hear the distant harmony of forests, groves, and fields."

Tears formed in Janina's eyes. Stillness wrapped the small group of people in the room together as Mira's lonely voice hung thick in the air. "The hope is forever. Like a child cuddling, it soothes this heartfelt pain," she went on, putting emphasis on the word "pain."

By then, everyone had tears in their eyes. As Mira ran to Janina's side, General Anders stood up slowly, leaned his tall body against his cane, and limped over to Mira. "Thank you for that lovely recitation," he said. Mira smiled a broad grin, one that she rarely displayed. Then she ran off to eat some of the baked delicacies that had been made from scarce rations saved for this special occasion.

"All I remember is how tall he was and how good the sweets tasted," she said years later of the event. And then, as if by com-mand, she and Janina would recite the poem in unison, never missing a word.

Religion

At some point I had to decide whether to take my children to Saturday Polish lessons and scouting or to the American soccer games that began early at the age of five. I decided on soccer, but I secretly wondered if I could accomplish both. It didn't take long for me to realize that Polish school involved more than just going there. It meant "being" Polish, which of course, meant "being" Catholic. As Unitarian Universalists, I sensed we would not be readily accepted. What would I tell my children when prayers took place at the start of each school session and they had to make the sign of the cross to bless themselves? I never taught them that! Would they behave with reverence at the Catholic masses they would be required to attend? I couldn't put them through that, nor risk offending devout Catholics—it would be hypocritical. Still torn between those two very different cultures, I opted to raise them as American and Unitarian Universalist and give them some lessons on their Polish and Lithuanian background myself, without heavily relying on religion. We were, after all, living in the land of religious freedom, and liberal religion was an important option for those of us who were alienated from traditional religions.

My own falling away from the church was precipitated in 1968, when the second ecumenical council of Catholic bishops met with the pope to decide on such personal matters as premarital sex and the use of birth control. I was in college and had stopped going to church on Sundays, a mortal sin if there ever was one! I wrote a paper in my philosophy class on "whether the statement 'God exists' is true or false." I labored on this topic, as it tore at the core of my being, and in the end I concluded that it didn't matter whether in fact it was true or false; rather what mattered was whether one *believed* it was true or false. I got an A for the paper and that cemented my decision—I was finished with a religion that even my mother did not practice, one that my boyfriend and future husband criticized, and one that I was relieved to leave. I felt brave to question all that I had learned during my exclusive American Catholic grade school upbringing, which seemed less welcoming than the Catholicism of my Polish community. I was grateful that I had gone to a public high school, where the majority of students were Jewish, unlike my Polish friends, who had attended Catholic high schools.

With her deeply Christian beliefs, my mother was sympathetic of all people and especially of Jewish people whose war experiences she understood well. Whenever anyone criticized the wealth of Jews in Poland, she reminded them of the poor ones she had witnessed scraping out a living on the streets of Grodno. In America, she made it her mission to visit with Holocaust survivors in our Jewish neighborhood, mostly women who had endured terrible torture at the hands of the Nazis. Perhaps it had helped her to reconcile herself to her own plight when she learned of atrocities greater than what she experienced. She also told me she thought that one of her great-great-grandmothers was Jewish. For the longest time, as a child, I confused her labor camp experiences with the Holocaust stories she repeated during our dinnertime discussions. She liked to cook Jewish food, as did many Polish families, and we ate bagels and cream cheese with lox after church on Sundays.

One day toward the end of the school year as we neared graduation, my eighth-grade teacher, a short, older woman clad in the black penguin-like habit of her Catholic order, called on me and asked me to stay after school to work on an art project for the class bulletin board.

"Why are you going to *that* school?" she asked, referring to my intended high school.

"What do you mean?" I answered bravely.

"Well, you know, it's full of those *bad* people," she continued.

"Really, who's bad?" I asked, feeling rather bold. I was dismayed that my parents would allow me to go to a school that might be unsafe, which is how I interpreted "bad."

"Don't you know? It's full of Jews?" she said averting her eyes as if trying to hide her comment.

"Oh," I said as I tried to think of what I should say next.

This old German nun stood up every morning from nine to ten boring the hell out of our very full classroom of fifty girls—the girls had to be separated from the boys in the minds of these puritanical thinkers in that German-Irish parish—with admonitions to live the life of Christ, to love our neighbor, forgive our enemies, and show kindness to all humans, and then she had the audacity to tell me in private that the high school that I was about to attend was "bad" because there was a predominance of Jews! That may have been the beginning of the end of Catholicism for me.

"My parents can't afford the tuition at a Catholic high school," I finally said.

"But you could work," she persisted.

"They won't allow me to work. They want me to concentrate on my studies," I interjected.

She didn't say anything more. I worked on the art project, sadly uninspired. Later, she tried to tell me that I would not get a good enough education at that high school to make it into college.

Years later, I ran into her once and told her that I was doing just fine at the University of Illinois. "I got a very good education!" I declared, glaring at her. Ha! I wanted to scream. See, you were wrong! I did amount to something. Those so-called bad people actually challenged me so much that I excelled!

With those thoughts in mind while my children were young, I was torn about cutting them and myself off from the Polish community entirely. I wanted them to feel like they belonged to the American culture to which they had been born but still have a connection to their Polish-Lithuanian heritage, so I stayed connected from a distance and visited Poland and my relatives with them a few times as they were growing up, experiences that proved to be a great lesson for them. We visited the churches my father had attended in Krosno, as well as the magnificent churches of Warsaw and Kraków, and discussed the importance of Catholicism in Polish history, especially its contribution to Poland's political freedom. They do understand and speak some Polish and are familiar with Polish traditions and customs, which we practiced during Christmas and Easter. Their Unitarian Universalist upbringing familiarized them with the world's other cultures and religions and taught them to appreciate their contributions to humanity.

The Guardian

Lieutenant Solecki rammed a wooden shovel into the hardened snow at the cemetery near the army camp at Tatishchevo. With temperatures at forty below zero, it was difficult to dig even a few inches for his friend's grave. Under his feet, the snow crunched noisily in the bleak January winter of 1942. Hundreds of graves now surrounded the camp.

"Poor Brodnicki. We can't even give him a decent burial in this horrible place," he called out to his friends.

Once the funeral procession began, the casket did not seem heavy on Lieutenant Solecki's shoulder. His friend's body had wasted away almost to nothing before his death, and four men could easily carry the pine box to the cemetery. With its many large crosses, the cemetery, standing out against the flat, gray, monotonous horizon, was a grim reminder of war. Lieutenant Solecki clasped his hands in silent prayer for the soul of his departed colleague as he listened to the priest's eulogy. He thought of the countless deaths and suffering he had witnessed on his journey to the camp only a few weeks earlier.

Upon his return to the barrack that housed a barber shop of sorts, he prepared for the end of his nightly duty supervising the guard patrol. The stove would need to be stoked again, so he poked at it lazily, trying to distract himself. His twenty-four-hour shift left too much time to think about the two years since his capture. Fortunately, the day's shift was just about over; he was looking forward to stretching out on his hard but comforting cot.

"I tried to be physically active because then I was so tired I could fall asleep without having to remember anything," he liked to say of those war years.

In the dimly lit barrack, in the darkness of early morning, he poked into the black iron stove that was keeping the few remaining coals of wood barely aflame. It was colder than any winter he had experienced in Poland. "One more time around the camp to keep warm," he said to a soldier on watch, trying to sound cheerful.

Not long afterward, he returned, rubbing his hands together, and noticed a young girl of about seven crouched near the stove. It was Mira. Her short dark blond hair peeked out from under her hat. The sleeves of her coat ended far above her wrists and revealed thin pale arms. She held a small wooden matchbox, which she was opening and shutting methodically when she noticed him looming above her. She looked up with pale hazel-colored eyes, her cheekbones protruding and her cheeks sunken. She reminded him of his two young daughters he left behind in Poland at the start of the war. He had been aching to hear children's laughter once again.

"Good day, young lady," he boomed. "What do you have there?" he asked.

She did not answer but continued to play with the box and to warm herself by the stove.

"Do you smoke?" he asked playfully with a twinkle in his eyes.

Mira tried to hide a smile. She was very serious most of the time, but she showed him the box. He saw two rubles inside. Then, he reached into his pocket and pulled out ten rubles. As he tried to put the money into her box, she pulled it away.

He reached into another pocket and took out a piece of hard candy, gently took her hand with the box and dropped the piece into the box. Mira unwrapped the candy and put it into her mouth, slowly rolling it around. Then she grinned and ran out of the barrack.

A few days later, Mira returned to the barrack when Lieutenant Solecki was on duty. Anticipating another piece of candy, she approached him.

"Well, good day again, young lady. Where is your mother?" he asked as he reached into his pocket for a piece of candy and handed it to her.

"Thank you," she said as she took the candy. "My mother is waiting in the bread line," she answered politely.

He was relieved to learn that there was a mother.

Lieutenant Solecki looked forward to seeing Mira again, but he had begun preparing for intense field maneuvers and so was no longer on duty at the barrack. He trained with his soldiers, who marched energetically, stepping high, puffing up their chests, displaying their new weapons and clean new uniforms provided by the British. As he was marching along with his unit one day, civilians gathered along the road, among them Janina and Mira.

"Look, Mama, there is the officer who gave me the candy," Mira pointed out excitedly.

"Please, Sir, please, Sir," called Mira as she started running toward him.

"Mira, stop! Don't bother the soldiers," yelled out Janina, but Mira ignored her and ran up to Lieutenant Solecki. He broke rank and leaned over to embrace Mira.

"Is that your mother calling to you?" he asked.

"Yes," answered Mira shyly.

"Then you must introduce me!"

Mira took his hand and pulled him toward Janina.

"Good day, Madame," he said, bowing from the waist and taking her hand, kissing the top of it in the traditionally formal gentleman's greeting of a woman.

Janina smiled and said, "Thank you for the candy for my daughter."

"I am pleased to meet you. You have a very delightful child. She was too proud to take money from me. I am very impressed."

They both stood in awkward silence.

"Do you have a place to stay?" he asked.

"We are in temporary shelter near some barracks."

"Then I will look for a better place for you," he promised.

Lieutenant Solecki was a man of his word. In a few days he returned to Janina and Mira's tent to tell them that he had secured a small cottage on the outskirts of the camp. Along with the good news, he brought them some bread and a little sugar. Soon, Janina and Mira settled into their comfortable new surroundings paid for by Lieutenant Solecki from his meager earnings and donations from other soldiers. Over the next few days, he visited them several times and always brought a small gift of food or clothing.

"Stay for tea?" asked Janina one day.

"Certainly," he replied, and they sat talking into the night until Mira fell asleep at the table.

As they carried Mira to a cot, Janina said, "I am very grateful to you."

"There's nothing to be grateful for," replied Lieutenant Solecki.

"You must miss your family."

"More than I can say. I only hope they are being cared for."

As a result of a new agreement between the Soviets and the Polish Government-in-Exile in Britain, many civilians enlisted to build a new electric power plant near the Aral Sea. Janina was still unable to obtain permission to join the Polish Army as a nurse, so she volunteered to work on the plant. In order to get to the work site she needed to travel to Chardzhou in Uzbekistan, some fifteen hundred miles away from Tatishchevo. In the meantime, Lieutenant Solecki prepared to leave for Tashkent, also in Uzbekistan, where a larger section of the Polish Army was forming. The day before he was departing, he brought Janina the last of the soldiers' donations of food and clothing.

"If you should return to Poland," he began, "please write to my family and tell them I am alive and what has happened."

He handed her a piece of paper with the address, again bowing to kiss her hand. Then he saluted with his hand toward his beret and mounted his horse. Expecting never to see him again, Janina waved good-bye. What a decent man, she thought. God bless him and keep him well, she whispered as she blessed herself with the sign of the cross.

A Man of Honor

The best gift I ever received was a promise from my father, whom I adored as much as I loved life, to get me a horse of my own. He always kept his word, his word being so precious to him that he could not live with himself if he were to ever go back on it. I anticipated the day when I would have my own horse and take riding lessons from my father, the expert horseman. If my father knew he could not deliver on his word, he never gave it. I thought of him as a rarity among humans. Even when I was a young child of four or five, he would shake my hand on a promise I had made, look me straight in the eye, and ask very seriously, "*Słowo honoru?* (Your word of honor?)" It was such an intense moment; I was totally captivated by him. I looked back into his eyes and just as seriously answered, "Yes, I promise." I kept my word to him always because I knew he would keep his word to me, and I never stopped believing him about the horse.

When I was a preteen, my father took me horseback riding in the park on every occasion possible and at his company's picnics or at the Native American powwows in Wisconsin when we vacationed at the farm. When I was an older teenager, he rented a horse for me during my visits to the farm, and I enjoyed the unrestricted riding in the woods. I was so excited about the horse that one day's ride kept me elated for days.

The best gift may be the one we are constantly anticipating, the one that never quite seems to enter our reality, but one that tantalizes us, makes us think about it, makes us dream. My father's dream was that he would be able to provide me with a horse and to share his expertise and love of horses that was a tenuous connection to Poland, which he seemed to constantly miss. I enjoyed listening to my father's stories of riding his horse in the woods in Poland before the war. It was time we had together that had a special quality, a young daughter and her hero father. I was mesmerized by his descriptions of a life that seemed so removed from mine. He told me of his many hunting expeditions for ducks or quail and about his position as chief forester for the wealthy count.

"One day, as I walking my horse, he warned me of a snake on the road by suddenly stopping and refusing to move forward," one of his stories began. "He reared up and wouldn't take another step. Then I saw the snake. I credit my horse for saving me from the poisonous snake."

Later, I learned how my father had escaped capture by the Soviets at the onset of World War II while he was riding a big brown horse that wasn't completely broken in. Eventually, the horse threw him off, something I was surprised my father would admit. I had not realized how serious a time that had been, as my father always relayed everything in a cheerful way. My imagination about what seemed like adventures enthralled me, instilling a desire to have my own horse someday.

My love of horses and my love of my father seemed to become one and the same. My father did finally keep his promise when I was twenty-one, but by then I was living too far away from him. I was newly married, working, and trying to finish my college education. I knew that he would have more work with caring for the horse than he could handle at the farm with the ten head of cattle, so I sadly declined the offer, and I guessed that he was relieved as well.

Had I actually gotten that horse when I was a child, I doubt I would have appreciated it. I would not have spent so much time thinking about it, imagining what it would have been like to own a horse. I would have taken it for granted, like I took many things for granted that my parents gave me to make my life more enjoyable, so different from Mira's early life. When I am in the presence of a horse, I sense this quiet majesty about it. I find myself unable to look into the eyes of a horse without feeling some connection, though fleeting, as if the horse knows me on some deep secretive level, like my father who always seemed to sense when something was on my mind or bothering me. Perhaps he acquired that ability because he spent so much time with horses. Perhaps by being with horses, this polite, well-mannered, army lieutenant and forester developed his deep respect for truth, a respect that made him forever a man of his word, a man of honor.

Under Naked Skies

After only a few weeks at the camp in Tatishchevo, Janina and Mira boarded a freight train that had been converted into a crude passenger train with rough wooden benches. Polish Captain Świetnik guided the hundreds of civilians on the fifteen-hundred-mile journey south to Chardzhou. With little more than a daily ration of bread and a watery soup, more children died each day from hunger and disease.

"We should not have left the camps! We're all going to die here!" someone lamented.

"Quiet! We're on our way out," said another.

"We are only going further away from Poland, not toward it."

For many, escape came in the form of death, and amnesty became a cruel illusion, but Janina held firm to her belief that the suffering would lead to her dream of freedom.

When they arrived, hundreds of people crowded into the station at Chardzhou. Uzbeks gave food in exchange for clothing. Underwear was especially valued, but by this time Janina had none to barter. Wearing only a simple dress that she had clumsily sewn from a rough wool blanket, she scratched herself and wriggled in discomfort from its itchy abrasiveness against her tender, malnourished skin, until red marks gave way to blisters on her shoulders, back, and waist. People were desperate to work at anything in exchange for food, and Janina and Mira waited at the station to board one of the barges that would take them down the Amu Dar'ya River to the Aral Sea, 360 miles away, where the power plant was to be built. The first set of barges had already left, but after two weeks, two Polish men returned to the train station from that trip. They were emaciated and dressed in ragged clothes, for they had walked all the way back with only water to sustain them. One of the men got up on a wooden crate and began to shout.

"Don't go! Don't go there!" he warned. "Don't let them take you there! Only death awaits you!" He gasped for air and tried to steady himself on the crate. "The conditions are terrible," he continued. "There are no accommodations. You will sleep under the naked sky. The climate is unbearable—cold, damp, and infested with malaria-carrying mosquitoes. You will have to make your own bricks for shelter. The only food is flatbread. There is not enough for everyone. Your children will die! The Soviets don't care—they will not help you."

The crowd grew restless, and people began talking among themselves. Janina spun around and grabbed the arm of a woman to ask what was going on just as some Soviet soldiers pushed their way through the crowd to the man on the crate. One of the soldiers pulled him down and commanded the crowd to disperse. "Get on the barge!" he ordered.

People hesitated, whispered to each other. The Soviet soldiers began grabbing women and pulling them aboard the barge. People resisted and small fights broke out, but because the soldiers were outnumbered, they soon gave up. Later, Janina learned that the two Polish men had sent a telegram to the Polish government in London, alerting them to the dangers to which people were being exposed, and the Soviets finally acquiesced to requests for better work conditions. People by then were waiting for days at the station to board trains bound for the closest collective farms. Janina and Mira eventually boarded one of those trains.

The old trains chugged back and forth across the southern part of the Soviet Union in Central Asia from Chardzhou near the Persian (Iranian) border to Alma-Ata near the Chinese border. Overflowing with refugees desperately seeking food, water, and shelter, the trains hissed and strained and crept into every small station along the way, stopping to unload as much of their human cargo as possible. The weather ranged from oppressively hot to numbingly cold. People succumbed to diseases that spread easily in the crowded, unsanitary conditions. Some even welcomed death as an end to their torment. The landscape became crowded with graves.

When the trains reached Alma-Ata, hundreds of refugees waited on them as others checked for possible placement on nearby collective farms. Janina hoped to settle at one of these, but she was apprehensive about whether she would be accepted.

"Get off! Get off!" insisted NKVD guards, but Janina hesitated, not knowing whether she would be better off riding the train back to Chardzhou.

"The train is our only hope," replied one of the passengers to the guards.

"Get off! You'll find places here," the guards said, but there were too many refugees, and the guards could not force them all to leave the train. No one really knew what to do.

Janina stared out at the countryside that seemed to stretch beyond any horizon, a bleak desolate flatland. Gray clouds gathered as if it were about to rain, and a cold breeze rushed past her seeming to whisper a message of forewarning.

The refugees traveled back along the same route to Chardzhou. When they arrived at the station again, they saw some of the same people who had been left stranded two weeks earlier on the bare ground without any shelter. These people again boarded the train, warning the others, "There's nothing here for us. There are too many of us."

As winter approached, the temperatures began dropping rapidly and it rained almost daily. Janina and Mira remained on the train back to Alma-Ata. The barren, harvested fields of the farm collectives were hidden from their view, as the boxcar had no windows. Only when the doors slid open at unannounced stops could they see outside. At each station, guards ordered the hundreds of people out into the surrounding fields. There was no shelter or food for them and little fresh water. Sometimes, a Russian or Uzbek farmer came to the station with charitable donations of food, but usually there was not enough for the massive crowds. It would be several days before another train arrived, and in the meantime more people would die. When a new train finally arrived, the remaining people quickly boarded it for shelter. When they reached the next station, they again would be forced off the train by the guards onto barren fields where there was no shelter from the wind and rain.

"They're hoping we'll die before we find a place to stay," muttered Janina to a neighbor.

Too weak to play, Mira sat with Janina in the boxcar guarding their few belongings. At another station in the open field, her doll held her attention most of the time and she ran her limp fingers through the tangled crop of hair and stared into the doll's face. Janina looked into the distance at the train tracks, while storm clouds gathered. People were strewn with their ragged belongings alongside the tracks, so Janina and Mira stayed on the train.

The next stop was at the larger city of Tashkent. Again they were ordered to leave the train. They settled on some barren ground near the tracks with their few remaining belongings. By this time, Janina and Mira were completely exhausted and desperate for any food. An Uzbek passing by stopped and threw them a piece of flatbread. Janina nodded weakly and took the bread, tearing at the pieces and giving the first of them to Mira. For several nights rain pelted them and the coldness of the barren ground stiffened their bodies. With her condition deteriorating, Janina became confused. All she could concentrate on was how to get food for Mira.

"I felt possessed," she would recall of the time.

At the station, she was relieved to find an abandoned boxcar on the side tracks away from the main ones. Several women had already settled in with their ailing children. In one corner, three men sat chatting amicably, seemingly unaffected by the depressing circumstances in which they found themselves.

"Good evening, Madame. How are you? Please, make yourself comfortable," said one man cheerfully pointing to the opposite corner of the car, as if he were inviting her into his living room. He had the manner of an educated man, polite with a tone of sophistication in his voice.

Janina smiled weakly at him, sat down across from the men and pulled Mira and their baggage close to her. She pressed her head against the wall and in between doses of fitful sleep, she heard fragments of the men's conversation.

"Yes, Sir, I agree with you."

"What did we have? Only this narrow passage to the Baltic!"

"Stupidity!"

Then there was silence for a long time, and Janina nodded off, but she was abruptly awakened again by the men's sobbing.

"Ah, Poland, my Poland. Such a noble power."

With the light of the next day, Janina awoke to find her companions right where they were seated the night before, still engaged in conversation. Though her thinking was foggy, she examined them closely. Their clothes were so worn that parts of their bodies were exposed through large holes. One man wore a thin shirt with large patches covering most of its front. His pants were filthy below the knee and only a rough rope through two remaining loops of his pants held them up. He said he had been an official for some ministry in Poland and was taken to Siberia at the outset of the war. The second man, younger than the first, was an engineering student, and the third one was a bailiff.

They continued their conversation in an incoherent train of thought—the greatness of Poland, what should have been, what could have been, what they would have done—to the point that Janina could not listen any more. Then, the bailiff leapt up in midsentence, walked over to a hole in the boxcar floor, dropped his pants and squatted over the hole to relieve himself, all while continuing with his conversation. Soon, the stench of his deposit filled the boxcar, and his companions wrinkled up their noses and swatted at the air laughing as if nothing unusual had taken place. Janina looked away, grabbed Mira's hand, and went outside to get some fresh air.

When she returned, she noticed the administrator scratching his armpits. Continuing with his lively conversation, he suddenly reached under his hairy armpit and pulled out a tiny, squiggly creature, and without stopping to examine it, he put the louse into his mouth. Without losing momentum, he picked another from his other armpit and casually flopped it into his mouth. With the next one, Janina stood up and yelled, "Ohhh!" The men looked at each other, and the administrator laughed, "What? If they can eat me, I can eat them too!" At that point Janina left the car.

It would be years before she could laugh at the incident.

The next day, Janina and Mira, the other women and children, and the threesome of half-crazed men were thrown out of the abandoned boxcar. On each of the next few days, as they waited for another train to arrive, Janina set out to look for shelter or for some food to buy with the last of her money, leaving Mira with another woman she trusted with children. There were a few isolated huts scattered in the distance around the station; she walked to a shed that housed camels that were outside at the time. The shed was surrounded with piles of fresh hay, and through the open door Janina saw huge woven baskets used to store grapes. The baskets were stacked high, one on top of the other, and there were only narrow passages between them. Janina approached the door as an Uzbek man rode up on his horse. Startled, she glanced at his face, focusing on his eyes, which were nearly hidden by a furry hat. As he dismounted, Janina noticed a bag of flatbread tied to his saddle. She held out her hand with her last five rubles, pointing to the bread with her other hand, and waited for his response. His unblinking eyes locked onto hers as he moved slowly toward her. Janina stepped back.

"I am very hungry. Please sell me some of your bread," she pleaded in fluent Russian. She spoke with a native's accent, rolling the sounds off her tongue as if the language had been her first. The Uzbek said nothing but continued to move slowly toward her, making no attempt to give her any bread.

"Please, I have a small child," she began again.

He smiled a toothy grin that exposed large yellow teeth and one missing front tooth. He slipped off his hat revealing long matted black hair with streaks of gray. Janina stepped backward and found herself inside the shed.

Suddenly, he lunged toward her, grabbed her arm, and pulled her further into the empty shed. Wasting no time, he ripped the front of her dress open, exposing her breasts. Janina grabbed his arm and held on tightly. Then, she started laughing. It was a hysterical laugh, haunting and interspersed with forced beguiling smiles.

"Wait, wait," she began. The Uzbek loosened his grip on her. "Give me some bread first," she said as she pointed to the bag, smiling all the time.

The Uzbek held onto her and forced her down to the ground among the baskets. Then he left to grab the bag from his horse, while Janina pulled the front of her dress together. She looked around the shed. The only way out was the door through which he had pulled her. She sat up and was about to stand when he returned with the bread. He threw one large piece to her.

The bread had just been baked and the aroma made her salivate, but she resisted taking big bites and broke off only tiny pieces, which she began to eat slowly. As she ate, she continued to survey her surroundings, all the time smiling at the Uzbek. He stared at her as he watched her eat. Her light blond hair, tall slender body draped loosely in the blanket-dress, and pale face were a novelty in this part of the world. By the time she finished about half of the large flatbread, he seemed to relax and said, "I have a black wife now, but I would like another wife . . . like you. So white." Then he smiled a silly, compromising smile, a crude attempt at charm.

Janina said nothing and continued to slowly finish the bread. As she held the last small piece, the Uzbek smiled wider, straightened up, and, anticipating his reward, pulled up his chest, and moved his large hands toward the front opening of his pants. Fumbling at the garment and the large protrusion behind the material, he smiled at her and moved toward her. As he was about to descend upon her, Janina swung out her right foot and with all her strength kicked him straight in the groin. The Uzbek yelled out in pain and jerked forward bending at the waist. With his knees held together, he grabbed himself and fell over. He seemed to have passed out and Janina ran out of the shed, grabbed the bag of bread and almost ran straight into an old Uzbek woman who was coming around from the side of the building.

"I saw everything," she said with a strange chuckle. "Oh, he will do terrible things to you if he catches you. You should hide in my house," she said, leading Janina away to her cart filled with large baskets.

Janina stayed in the woman's hut for almost an hour, sipping aromatic tea and waiting anxiously to return to Mira. Later in the morning, the woman escorted Janina back to the station along another route.

At the next station, the conductor motioned to Janina and Mira to get out of the train. Again they settled down among hundreds of desperate people on the barren fields outside to wait for further transport or a place to stay on a collective farm. When a train approached, people began shoving each other trying to get to a place where they could board. Janina jostled with them and managed to reach an open door. She put the basket down on the ground, swung the suitcase up onto the car platform, and then pulled Mira up next to the suitcase.

"Guard the suitcase, Mira!" she commanded. She tried to reach the basket, but it had been moved by the crowd several feet away. She pushed people aside to get to it. She grabbed it and tried to push her way back to the car, but people clamored with equal desperation. Janina pushed past arms, shoulders, and entire bodies to reach Mira, but the more she pushed the more people resisted and worked their way in front of her. She was pulled further away from Mira.

Mira watched as Janina disappeared into the crowd, which had become more agitated and noisy from the struggle to find a place on the train. The train's whistle blew and the train slowly began to roll away. Mira bounced up and down on her toes, jockeying between large adult heads, trying to catch a glimpse of Janina. At one point, she lost sight of her entirely and bellowed out screams that brought nearby people to a halt.

"Maaah-maahh!"

She began to cry, tears rolling down her cheeks.

"Mira! I'm coming," yelled Janina.

Janina was not certain that Mira heard her and she pushed forward through the crowd, which was now running after the departing train. The stronger ones managed to pull themselves up onto the car, and that opened up space along the path for Janina to make a dash for the train. When she reached it, she pulled herself up with the help of a man who grabbed her arm, the basket still in her other hand.

"Mira, Mira, stop crying. I'm here, I'm here," she said, trying to comfort her. Then she looked around and shouted, "The suitcase! Mira, where's the suitcase?"

Janina began frantically looking under people's feet and in between the bodies that were squeezed tightly together in the crowded car. She saw only dirty rags wrapped around feet with bloody toes peeking through holes, dust, and some dry hay scattered on the wooden floor. There was no room to search the corners or any part of the car. Mira continued to cry softly. When Janina noticed Mira, she moved her away from the open doorway of the car and rocked with her in her arms, stroking her hair which had become matted and dry from the weeks without a bath. As she rocked, she thought of the things that were packed into their suitcase—the family portrait with her parents, Walenty, Natalia, and herself as a precocious young girl dressed with a satin bow so large that it nearly covered her entire head, the family documents, especially Walenty's underground service certificate presented to him with the large parcel of rich farmland outside Grodno. The certificate was a stiff cream-colored paper with a large imprint of the Polish eagle proudly displaying the symbolic crown of freedom. It was proof that the land belonged to Janina. Mira's birth certificate was among the documents as well, but most importantly, their passports were inside the suitcase. Many years later, Janina and Mira both lamented the loss of those documents as if the documents themselves were the very family members whose images were imprinted on them. Those precious documents were proof of their wealth and their identity, their very existence. The suitcase also contained the last of their underwear and clothes for Mira, including that favorite navy blue velvet dress that she wore for General Anders. There was also a shawl and a sweater that could keep her warm, but the loss of Walenty's certificate was the greatest loss.

At the next stop, NKVD guards again ordered the people off the train and Janina and Mira scrambled out into the open fields. Janina quickly found a steam jet from the engine and collected hot water into her teapot. By now the temperatures had plunged to near freezing levels, and the water cooled quickly. It cost ten rubles to buy a handful of dry twigs, which was a rarity in this barren part of the world, so Janina gathered dried tufts of wadded hemp-like weeds that blew in round balls across the plains. Clouds began to gather into tight packs of darkness, rolling low and steady across the horizon. Fat blades of light cut through the cloud mass, extending in long flashes to the ground, as if some demonic gods were fighting in an unending dispute. As the storm neared, Janina covered Mira's head with a small woolen blanket and tried to shield herself as well under the tent she created with her arms raised above both of their heads. Janina's stomach growled loudly in the heavy, moist air of their makeshift shelter. It sounded louder than usual, almost comical. She laid her hand against her stomach, pressing lightly to relieve the pain and the sounds. As she did so, the blanket fell down around them and she noticed how her arms ached. Finally, she gave up and wrapped Mira with it instead, letting the rain pelt her.

The dark clouds moved closer, and booming thunder followed bolts of lightning. Children whimpered as mothers gathered their belongings into ever smaller piles. Janina took short, shallow breaths, forcing air through her flaring nostrils, her warm air jetting into steam when it hit the cold outside air. The storm passed quickly. She uncovered Mira; her shoulders were wet, so she changed her into a sweater. As rainwater dripped off her hair, Janina pulled out a half-eaten piece of flatbread. Its aroma had long evaporated, and only a hard cracker remained, protected from the dampness by a tightly woven cloth. Certain that there were more pieces in her sack, she broke the small piece in half and handed one half to Mira. Taking only a small bite to savor it, Janina reached into the bag for another, only to discover it was empty. She looked over at Mira, who was busy breaking off small pieces and hungrily chewing them up. Janina stared at the piece of bread that barely covered the palm of her hand and slowly took another bite. Suddenly she lost her appetite. Mira looked up at her, anticipating another piece of bread. Janina gazed at Mira's small face with its sunken cheeks, protruding jawbones and taut skin and was struck by the total lack of healthy plumpness in her child.

"The bread I was chewing felt like it was my own dead skin," she said years later.

Then Janina removed the piece of bread from her mouth and gave it to Mira along with the rest of the bread in her hand.

"I will never forget what Mother did for me that day," recalled Mira.

That one unselfish singular act seemed to cement Mira's attachment to Janina forever.

Not Me

In early 2002, I stared into the mirror at my contorted, horrified face, unrecognizable in the absence of the normally smooth skin and outwardly congenial smile, and it reminded me of my mother. I was in the changing room of Northwestern Memorial Hospital's Lynn Sage Cancer Center following my diagnostic mammogram. I had just been given a preliminary diagnosis of breast cancer, but not the type, stage, or the extent of any spread. That would be determined with a biopsy and surgery a month or so later.

I didn't recognize myself. I looked like my mother had so many times while I was growing up, when she recounted some painful story from her past—that contorted, desperate expression that I grew to associate with her. Now it's me, I thought to myself.

I had begun to think of myself as invincible. I had been caring for my old sickly father, my sickly father-in-law, juggling work and the responsibilities of a household with three teenage children. I thought I could do it all. I could not afford to get sick.

I spent the next month researching cancer and cancer treatments and getting second and third opinions until I could no longer postpone the surgery. At the same time, my younger son was about to leave for a special therapeutic high school in West Virginia. As a home-loving person, disliking change, he was distressed about leaving and living hundreds of miles away from home.

My husband and I agonized about how to tell the family about my health situation, so we decided to take a short family vacation to a Wisconsin resort before my younger son had to leave for school. I tried to be as jovial as I could during the day for the sake of the kids, but I was very depressed and wrote in my journal every night. I reminded myself of my mother in her constant agony with life. I hoped that I was not developing the same anguished frown on my forehead.

April 12, 2002: What if I could pass each moment in life as if in re-play mode? . . . Being present to my presence? . . . What power to live in the exact moment of my own observation, as if the mirror of my existence moves in utter truthfulness and honesty? . . . And then, in that moment of accidental freedom, to have that buried, secret self emerge? . . .

I have always loved secrets . . . to empower myself . . . Where once I saw my body as powerful . . . where there were no secrets . . . That body that brought life to others, . . . joy . . . is dying. And die it must . . . It is now time to test my belief—the inescapable truth that for there to be life, there must be death . . . And, it has been great, a life of chosen intention, not mere accident, a life lived and loved . . . never to look back, only forward, only with hope and joy and possibility.

I read the ramblings of the passage to my husband, and we talked quietly long into the night so not to waken the kids in our shared resort hotel room. We talked about the possibility that my body was full of cancer and that my end was near. I cried, trying to stifle my sobs as my husband consoled me. Little did we know that our younger son was listening.

I had a pre-surgical biopsy to determine whether cancer was present and if so, what kind. On the night before I was to accompany my son to his new school, I was given the confirmation that the lump detected during the diagnostic mammogram was indeed cancerous and that surgery would be required to remove it and nearby lymph nodes. Only then would we know the extent of the disease. If the cancer was localized, only a lumpectomy would be performed. If there was a larger spread, a complete mastectomy would be done.

I agonized about how to tell my son, or whether I should tell him at all. For the first month of his new school he would be camping in rugged terrain in the nearby mountains, and no communication would be possible. What if I never emerged alive from the surgery and he learned of my death when he came down off the mountain, most likely feeling healthier and happier? How would he react? I could not risk that, so on the way to the airport,

I told him. He answered, "I know. I heard you and Dad talking." After that he said little else about it, as the whole experience of going away was overwhelming to him.

Surgery revealed a borderline stage 2 cancer that had not spread. I began several rounds of chemotherapy. Meanwhile, my son improved with each passing month. I bought a nice brown leather journal whose pages had gold-painted edges, and I wrote to him in it daily as if we were talking, as both of us were in a new, scary place in our lives. I wrote mostly positive things, covering all the pets—Sarah the wonder dog, Izzy ("Izzy busy" as we liked to say) the sweet but dumb cat—his older brother's antics, his twin sister's accomplishments in school and sports, the weather, the garden, anything so not to reveal how sad I was really feeling and how much I missed him.

During one phase of the chemotherapy, after my fifth or sixth round, I refused to go to the clinic. I felt as if my mind had abandoned me. I felt so sick to my stomach; every cell in my body ached, and my body seemed to be completely out of whack. I couldn't sleep, and I downed bottles of wine every night trying to forget the pain. I had had enough. My husband came looking for me to drive me to the clinic. I had hidden on the floor of my bedroom closet with the door closed. I was crying quietly, wishing I would just die right then and there. It was all so reminiscent of my mother that I hated myself.

"What's going on?" he asked quietly as he opened the door. Compassion was oozing from his voice and even that annoyed me. I wanted no pity.

"I'm not going," I declared through the tears streaming down my face.

He knelt down and then sat on the floor next to me. The two of us sat in silence in my tiny closet with shoes and laundry surrounding us. After a few minutes, he got up and took my arm and tried to pull me up.

"I'm not going," I shrieked at him in anger. "I want to die. I want to die!" I threw myself against the wall hoping to crack open my head.

I surprised myself with such a suicidal proclamation, but by this time, I really had had enough of everything in my life. The image of my mother flashed across my challenged "chemo" brain. She'd thrown herself up against a wall in frustration during one of our many fights when I was a teenager. With that image in my mind, I calmed down. I did not want to be like my mother in that regard.

I don't remember exactly what my husband said to me afterward, but it was probably a declaration of his love and how much I was needed by the family. Reluctantly, I cleaned myself up and went with him to the clinic for another treatment of the poison.

By the end of the year, in addition to the chemotherapy I had undergone daily radiation treatments for six weeks. I was exhausted. The doctors and nurses began referring to me as a cancer survivor, but I didn't think of myself as such. I still had five more years of daily oral medication to take. I started going to a support group, but the daily reminder of my situation and the detailed discussions about the disease made me realize that I didn't want to be treated as "special." I wanted to live life like a normal cancer-free person, but I thought about death and my death every day. I thought about my mother. I envisioned her nodding and saying, "Now you know."

Death in Small Doses

At the next train stop, Janina and Mira found refuge in a local farmer's hut that was part of a collective farm. They had been traveling back and forth across the southern Soviet Union through Uzbekistan and Kazakhstan for six weeks. The hut was made of mud bricks and there was no stove, but an open fire burned in the corner, the smoke curling lazily toward a hole in the roof. Two other families were crowded into the cramped quarters; all together there were eight people in the hut. Without noticing the conditions, Janina collapsed onto the dirt floor and slept for two straight days. The hut was so small that lying fully stretched out, she touched one wall with her head and her feet just missed the open fire on the opposite side. When she awoke, the Uzbek farmer's wife brought her a bowl of freshly made tripe soup with rich egg noodles. She and Mira gulped down their first hot meal in weeks and then dropped back to sleep for another day.

The following morning, Janina noticed the warmth of ashes at her feet as she slowly awoke from her long rest. She lifted her head and looked around the hut. It was still dark outside, and Mira and the others were sound asleep. One of the other women and her two children were covered with a blanket that was crusty from accumulated dirt. Part of the blanket covered Janina and Mira as well. Janina saw familiar insect movements across the stiff blanket silhouetted by the light of the rising sun peeking into the hut through the small open doorway. She blinked, hoping that she was only imagining these creatures, but as she examined the blanket, she confirmed that there were hundreds of lice crawling all over. She roused Mira and with one fluid motion threw off the blanket.

Mira asked sleepily, "Do we need to leave again, Mama?"

The conditions at the collective farm were far better than those they had endured on the trains and at the unsheltered stops.

The refugees were given flour, mostly with peels and bran from poorly milled grain, rough and difficult to digest, but they could still make a nourishing porridge. One time, Janina threw a handful of the flour into a pot of boiling water. It splashed heavily, which surprised her. When she stirred it with a wooden spoon, she noticed grittiness on the bottom of the pot. The porridge contained mostly sand. She continued to stir the gruel, hoping that there would be enough nourishment for the day.

Though she was delirious with fever, she recalled Lieutenant Solecki and their last farewell. He seemed to be her only hope, as she believed by this point that she and Mira were at the end of their lives. On a gray piece of wrinkled paper, she wrote, "Please, Sir, do you remember me from the camp in Tatishchevo? You gave my daughter candy and were so kind to help us. The situation here is terrible. I am sick with malaria. We have little food. I worry for Mira. If I should die, please take care of her. I beg you." Janina gave the letter to someone who could get it to the Polish Army, but she had little hope that it would arrive in time or that it would reach him at all. Lieutenant Solecki was somewhere preparing to fight a war. Yet in this singular act Janina managed to restore her hopes, and for a while it lifted her spirits.

By this time, Janina had become so weakened with malaria fever that her actions became mechanical. Her only goal was to provide food for Mira. So when a letter arrived one day, she was initially completely unmoved. The letter addressed to her was written in a fancy penmanship, words with rounded loops. Janina ripped open the tissue envelope and pulled out an unusually thick letter. From within its folded pages, several large denominations of rubles fell into her lap. She stared at the money in disbelief and then quickly hid it in her pocket as she read the letter.

"My dear Madame I was moved by your letter which I received as we prepare to depart for Dzhalal-Abad. Enclosed are 367 rubles that I collected from the men. I hope that it is enough to help you and your little Mira through this difficult time." It was signed "W. Solecki."

Several days later, during one of her delirious fevers, Janina dreamed of herself at about the same age as Mira during the First

World War, when her own mother lay sick in bed. She was jolted out of the dream when two pairs of large arms lifted her from the floor of the hut.

"Stop! Where are you taking her?" screamed Mira. A neighbor held Mira in place and said, "To the hospital. Your mother is very ill. They will take care of her there. Stay here. We'll watch over you."

The two men packed Janina into a wagon and covered her with two blankets as another attack of malaria shook her. She lifted her head and saw Mira standing in the doorway to the hut, the other woman holding onto her, but Janina was too weak to call out.

As Mira followed the woman into the hut, she heard the others talking about Janina and her chances of surviving malaria.

"Mostly, they die from it."

"Death" and "dying" were not new words to Mira. She had seen enough of death in the past several weeks to know its bitter meaning. She feared now that her own mother had been taken away to the hospital to die.

After four days, Janina returned from the hospital. Her head had been shaven in an effort to control the spread of lice. Mira almost did not recognize her, but she ran to her arms, embracing her for a long time, trying to hold back tears.

"It's only a mild case of malaria. They gave me some medicine. You needn't be alarmed," Janina assured everyone in the hut.

However, the short stay in the hospital proved to be disastrous. Janina brought back typhus-infested lice. Unaware of their presence, she took Mira to bed with her and wrapped herself and Mira with a blanket. In a few days, Mira developed symptoms of typhus. Typhus was what they all dreaded. It could spread quickly, devastating life in crowded, unsanitary conditions. Mira and another woman and child in the hut were covered with the typhus rash, and all three were sent to the hospital.

The one-room hospital was several miles away. There were forty beds with one nurse and one doctor to care for all the patients. Several broken windows were sealed up with only thin cardboard. Mira lay in a bed against one of the broken windows and Janina worried about her developing pneumonia. Because typhus is so contagious and potentially fatal, Janina was not allowed to stay with Mira. A young woman lay in a cot covered with a fluffy warm comforter next to Mira. She told Janina, "I will take her to bed with me. Don't worry."

The next day, Janina returned to the hospital to visit Mira, but the nurse stopped her at the entrance. Other parents and family members had already gathered outside and stood silently milling around, waiting for any word of their loved ones. After two hours, the doctor stepped out onto the small porch and closed the door behind him. Several shovels leaned up against the wall of the hospital. He read names of those who had died overnight from a list on gray paper attached to a clipboard and handed shovels to the waiting family members. With each name, Janina heard a quiet sob. She stood frozen listening, dreading to hear Mira's name. The doctor came to the end of his list and went back inside the hospital, while the nurse instructed family members to remove the bodies from the back of the building.

Few survived typhus, and Janina was familiar with its devastation from her brother's death. She began to imagine Mira coming to such a dreadful end.

"Please, won't you let me see my daughter?" she pleaded with the doctor the next day. He nodded to the nurse beside him.

"You can come in and look from the doorway," said the nurse. Janina looked. All she could see was an immobile body.

"Please, let me go up to her."

"No, I'm sorry. Please leave."

Janina returned again the next day and the day after and the day after that. It was the same each time—the dread of hearing Mira's name read off the list that seemed to grow longer each day, the exhausting walk back, the few hours of tense sleep, the rush to return. There was no time to dress, to wash, or to eat.

It had been seven days since Mira first entered the hospital. For three more days, Janina dragged herself there. Malaria fever and chills still gripped her, but she didn't notice them so much anymore. By then, she knew the path so well that she could have walked it in her sleep.

"Today, he will hand me that shovel," she thought on the twelfth day, but again she was relieved to learn that Mira was still alive. On the way back to the hut, her head felt light, as if it had been lifted from her shoulders. The whiteness of the sand blended with the horizon and blinded her, and everything seemed different as the sound of the wind masked the occasional bird's song. Soon, she heard nothing as she dropped onto the ground.

Because of a rainstorm, the collective farmers finished their work early that day and were returning home when they came across Janina's body nearly frozen on the road. They lifted her onto a wagon and took her back to the hut. One of the women poured spoonfuls of warm soup into her mouth, and after a few days, Janina regained enough strength to return to the hospital.

This time the nurse allowed Janina to enter the room and escorted her to Mira, who sat up alert in her bed. She was pale and thin and her beautiful hair had been completely shaved off, making her look very boyish, exposing the thinness of her small neck and the square shape of her face.

"Mama, I'm hungry!"

"Oh, thank God," Janina responded. She smiled at the nurse, who told her that Mira could leave that day.

When the door closed behind her, Janina sat down on the steps next to the dreaded shovels and began to cry. "I thought by that time, I could no longer cry," she recalled. With death, tears had brought her no comfort, but with life, they became a welcome relief.

Like No Other

Almost two years to the day from my own cancer diagnosis, my younger son was diagnosed with cancer, a far more serious neuroblastoma that was the size of a grapefruit surrounding his sciatic nerve and causing him great pain. It seemed that my ordeal had been preparation for what awaited us in this new dreadful phase of life. I felt as if I were reliving my mother's ordeals with Mira. My father lay dying in the nursing home where I had to put him because I could not take care of him during my treatments, and there he remained as old age continued to deplete his strong body.

Death never comes at convenient times. I rotated duty at the nursing home with Mira and my father's first daughter, Luta. She had moved to America years prior after her retirement from a medical research position in Poland and lived in Florida with her cousin. From the nursing home, I rushed with my son to get medical tests done and prepare for the biopsy. Then I rushed back to the nursing home to be with my father. He was slowly dying while my son was trying to cope with this unforeseen enemy invading his seventeen-year-old body. A few days later, on May 6, 2004, my father died while I held his hand, stroking it as he had lovingly stroked my hand through my many days of illness as a child. We postponed my son's tests, my older son obtained a release from his duties at the Air Force base he was stationed at in Florida and flew in, and we held the short funeral, all too brief to allow for proper mourning.

Weeks later, I begged the oncologist not to rush into the surgery to remove the huge tumor from my son so that we could take a family vacation after those intense weeks of chemotherapy at our favorite wilderness camping place in northern Minnesota, far from the intrusions of urban life and the reality of my son's cancer.

The doctor finally agreed to postpone the surgery. I was so looking forward to our trip, but then, my son ended up in the hospital once again, and only my husband and daughter were able to go on the trip. I stayed in Chicago, mourning the loss of what I thought would be our last time together.

It was like an endless nightmare, like a scene from a horror movie that could choke me to death with fear. After the initial scans before the surgery, I talked with the surgeon over the phone, when he caught up with me as I was grocery shopping, like a robot in a numbed state of mind. Needing privacy, I abandoned my shopping cart that was already filled to the top. I felt as if I were going to faint or be sick, so I ran to the car while I stayed on the mobile phone with him and put the air conditioning on full blast as I tried to absorb what he was telling me—tumor hardly shrunk from all the chemo, intertwined within muscle and the main nerve down the leg, would be extremely difficult to remove, would have to discuss further options—more chemo, bone marrow transplants, radiation with potential for partial or full paralysis. I thought I was going to pass out.

My brain just kept screaming, I want a normal life for him! The surgeon was matter-of-fact and said that my son should be given the options. Then, I wondered in fear, what would we be saving him for? An existence as a paralyzed beggar on the street confined to a wheelchair? A lifetime of mind-numbing painkillers? The surgery would leave him a cripple. The drugs would be his escape.

After the surgery, I buried my head in the white hospital sheets draped over my son's body as he lay recovering in the post-operating room of Children's Memorial Hospital, still unconscious from the general anesthetic. I was bawling my eyes out and trying to muffle the sounds by stuffing the wet sheets into my mouth. I had just learned that they could not remove the cancerous tumor. The young nurses in the room were chatting away amicably, seemingly unaware of my distress, and that annoyed me. Someone should have come up to me to console me. Someone should have tried to reassure me that my son was not going to die. I wanted to scream at them, "Don't you know that they couldn't save him?

Don't you know that he will probably die?" I needed my mother. She would have understood, but she could only be there in my thoughts. I called my sister and stifled my tears because in situations like these, she had a tendency to launch into a tirade about how doctors "manipulate" things. I didn't need to hear that. I called my husband who was forever calm in such heart-wrenching circumstances.

My son and I had said good-bye to each other just before the surgery, both hopeful that the giant tumor intertwined with his spine—almost another organ itself with its own blood supply—would be gone when he came around. The surgeon had cut him sixteen inches down the middle of his abdomen but sewed him right back up as soon as he determined that the tumor was inoperable. How was I ever going to let my sweet son know that the tumor was still there? I worried about his fragile mental health.

I didn't want to believe it. He had just gone through several rounds of intense chemotherapy over the summer, and each time, he had been hospitalized for days. He had become violently ill after the first round and had to be hospitalized again. He had a complete mental breakdown—what more could happen to this seventeen-year-old just on the brink of manhood? He had lost all his hair. He slept most of the time, vomited often. When other teenagers were out enjoying their last summer before senior year in high school, my son was confined to a bed, nauseous from the chemicals that were supposed to attack the cancer cells, medicated to the point of numbness. I knew what he was going through, and each time I looked at him, I wanted to cry, but I knew I had to be strong, to be as strong as *my* mother.

I was fretting about telling him that none of the tumor could be removed, so I said that *some* of it had been removed, since the doctor had taken a small sample for another biopsy. I think that he believed he was going to die and that caused him to panic and break down. I thought of my sister's mental health problems years earlier, when her doctor commented that we all walk a fine line between sanity and insanity. My son was in so much pain from the surgery it was not surprising that he caved in under the stress.

We talked a lot about death and dying that summer. I remembered my mother's conversations about death, how matter-of-fact she seemed about it. I tried to be the same, but I was still trying to grieve for my father. It was difficult for me to keep the tears back or control my quivering voice. It was all too much. I was glad that my father never learned that his grandson was ill, the grandson who bore his name and was so much like him—intelligent, gentle, caring, and sensitive. During our talks about death, my son said he wanted me and his father to die before him, so that we would be there in the afterlife to greet him, like the Romans believed, like he had seen in a movie. I told him that I believed our spirits lived on with those on earth. I really didn't know what to say. That God would take care of him? My mother would have said something like that. That we should pray to God? My mother would have been praying day and night had she been there. I found myself praying, "Oh God, if there is a God, please help my son. Please don't let him die."

A couple of months later, at lunch after one of his intense radiation treatments, he seemed to be more talkative than ever, so I asked him how he was feeling about having the tumor that was still cancerous inside him. We had just learned that the intense radiation, which was further depleting his energy, was doing little, if anything, to defeat the cancer. He was agitated and got impatient with me, suddenly saying, "Look, Mom, I'm not afraid to die." His appetite had returned, and he was hungry. I was happy to watch him wolf down his sandwich. Then he went on to tell me a story he had read about how a father and his two young sons had been killed at an amusement park. Now that was really unfair, he said, as if he accepted his own situation. He seemed so wise for his age. I was the one who was afraid of his dying, of losing him. I tried not to grimace like I remembered my mother would do in such circumstances. I didn't want to be the alarmist that my mother had been, constantly pointing out the dangers, the bad things that could happen. But as much as I tried, I was that alarmist, that same frantic woman bracing herself for the worst, putting on a poor front of composure.

As my son continued to battle his cancer, I no longer found joy in life. I was only going through the motions of living. The minutiae of daily life were becoming a chore, like a heavy yoke around my neck. I began to realize that it was no wonder that my mother seemed to receive so little pleasure from so many things in life, with all that she had gone through with my sister. She must have been annoyed at my childish exuberance, just as I was at those young nurses at the hospital.

Numbing Existence

Janina brought Mira back from the hospital to the hut and decided to leave the kind Uzbek's collective farm once she regained her strength. I'll pose as Lieutenant Solecki's wife, she reasoned. That way, Mira and I can join the army and be safe. She was hopeful that her guardian would not mind the small deception.

A few days later, Janina surveyed the few possessions she still had and went out to look for the Uzbek woman who had asked if she could buy her goose down pillow.

"I made it myself from the fine down of my own geese. You can have it for a kilo of butter," Janina told the woman. The old woman grinned a toothless smile and quickly retrieved the butter. Then she asked, "What about your wool blanket?"

Janina nodded and replied, "For a bag of flatbreads, you can have it."

After the exchanges, Janina hurried back to Mira with her prized possessions. Mira's eyes lit up at the sight of the sweet butter. Janina spread the satiny smoothness across a large piece of flatbread and handed it to Mira, saying, "Now listen carefully. I must return to the village where you stayed at the hospital to get some important documents. The Polish Army has moved to a place called Dzhalal-Abad, and we're going there. I'll be back, maybe in a few days. There's a Polish delegation there and I'll find out what I need to do. Don't cry. Just stay here in the hut with the other family and eat this bread."

When Janina returned to the village, she was told that the delegation had moved on, so she boarded a train for a place that was some forty-three miles away. She knew little about it but hoped to find someone there to help her. When she arrived at the delegation's office, the man in charge said to her sternly, "You need a photograph, but the photographer has gone. You will have to wait."

Instead of waiting for the photographer to return, Janina decided to follow him to where the delegate thought he may have gone. It was a risky undertaking, as the city was farther away from Mira, and the train ride was through rough mountainous territory. Janina climbed aboard a train, but there was no room inside the passenger car so she stayed outside on the open platform, hanging onto a handrail at the top of the steps between the cars. The gap between the cars was dangerously large enough for a person to fall through. Another Polish woman stood across from her and faced in the direction of the train's path while a Russian man leaned against the door close to the warmth of the compartment. The cold wind blew against the woman's face, loosening her unusual white woolen shawl from her shoulders, forcing her to keep adjusting it around her head. The man stood admiring the shawl, never once offering her his wind-protected place. Then, in Russian he said something garbled to the woman. She ignored him. The train sped through jagged mountains, over deep valleys, steep passes and through long, dark tunnels. The clatter of the train's wheels along the cold bumpy tracks over the rugged terrain was deafening. Janina clung to the railing knowing that if she lost her grip she might fall into the precipitous valley below and to certain death.

The Russian said something again to the woman that sounded like a demand for her shawl. She shook her head, dropping it to her chest to keep the wind out of her face. The Russian moved closer to her. Suddenly, he reached for her shawl and began pulling it off of her head. She struggled to keep it from him, and the two danced unsteadily on the narrow platform.

Janina stood watching, unsure of what to do, but she was certain that the woman would freeze to death without the shawl. The man grabbed the handrail near Janina and was about to pull the shawl completely off the woman when Janina stiffened her arm and with a swift punch hit him across his forearm with the side of her hand and then pushed him away. He dropped his arm and grabbed it with the other. At that moment, the train rolled over a rough portion of track and bounced. The man lost his balance as he stood at the edge of the platform. He tried to catch the railing, but he fell off, tumbling into the jagged, rocky valley below.

Years later, she recalled the incident in a detached manner, as if it had been nothing. She would say, "I felt nothing, nothing at all." It was hard to believe that's how demoralized she had become.

After obtaining the necessary travel documents, Janina began her trip back to Mira. In order to obtain a train ticket for any destination, all passengers were required to take special showers to disinfect their bodies. Typhus was now an epidemic, and no one was exempt from the meticulous cleansing at every station, no matter how short the trip. The population of refugees had by then risen to thousands in the remote mountainous regions of southern Uzbekistan. On the return trip, Janina came across hundreds of these displaced Polish people begging for food, sleeping on benches, trying to stay warm with the remaining shreds of clothing on their backs. Janina's only conscious thoughts were of Mira—how to reach her, to save her.

She finally got back and found Mira in better condition than ever with the care provided by her neighbors and the old Uzbek farmer and his wife. Concerned that their situation would become as desperate as the ones she had witnessed, Janina prepared carefully for their next trip. She bought thirty-three pounds of flour and used part of it to make large flatbreads, a skill she learned from the Uzbek woman. She filled most of her basket with the bread and poured the rest of the flour into a bag that she slung over her back like a knapsack. With the basket in one hand and Mira's arm in the other, she set out for the village.

At the train station, the cashier refused to sell Janina tickets for the trip.

"The trains are overcrowded," he explained.

"But I must get to my husband," Janina pleaded.

"I'm sorry, but I am not permitted to sell any more tickets until further notice."

Janina was stunned and could feel her stomach turn into a tight knot as panic set in. She looked around and noticed a man standing beside her.

"Pardon me," he interjected, speaking in strong, fluent Russian. The cashier turned away from Janina and nodded to the Ukrainian as he approached him. They spoke to each other in soft whispers. Janina grew more nervous with every passing minute.

"All right. I'll sell you the tickets," said the cashier as he turned back to Janina.

Outside the ticket office, Janina waited for the Ukrainian.

"Thank you for helping me," she began.

He looked down at Mira's thin, pale face.

"Do you know that your train is not due for another day? Do you have a place to stay?"

"No, but . . . ," Janina answered unsure of what else to say.

"Then you must spend the night with me and my wife." Janina was hesitant but followed the man to his hut. That night, she learned that he had been one of the early deportees to the labor camps in Siberia and now worked at the train station.

When the train finally rolled into the station the next day, it was overflowing with people. A Russian conductor stood guarding the main entrance, preventing anyone from boarding the train.

"This woman is with a sick child and she is trying to reach her husband. Can't you make an exception?" begged the Ukrainian. The conductor stood high above them on the platform of the passenger car and shook his head in silence.

Janina could see that he was steadfast in his decision. He looked past them, far above their heads, pretending to be preoccupied with the other passengers. Almost without thinking, she heard herself say, "I'll give you some flour," and pointed at the knapsack. With those words, Mira began crying. "No, Mama, not the flour! Don't give away our flour!"

"Mira, quiet!" scolded Janina. With that, the conductor relented.

Once aboard, she said to the conductor, "Here are about four pounds," as she scooped flour into a bag and snuck it to him so that no one would see the exchange. The conductor quickly walked off with it. Later, with a much humbler demeanor, he returned to thank her in a whisper so not to alert the other passengers.

After five days of exhausting train travel, rounded mud bricks forming the walls of the city of Dzhalal-Abad appeared through the dusty windows of the train. Janina and Mira left the train with their few belongings but no more food. Janina's burlap dress had become even more ragged from sleeping in it. She was completely disoriented. She and Mira followed a group of passengers down a narrow street, trying to find a place to stay. Groups of Uzbeks in their customary squatting positions negotiated the sale of their livestock. Dressed in quilted jackets which extended to their knees, they lowered their dark faces in concentrated debate, heads covered with intricately embroidered caps with paisley designs. They did not seem to notice Janina, Mira, and the other passengers passing by.

Janina approached an old Uzbek woman and asked her in Russian for a place to stay. The woman led her and Mira to a small shed where she kept her pigs on the outskirts of the village of Blagoveshchensk near the army camp. There was a dirty, sticky, food-encrusted tub filled with cooked potatoes and dishwater for the pigs. Janina told Mira to lie down next to it and rest while she searched for Lieutenant Solecki.

At the entrance to the army camp, Janina left word for him and returned to Mira who was sound asleep. A few hours later, he entered the pigsty.

"You came," said Janina with tears in her eyes. Lieutenant Solecki looked around and nodded toward Janina in acknowledgment.

"I didn't recognize her," he said years later. "She was just a shadow of a human being—thin, frail, her body wavering as she stood looking at me, rags hanging off her, her hair sticking out in dirty clumps. I thought I knew what she must have gone through. I had seen the multitudes with outstretched hands, mostly women and children, begging for any scraps of food as we passed them on the trains. I pitied the children the most," he recalled until he could not speak anymore, tears welling up in his eyes. Lieutenant Solecki looked at Mira sleeping, silent in the world of childhood dreams. What was she dreaming? It seemed it wasn't what would later plague her in her sleep, the unsavory memories that years later still pierced her heart and made her scream out in the middle of the night.

"Come, sit down," he said in a whisper to Janina, who was about to keel over. He tried not to stare at this skeleton of the person he had met only a few weeks earlier.

"I didn't write to thank you for the money . . . ," began Janina, breathing as if lifting a heavy stone off her chest. "It saved our lives! If it hadn't been for that . . ." Janina stopped, feeling as if she were ready to burst into tears. She swallowed hard, wanting to keep her dignity. She realized that her pitiful appearance must have alarmed him. It was the first time she admitted to herself that she needed to rely on someone else to survive, and she was glad that it was Lieutenant Solecki. They sat down together on the dirt floor of the pigsty.

"I was next to my 'guardian,' and it was so tempting to just cave in, to embrace his care, to stop having to think altogether, for thinking had become such an unbearable chore. How good it would feel to collapse into this compassionate man's arms, to be cared for like my father had cared for me as a child. I could then just concentrate on taking care of my child and leave the worries of the harsh world to someone stronger."

"I will find you a better place to stay," said Lieutenant Solecki. He handed her some money for milk and left the pigsty. Janina dropped her head to her chest, closed her eyes and rolled over onto her side, not even bothering to hide the money. She was asleep almost before her head hit her folded arm.

Lieutenant Solecki returned later to tell Janina he had secured a small house for them in the beautiful Fergana Valley. After several weeks, Janina and Mira regained their strength and were able to enjoy the early emerging spring weather. Lush green gardens began sprouting from the seedlings of melons and other exotic fruit. Hundreds of canals crossed the valley connecting adjoining rivers and creating an intricate irrigation system. The view of the surrounding hills and distant white-capped Pamir Mountains was breathtaking. Janina and Mira strolled along the path from their house to admire the scenery and to forget about the war, if only for a few precious moments. As they walked, they came across poor Uzbek men and women riding on their horse-drawn flat carts with huge wheels or on camels packed with goods for sale.

Women in complete head coverings balanced baskets and earthen bowls and jugs atop their heads. Their dark slanted eyes peered out from brown-skinned faces.

The land's fertility seemed unbounded. Before the collectivization effected by the Bolshevik Revolution, it was overflowing with resources. Now the people lived poorly on the mismanaged farms, herding sheep and shearing them for their wool. Janina watched as Uzbeks who had tried to escape conscription into the Russian Army were rounded up by the NKVD, tied to camels and dragged to the train station in Dzhalal-Abad. She later learned that they were then transported to detention centers where they were outfitted with uniforms, briefly trained, and sent to fight the Germans at the Front.

Lieutenant Solecki and Janina were on familiar terms by then. They became Janina and Wawrzyniec, and Mira was delighted with Wawrzyniec's amusing stories of strange animals—elephants and camels and his dogs in Poland and how he would hunt for ducks with them. Best of all were his games. "Give me your paw," he laughed as they held their palms joined lightly. Then they would wait to see who could first pull out their hand and gently slap the other's. "Ah, I have you!" Wawrzyniec would say, as he quickly won. Mira giggled so hard she had to gasp for a breath. Janina was thrilled to see her daughter laughing again.

"You are so good with children," she said, admiring his thick bright blond hair and eyes so blue they seemed to blend in with the clear sky.

"I am at your disposal," he joked as he lit a cigarette.

Wawrzyniec visited Janina almost daily at the one-room house, which had a small kitchen that she shared with another family. It was difficult to find a private place to talk, but on occasion they managed to get away and share their longing for Poland. He brought her portions of his ration of sugar, bread or flour, and milk for Mira. He also brought money, which he continued to collect from the other Polish soldiers to help some of the displaced civilians.

"You are our savior," said Janina one evening as they sat together at a small table in the cottage.

"It's our duty to help those in need," he asserted.

"I think I must have fallen in love with him then, but I knew he had a wife and two daughters in Poland, so I only talked with him, admiring him from a distance," said Janina of that brief time, years later. "I was so grateful to him. He had saved us. What else could it have been if not love?"

In the weeks that followed, Janina and Mira continued to recover from their malnutrition. Wawrzyniec visited them as much as he could between preparations for fighting the Germans. During his visits, he spoke of his own experiences since his capture and release. He told her of his orderly, Antoni, during the days before amnesty had liberated him from a Soviet prison. "At first they gave them a handful of dry buckwheat, millet maybe, but no pot in which to cook the grain. It was a place called Szepietówka . . . ten thousand soldiers there! Later, they moved them to Siberia, where Antoni had to dig coal in some unknown place. They told them that if they worked hard for three months, they would be released and sent back to Poland. They worked hard, but after three months, the Communists didn't let anyone go. They promised again that in another three months they would be released, but it never happened. A group of about thirty of them, Antoni among them, formed a delegation and went to the commandant to complain. Instead of treating them as prisoners of war, they threw all thirty into solitary confinement. He was there for three weeks with little water because it would freeze. They gave them only some bread. He lost his hair when he rested his head against the walls and it froze to the wooden surface."

The next day, Janina approached a small desk that was set up near the army camp to help the refugees get out of the Soviet Union.

"Your name?" asked a man whose head was bent over a long list of names. Janina wasn't sure whose name to use, so she answered, "Ślarzynska, my father's name."

The man dropped his pen and with his mouth agape looked up at her. "Janina, is that you?" he asked.

Janina stared at him but did not recognize the face.

"I am your cousin, Antoni Manturzek, Father Manturzek, now," he said.

Janina thought for a moment as she stared at his priest's collar and then said, "My cousin Antoni?"

"Yes, yes. It's me. We met a very long time ago when you were a young child, but I know the name!"

Janina had assumed that she no longer had any remaining relatives. When her family moved to the far eastern regions of newly formed Poland, they were separated from their distant relatives, but she remembered Antoni's name and that he had been spoken of at home as a kind and gentle man.

Her cousin said, "Janina, the army has received notice to evacuate to Persia, then to Kirkuk, to protect the oil fields against the Germans. I can get you out of here through the help of soldiers without immediate family who have volunteered to sign documents for women and children."

Janina was relieved to learn this because Wawrzyniec would never be able to sign such a document for her as his wife, and she had decided she could not ask any more of him after all his generosity.

In June 1942 Lieutenant Józef Ciot, a young teacher and son of a coal miner from Śląsk, signed Janina's travel documents saying that she was his sister. Janina immediately prepared for the journey to follow the army to Persia. She packed a few pieces of clothing, mostly donated by the army, and some food for the trip.

On their last day together, Wawrzyniec rode on his magnificent brown horse along the river by Janina's rented house as she and Mira walked alongside. To Janina, he could not have looked more gallant with his cavalry beret slanted across his thick, wavy hair and his sturdy broad chest covered with his uniform displaying various insignias. His eyes were covered with sunglasses clipped on to round eyeglasses that seemed too small for his large face.

There was really very little to say. What occupied Janina's thoughts was her deep desire to return home to Poland with Mira. Wawrzyniec was her guardian. He had helped her heal, given her the strength to continue, to be unafraid, to save Mira. In the grip of war, there seemed to be no future for two people in those circumstances, no commitment that could be kept, no declarations of love that could be honored. What more could she say to him than simply thank you and good-bye? You saved my life and that of my child, and now you are going to fight for peace and for freedom. Who knows if you will live. But she did not say any of that. There was no need for words. It was all understood.

"Good-bye," he said. "Take care of yourself and little Mira."

"Thank you. May God keep you in His care," she replied and took both of his extended hands, which were warm and inviting to the touch. They stood holding each other's hands. Janina looked down at their hands, and Wawrzyniec stared at her. She resisted the urge to hug him and instead grasped his hands harder until she felt self-conscious. Then she released her hands and averted her eyes from his penetrating look.

"Well, it's time," he said.

"Yes," she nodded, trying to smile.

As he departed, she waved. Mira mimicked Janina and waved her small hand. Wawrzyniec rode away in the manner in which he arrived, slowly, deliberately, turning back only once to smile.

Believing that she would never see him again, Janina watched him for a long time, until she could no longer see his figure in the distance. "Farewell, my guardian," she said out loud. Then she remembered an old proverb and quietly repeated it to herself. "Whosoever takes the child by the hand takes the mother by the heart."

War and Mental Illness

Was my mother really crazy, or did I just think so? In 1978, when my sister was first hospitalized, long before I had children or had begun to write my mother's story, I asked my sister's psychiatrist that question. The reality of my sister's situation was difficult for me to grasp. It was as if she had died. This person I thought I knew became a total stranger to me.

For my part, I had enrolled in graduate school and was desperately trying to prove myself after six years away teaching high school biology, first to pregnant inner city girls in a public school and then to privileged suburban girls in an all-girls Catholic high school. I was not prepared to deal with this new ordeal of my sister's illness in my rather cozy life.

"Oh, my God, will they think I'm crazy too?" I would ask my husband. He assured me that I was not crazy but said that maybe I should not mention anything about my sister to anyone. In those days, mental illness was still swept under the carpet. I didn't mention my sister's hospitalization to any of my colleagues. Only a few trusted friends knew.

My mother's daily hysterical phone calls to me did not help me cope with the situation. "She needs to stay in the hospital. She needs medicine. Don't let them let her out!" she'd rail at me over the phone from the Wisconsin farm.

Well into her sixties by then, my mother had her own health problems, so her words came in spurts. I could hear her labored breathing. When we were together, she always besieged me to open the windows. "I feel as if there is no air in the room," she'd say, gasping. She had cut away the necklines on all her dresses, which she had carefully sewn herself, leaving the raw edges exposed. The mere brush of cloth against her throat made her feel as if she were suffocating.

"Oh my God, oh my God!" she'd say over and over again to me on the telephone. "What am I to do? What am I to do?" And I thought to myself, what are *you* to do? What am *I* to do?

She kept me on the phone like that for hours. It was my turn to comfort her, but I was at a total loss.

I endeavored to navigate the system by making phone call after phone call to anyone in the medical profession who would listen—my sister's old internist, who seemed to be in tune with what was going on with her, the overworked social worker at the hospital, the volunteer woman at the self-help organization, the National Alliance for the Mentally Ill, which had formed in the wake of new mental health laws. These laws were designed to protect the rights of hospitalized mental patients. Instead, they effectively put mentally ill people on the streets to fend for themselves, as their families stood by helplessly watching them disappear into homeless shelters and to distant street corners, begging from strangers.

I began to imagine my sister among them. Though she was only in her forties and had always been an impeccable dresser, I envisioned her as an old bag lady like the one I'd often see on the streets of Chicago—pitifully overdressed in layers of clothing in the heat of summer, with heavy smeared eye makeup, long disheveled gray hair covered with multiple hats, hunched over and aimlessly shuffling in worn shoes too large for her, the cracked heels of her feet hanging over the smashed down backs of the shoes, and struggling with several old plastic shopping bags, bulging with rags and a few precious worldly possessions. I'd given food and money to such people, but would someone do the same for Mira someday? Would this be the war story all over again?

I tried as best as I could to explain things to my mother, whose attention was difficult to maintain. "Why can't they do something? Anything? So, what's supposed to be wrong with her anyway?" she asked, challenging me in her hysterical voice that made my heart palpitate and brought back painful memories from my childhood when she'd rail at me for something I had done. After I explained to her in Polish again to the best of my abilities the nature of Mira's diagnosis, at least the diagnosis according to the doctors, described her symptoms of delusions and incoherent talk, listed the medications with their mind-numbing side effects that she'd been prescribed, outlined the long conversations I'd had with her understanding doctor, I finally shouted into the phone, "There's only so much they can do! She has to let them help her!"

I tried not to slam down the telephone, as was my inclination at such times with my mother. It had been a couple of years since we had had a serious fight, and I tried to avoid the upset that usually left me depressed for days. It was completely typical that my mother should be in such turmoil at just the moment when I was stressed out about how I was going to prepare for my upcoming final exams. I thought I was losing my mind.

Maybe my mother is crazy, I asked the psychiatrist. "No," he said definitively. By then, he had learned the whole family saga—the war story—the arrest in Poland, the deportation to the labor camps in Siberia and Russia, the long dangerous journey through Central Asia to safety in India, and finally to a fleeting resemblance of a normal life in America, where my mother, still fiercely patriotic, always longed for Poland.

"If your mother was mentally ill, she would have broken down by now," he assured me. "You see," he went on in his detached, scholarly tone, "every one of us walks a fine line between sanity and insanity. It only takes some stressful situation, some extremely difficult event, to push us into insanity. From what I have learned, your mother is a very strong woman."

I was unconvinced that she was sane. It seemed like the war and the daily reliving of those horrible episodes would be enough to make anyone insane. I realize now that all my mother's detailed recollections and all those explicit war stories she told at numerous family dinners could not have helped my sister maintain her sanity. The school of thought that preaches we should confront our fears and lay them to rest, in order to become "complete" as they say in some circles of pop psychology, did not seem relevant. My mother never seemed to lay anything to rest.

My sister's mental breakdown could not be explained with pop psychology. It occurred shortly after my mother's near death from heart failure, when she had gone into the hospital for varicose vein surgery. Was that the stressful event that pushed my sister over the edge? Still thinking there had to be a connection between my mother's psychology and Mira's mental health problem, I asked the psychiatrist if mental illness was hereditary. Secretly, I wanted to know where my breaking point was, whether I had inherited any such thing, whether I should even ever have children. "It was probably her father, based on what I know of him—an alcoholic, prone to violence, but we'll never know for sure," he casually replied as I hung on to his every word, relieved to learn that I may not have inherited any such disease. Though I had thought of it as one and the same, maybe being "crazy" was not the same as being "mentally ill."

It was the War, I finally concluded. Only the war could have done this. The damn, damn war.

"What 'they' did to me, to Mother, to us," my sister would repeat when I visited her in the hospital. It seemed to me that she mimicked my mother's obsession with pain and suffering, the victimization that plagues many war survivors.

"There's nothing wrong with me," my sister declared. "I don't need any of those shit drugs. You go take them!" I gave up trying to convince her to take the medication.

Once she was stable enough to leave the hospital, she settled into her hermit lifestyle in her house, unable to work, dependent on government disability payments, under the watchful eye of my parents until they became too old and ill to oversee things for her. Many years later, I had to take over, and the experience of dealing with her helped me later in dealing with my son.

The effects of World War II on my family were extensive and long lasting. As in all families who have survived wars, the scars ran deep. Would I have been a different mother if my mother had not been preoccupied with all that happened to her and my sister during the war? It was a nagging question that emerged every time I lost patience with my own children, every time I felt frustrated with my own inabilities to cope with them, with my own rage, which surprised me. Was I becoming the mother from my childhood? I had hoped not, but I also was not the kind of mother that

I idealized—the kind that was always cheerful, always patient, always adored by her children.

I was angry with my mother for not being that perfect American TV mom of the 1950s. My mother was the raw, bitingly direct character who took no bull from anyone, whose lifelong ordeals made her the survivor she had to become. Every time I saw myself in her, I shuddered.

"No, no, I don't want to be like her," I would cry to my husband.

"Then, from where does your strength of character come?" he would ask.

When I continued writing my mother's story, conducting a new round of interviews after my twins were born, three years after I had begun the project, my mother often stopped in the middle of a story that involved Mira.

"You will take care of her, won't you?" she would plead, her voice bearing none of the power I had been accustomed to as a child. By then, her health had deteriorated so much that it was difficult for her to get out of bed most days. She stopped her routine walks, which she used to love. My father cooked all their meals, and it seemed that she was simply waiting for the end. My sister had managed to stay out of the hospital for several years, and my mother stopped talking about death, but it seemed that there was still some unfinished business that made her restless. Our sessions by then had to be short. She tired easily, and my twins slept only for short stretches in between nursing. But we were both determined to get her story written no matter what.

One time, I let the tape recorder run longer than usual as my mother digressed from the chronology of war events. Usually, she asked me to turn it off, but this time she went on about her first husband, Mira's father. I found it curious how she managed to find so much to say about all the other events in her life, but not much about him.

Mira once told me, "He bought me dinner once in the camp restaurant when I asked him, when I was very hungry, and Mother was still working. It was soup and stew of some sort. And then he told me to never bother him again. I never went up to him after that and then we were separated. He was sent to prison." Mira was five years old at the time and would not see him again until many years later, when she was a teenager.

Mira was attached to her father in spite of all the rejection, like most children, who tend to forgive their parents' transgressions, however egregious. She mentioned him sometimes in a quiet moment when I was a child and showed me the ring (which she still wears) that he had given her after the war, when they were briefly reunited in England, shortly before he died.

"He never helped us, and Mother had to use what little money she had from the fruit farm to exist. Later, in England, after the war, he was different. He had been in a hospital, but I don't know why," she said.

I noticed tears forming in her eyes as I asked her about some details recently when I was visiting her at her nursing home. "I can see that you are getting upset, so I'm sorry to ask you about him," I said.

"It's just my eyes. My eyes tear up sometimes," she answered, as she wiped them away.

"So, it was good that you had my father then," I said trying to cheer her up.

"Yes, that's why I called him 'Father,'" she smiled.

We did what we had to," my mother would say. My sister repeated that refrain. "Mother did what she had to do." Sometimes I wondered if that meant something terrible, something unspeakable.

From Here to Hell

The familiar clatter and jarring of the freight train heading to the port city of Krasnovodsk on the Caspian Sea comforted Janina—they were on their way out of the Soviet Union. As they rode, she was oblivious to the hardness of the raw wooden benches and the stifling heat. Even the lack of fresh water was bearable. Time seemed to move like lightning across clouded skies. When they arrived at the station, Janina and Mira walked a few miles with groups of other passengers to the port where they boarded a hot, stuffy ship that would take them across the Caspian Sea to the Persian port of Pahlevi. Janina could breathe easier. No longer did she need to look over her shoulder for any NKVD soldiers. No longer would she feel desperate for food. Mira would not go hungry again. She would have a proper dress and shoes and even a new doll to replace the one she lost. She would be able to go to school.

After twenty-four hours in the stifling heat of the crowded ship, they emerged feeling rejuvenated, elated by their new sense of freedom. They were finally out of the Soviet Union. At the port, older children jumped into the sea as if to wash off the stench of that horrible land, and everyone rejoiced at their first taste of real freedom in more than two years. Janina and Mira took the obligatory disinfection shower and were administered required immunizations. After receiving a packet of dry food, they boarded open trucks driven by Persian men hired for the journey to a temporary Polish camp near Tehran.

As the caravan of trucks traveled along narrow, rocky roads through the precipitous Elburz Mountains the passengers looked down into narrow valleys so deep that the bottoms seemed to disappear. Temperatures reached such heights that Janina felt as if she would shrivel up. She adjusted Mira's head scarf and fanned her flushed face trying to keep her from the sun's burning rays.

At a rest stop, some of the passengers, mostly women, jammed into a small restaurant that sold baskets of exotic fruit, but Janina could not afford to buy any so she and Mira stayed outside and ate their dry food rations with some water from a local well.

"Would you like some grapes?" a local woman asked Mira. Mira looked at Janina, unsure whether to accept them, but Janina nodded to her and thanked the woman.

The caravan was soon on its way again along the steep serpentine road. The passengers learned that two trucks had fallen into the ravine and disappeared in a blur of dust and smoke, killing all aboard. At the end of two days, they reached the outskirts of Tehran, where they stopped for rest and food at a small kiosk. A shiny, clean and elegant automobile stood near the kiosk, and a man who looked like an Arab sheik dressed in a clean white flowing gown stood next to it, but he could've been Persian, as it was all confusing to the Poles who were unfamiliar with such people. As the women stood admiring the enticing fruit for sale at the kiosk, the vendor approached them with a large basket and motioned to them to take the melons and other fruit. He pointed to the man and said something in what sounded like Arabic.

"The Arab must have paid for the fruit," said one woman. Janina cut into a melon, and pink juice trickled along the tabletop. Mira smacked her lips at the sweet delicacy. When they had finished their portion, Janina approached the Arab, who was seated at a nearby table, and attempted to thank him in broken English, which she was beginning to learn from the British, who were in charge of setting up the resettlement camps. He smiled a wide, humble smile and bowed his head.

Ten thousand women and children and some old men settled into three units in the camp, assigned to either flimsy bamboo-mat barracks, windowless brick houses without doors, or simple tents. Nights were cold in this desert climate, and the brick houses that were once used as stables for German horses allowed the cold night air to blow in with ease. The refugees' only protection was the wool blankets that had been supplied by the British.

Though they were under British care, the camp was operated by Polish authorities who were refugees from Siberia. The barracks were crowded but clean and modest, and each family had a separate space. Soup, tea, bread, butter, and some fruit for the children were regularly provided. Janina took an administrative job managing the dry goods and clothes that were sent from America for distribution to the families. From one blanket, she made a coat for Mira. There was even silky hosiery that was a luxury, but the real prize was a flannel nightgown.

"I ran my fingers over the soft fluffy fabric and could not get enough of its comforting softness against my abraded skin. I prayed for the American woman who must have donated it—I prayed that she would always be in good health for all her kindness." For many years, Janina's favorite sleeping garments were those made from soft, warm flannel.

Although the facilities were the best they had seen since leaving Poland, the winter of 1942–43 was particularly cold. From the American donations, Janina received a warm winter coat, which proved to be lifesaving. Diseases were emerging once again in the crowded conditions, and this time Mira contracted scarlet fever, which was considered very serious when left untreated. Much to Janina's relief, the form of the disease was mild but she was concerned that Mira might develop pneumonia, and every day as she walked back from the hospital she cried the entire way.

By then, they had been in Tehran almost eight months and Janina wondered if they would ever be able to leave, as war raged on in the world.

Janina regained much of her strength, and her hair became thick and lustrous once again, even lightening with the bleaching effects of the bright sun. She combed and twisted it into a roll that framed her delicate face, and a certain peace of mind turned her persistent frown into radiance. She had gained a few pounds, which filled out her sunken, emaciated chest and legs, and she was beginning to feel like her old self once again. One day, a Polish officer invited Janina to lunch at an expensive restaurant, one reserved for those with certain connections, and presented her with a proposition. He was a short man, and he had a constant sweat over his face that he nervously wiped away with a white handkerchief.

"Madame, please. I want to tell you about this 'Arab' gentleman. He is rich, old, but handsome. You could be secure for the rest of your life!"

"What are you proposing? An arranged marriage?" she asked.

"Yes, of course!"

Janina hesitated.

"Madame, think of your child."

"It is only for my child that I would ever consider such a thing," Janina asserted. She smiled modestly at him as she sipped her tall glass of cool water. She had heard of this before; these wealthy men seeking to enlarge their harem with tall, blond European women.

"Really, Sir, I do not want to become isolated from our people. I am honored by the proposal that you so enticingly deliver, but please tell your 'sultan' not be offended that I must decline his offer. I am still hopeful that Poland will someday be free and that we can all return to our homes."

By March 1943, activity in the camp began to mount as the authorities made preparations to permanently resettle the Polish refugees. As the war continued in Europe with little end in sight, volunteers from the camp were being trained to assist the Allies. Janina began a nursing course offered by the Red Cross along with an English language course. In the meantime, Mira attended school under one of the larger tents. In addition to working all day, Janina stayed up late into the night studying the difficult English language, but she was determined to master it, as she sensed that somehow this language would one day become crucial to her and Mira's well-being.

As she pushed herself, Janina did not notice her own health declining. One night she noticed small blotches of red-streaked mucus in her white handkerchief during one of her frequent coughing fits. The last one took several minutes to subside, and her chest felt as if it were going to explode. She tried to hide the bloody handkerchief from Mira and everyone else, for she feared what she knew led to her sister's death. Tuberculosis, they had said, but they were never sure. It all seemed like some distant, timeless, foreign past. She was fearful that she might be dismissed from work, but after a few weeks, her cough subsided.

After completing the nursing and language courses and getting some practical experience at the local hospital, Janina was sent to another transfer camp in the desert near the Persian city of Ahvaz to work as a Red Cross transportation nurse. Janina and Mira lived in a tall brick building that had once housed horses or camels. The building had been converted into makeshift compartments with sleeping benches for the crowds of refugees. In Persian, the name Ahvaz refers to hell, and when the heat of summer reached its oppressive peak, Janina understood its meaning. The scorching sun pounded down on them incessantly. Even in the darkness of night, they could not escape the heat. Never had she experienced such dryness in her throat or the debilitating weakness that breathing in the hot air brought on. She performed her nursing duties with difficulty, having to stop often to rest at midday when it seemed the ground was aflame.

Janina's duties included circulating among the camp refugees who were arriving weekly and identifying those who were suffering from serious illness and so needed to be sent to the hospital. People were malnourished and easily fell prey to various diseases. Accustomed to bland, watery food and bread from their recent stay in the Soviet Union, they became ill from the fatty sheep's meat because their starved and delicate systems could not properly digest it. Dysentery, diarrhea, and malaria were widespread.

Due to the crowded conditions in the brick building, Janina and Mira were moved into a tent along with one other family. As summer progressed, they developed techniques for surviving the relentless sand storms of the region. During one storm, Janina and Mira huddled inside the tent as wind howled and pounded sand against its heavy canvas walls. When it was all over, they shook sand out from their hair, clothes, and every article of their belongings. When she tried to open the flap of their tent, Janina discovered that more than four feet of sand had piled up against it. She and Mira began digging out. The imprints of camel hoofs had been replaced by a beautiful wavy smoothness. Large jugs and mats, rocky clumps of dirt and piles of goods were completely covered up with sand. The wind began howling again, and Janina and Mira quickly returned to the safety of their tent.

Janina often thought of Wawrzyniec, wondering where he was, whether he was even alive, during the monotonous hours she was confined to the tent. She decided to write a letter to him after an officer from the Fifth Division stationed in Kirkuk, in Iraq, arrived to visit his wife and family and offered to take back letters to the other soldiers.

"Dear Sir," she began. That formal opening seemed strange to her.

"We arrived in the camp after a long, hot journey, but we are grateful to be free. There is plenty of food and adequate shelter. Although we are living under tents, Mira is in school for the first time, and I am happy to be out of the Soviet Union. I am working for the Red Cross. The conditions in the hospital are depressing. Children die daily. They stare out from sunken eyes, lost in thoughts of their deceased parents and siblings, and when they close their eyes, many do not open them again.

"I will be forever grateful to you for all that you have done. Without you, we would not have survived. May God repay you for your kindness and generosity." Janina picked up a photograph of Mira and stared at it for a minute before putting it inside the envelope. Mira seemed much older than her eight years of age in the photo. Her long thin arms extended from the short puffy sleeves of a dress that seemed too small for her. Only hints of adversity could be detected on her unsmiling face, half hidden under a large brimmed straw hat.

A child's face never lies—one can see everything in the eyes, thought Janina as she stared at Mira's image.

Part 4

Bittersweet Lessons

I, as Savior?

In the winter of 1998, I sat at my desk, finally relaxing after several months of dealing with my younger son's broken leg, my father's cancer treatments, my ailing mother's transfer to a new nursing home, and my older son's school anxieties. I had finished a first full draft of my mother's story the previous spring, and that summer I took a long road trip with my three children, who were thirteen and ten at the time. I needed to become reacquainted with them after several years of intense consulting work that often kept me away from home for several days each month.

That fall, my fiercely independent father had been diagnosed with cancer, so at ninety-three, he finally agreed to live with us in Chicago under my care. As a result, I had to put my mother into a nearby nursing home as her health was very poor, and I simply could not take care of her. I felt very guilty. At the same time, my younger son required a wheelchair while his severely broken leg healed, and for four months I had been chauffeuring him to school and other activities. My older son was falling apart mentally under the pressures of his last year of elementary school in preparation for high school, and my daughter had just suffered a serious burn to her hand. The whole family was in crisis mode. Somehow, my level-headed husband was able to maintain some semblance of order in his work, and I was very grateful for his emotional support.

That Monday morning in late January, I breathed a deep sigh of relief. All the kids had gone to school with my husband, the first day back for my younger son after having had the five external pins that kept his leg in place removed. My father was quietly tucked in bed for his morning nap. I planned to visit my mother in the afternoon at the nursing home after I picked the kids up from school, so I was looking forward to a few precious hours to write without interruption.

Then the phone rang. It was Mira. "Oh, hi there," she began with an unusual hesitance in her voice. It was odd for her to be calling me at that hour, and I was rather put off by the interruption.

"Do you happen to know a real estate attorney?" she asked without first trying to engage me in the usual chit-chat about trivial things. Right away, my brain went on high alert, and I felt my stomach knot up.

"Why do you want to know?" I asked slowly.

"Well, I don't know," she began again, and I sensed her confusion. "I received this letter and supposedly, I have to move out!"

"What? When?" I shouted into the phone.

"Ah, in two days, it says . . ."

"What happened?" I interrupted.

"I don't know, all this psychotic shit. They manipulate everything," she went on, revealing the paranoid side of her, which I usually tried to ignore.

"OK, bring me all the letters you received," I told her. Within the hour she arrived at my house with several letters from a real estate agent and the sheriff's office. I reviewed the letters and called the agent.

"You are not getting my sister's house," I said in as calm of a voice as I could muster. What I really wanted to say to him was, "You scumbag—how dare you take away an old woman's house!" My sister was sixty-three.

I dropped everything I was doing and stayed on the phone nonstop for the next two days trying to determine if there was any hope of reclaiming Mira's house. But all the answers I received were the same—it was far too late to do anything about it, and she would have to move out. Move out to where? My house was already overflowing with six people, and my sister with her strange ways would add a layer of stress that we did not need or want. Luckily, the outside temperatures were below freezing and the sheriff could not legally evict her, so within the week I went to probate court. With her surprising but reluctant agreement, I obtained full guardianship of her and took over trying to resolve the matter. My father had found the house for Mira in 1972, and she bought it very inexpensively as part of an estate sale. He fixed it up for her, and for many years he and my mother would come down from Wisconsin for the winter to stay with Mira. After Mira had her breakdown and lost her job, my father kept a vigilant eye on her affairs until his own health prevented him from watching over her.

In between taking care of my father, the kids and the house, working, and visiting my mother daily, I tried to find a way to get Mira's house back. We found an attorney who gave us hope, paid him a hefty retainer fee, and backed off only slightly while he worked on the complicated case. A judgment lien had been recorded against Mira for an unpaid medical bill. She had had foot surgery some years back, and there was an outstanding bill for four thousand dollars, which she insisted should have been paid by her insurance. When the bill was never paid, unbeknownst to the rest of us, the medical provider slapped a lien against her house. The real estate agent had then bought the house in a judicial sale for the four thousand dollars that was owed. He paid Mira's ten-year-old water bills—which she had refused to pay because she believed that the city had wrongly assessed her when they installed new water lines and she insisted that the water was tainted—and then resold the house, sight unseen, netting over seventy-five thousand dollars on the deal. I was furious. Not only did the house have sentimental value, but my sister would have no place to live.

It seemed that one thing my mother and I had in common was our commitment to saving Mira one way or another. This time, my mother was incapable of understanding what was going on, and on February 23, 1998, almost sixty years after her arrest in Poland, my mother died. We put Mira's house matter aside for a few days as we mourned and prepared for the funeral.

The battle over the house lasted for nearly four years, partly because of my dogged persistence and partly because of the bureaucracy of the legal system. Critical assistance came from the Cook County Office of the Public Guardian's attorneys who stepped up to help in this age-old battle of the opportunistic over the weak. The final day of the week-long trial took place one day before the terrorist attacks of 9/11, and we were victorious. After that, I hid out at home on my couch for the next week watching TV news coverage of the attacks and crying at the tragedy, trying to recover from the ordeal of the trial, but feeling vindicated. I was grateful that my husband could keep things going otherwise. Mira was relieved, but I always felt she never fully realized how close she came to losing her house or the massive efforts it took to regain it for her. She could not attend the trial, as the whole ordeal had reactivated her paranoia.

The story of my sister's case was reported in the *Chicago Tribune* and the *Chicago Sun-Times*, and she and I were interviewed together for the local evening news, as the reporter, who also had a family member with mental health issues similar to Mira's, decided to make an example of the real estate investor. As a result of Mira's case, the law in Illinois was changed to require another step in the sale process before someone could be evicted from their home.

I was not able during this time to reflect on all that was happening in my life to make sense of it. I only moved numbly forward, somewhat like my mother had done in the midst of crisis. I became a stronger person, satisfied that I too could stand up to adversity, although of a different kind from what my mother had experienced. I had kept my promise to my mother to watch over Mira. The whole ordeal exhausted me, and a few months later I found out I had breast cancer and had to summon that strength once again.

From where did that strength come? I ask myself. I could easily say it came from my father. "Don't give in," he would respond. "Be strong," he would say, rallying me onward. But I see now that my mother's influence must have inspired the determination that moved me forward. I never thought that she would be the one to give me strength. I never thought I'd give her credit for something so critical to my life and my family.

"I took her in my teeth and dragged her through it all, and we survived," my mother would say of her efforts to save Mira during the war. I imagined a mother cat carrying her litter to safety. That remark alone must have influenced me more than I realized. And, then, there was my mother's pleading question that rang clearly in my mind, particularly from one visit with her at the assisted-living facility in Wisconsin years earlier. "You will take care of Mira, won't you, Danusiu?"

Who was I, this person who once resented her mother's imposition of Mira's problems on her? I'd ask myself. The threat to Mira's house, which I viewed as an attack on her well-being, was a call to action for me. Several years later, I was called to action once again in a fight against another invader over which I had no control. My son's cancer proved to be a true test of my strength, just as my mother's hardships during the war proved to be for her. I finally understood my mother. My motherly instinct to protect my family emerged stronger than I could have imagined possible.

My mother's ordeals did define me and her stories proved to be precious, albeit bittersweet, lessons that became critical to my own survival and that of my children. As I watched my young son, not quite two when I first began writing my mother's stories, I wondered what it must have been like for her to lose her first baby, then another, and then to try to save Mira. Years later I found out what it was like as my younger son battled cancer. I began to understand why a prevailing sadness overshadowed any joys in life for my mother. I puzzled over it, wanted it to disappear, but it never did for her, and I feared it would not for me.

I finally became philosophical about such things, about my son's cancer, having become exhausted by the emotional turmoil and not yet having arrived at a spiritual understanding of it all. Was my philosophical resignation similar to my mother's emotional distance, the result of numbly moving forward in an attempt to survive? My mother never seemed to push her memories away from her consciousness, beyond emotion, as many people do in response to such tragedy. Rather, she seemed to relish her memories like some unbearable sadness of being, not knowing how to stop dwelling on them or how not to talk about them. Perhaps she believed that they could give her life validity by eliciting pity from all of us, in some half-crazy evocation of induced suffering. Trying to have a "normal" life around my mother seemed impossible for me. She had repeated her stories so often she never forgot them, and always they were the same, as if they came from a script that she had merely incorporated into her own life and into mine.

So, why did I keep coming back to her story when I had tried so hard to get past it? Was it because I had begun to understand her plight during those war years, trying to save her child and herself? As I feared losing my own child, I sensed the heavy sadness that must have weighed on her.

"Where does one go once one has been to hell?" my mother asked out loud sometimes.

For her, simple joys were ludicrous reminders of a life not lived—the preoccupation of others with insignificant events such as birthdays and anniversaries was laughable. At one time, I had no answer to her question about hell. I now understood. My own sadness had brought me to this insight. Having gained a sense of her ordeals, the trivialities of life indeed seemed inconsequential.

I have learned through my children that children teach us to be real human beings. As caring parents we are ready to lay down our own lives for another—that is the greatest gift—to become lost in another without regret or resistance or care—that is true love, though my mother's unconventional ways of trying to show how she loved me was not apparent to me as a child. It saddens me to realize that only as an adult.

My mother would say that belief in God provides redemption, and she prayed a lot for that relief. My father too sought such redemption in prayer, although he once asked himself as he watched a German soldier in a small military plane shoot down an innocent peasant walking his horse through an open field during World War I, "Where is God? How could He let this happen?"

Oh God, if there is a God, I have prayed, help me get through my child's ordeal without losing my mind. Help me help others, for in helping others as my mother always did, I can, perhaps, find myself, and this sadness will be lifted. That I did learn from my mother.

India

In mid-1943, Janina and Mira boarded a British ship in Ahvaz, along with hundreds of other refugees. They were bound for India, a British colony. Britain's agreement with the Polish Government-in-Exile in London was to help the thousands of Polish refugees displaced from the Soviet Union. There was a resettlement camp in India that was to become their final destination while the war continued. Other refugees traveled to Mexico, Africa, and New Zealand. The British arranged for the transport, but the ship had to be escorted by British military ships through the Arabian Sea owing to the ongoing fighting. At one point, sailors began to shout to the crowd of refugees but Mira did not understand the English spoken. One of the sailors ran up to her, and as he put a life preserver on her, he tried to explain, as she later understood, that a German submarine had been spotted nearby. Luckily, the sub was avoided. At another point, Janina saw a floating round mine with its large spikes extending from the water. Again the ship managed to avoid that. The ship also had to avoid the masts of sunken ships bombed in the fighting that protruded from the dark waters and threatened to capsize their ship. Throughout the two-day trip, the tension among the passengers aboard the ship was clearly visible in their eyes as they stared out in anticipation of land on the horizon. Mira remembered not feeling hungry.

When they arrived in India, they first landed in Karachi (now in Pakistan). At the port, they were escorted to a camp where hundreds of large tents were set up for them. Unknown to Janina and Mira, they were located in an area often frequented by striped hyenas. One night they absentmindedly had left some food in their tent. Toward morning when it was still dark, Mira awoke to some rustling noise. As she opened her eyes, she came face to face with one of the hyenas. She was about to scream when the hyena turned quickly and ran out of the tent.

On another occasion, Mira and a group of other eight-year-old children crept into a very large empty tent. One of the boys called out to them to follow him and waved in the direction of a small hill behind the tent. Then he suddenly jumped up onto the outside of the tent and slid to the bottom, giggling the entire way. That afternoon Mira and the other children enjoyed themselves on their newfound slide.

Soon Janina and Mira boarded a passenger train to Jamnagar. After settling in on a bench in the crowded train, they stared out of the window. The landscape changed from flat prairie to rolling hills. The temperatures rose dramatically by midday, and the sweltering moist heat made it difficult to breathe. At one point, the ground shook as if an earthquake was about to heave them up, but it was just a large herd of elephants stampeding along the railway tracks on the open plains. Janina marveled at the massiveness of these creatures she had never seen before. As the train next passed through thick, lush jungles, hundreds of monkeys shrieked and scampered running directionless, fleeing a group of completely naked natives on a hunt.

At a stop in a village, young women dressed all in white danced silently around sacred cows lying in the streets. The women fanned the cows and adorned them with wreaths of fresh, colorful flowers. The strange beauty of this land was beginning to intrigue Janina and Mira, and they looked forward to what other mysteries they might witness.

There were several camps for Polish refugees. Near Jamnagar in Balachadi, orphaned children were confined within restricted campgrounds, while the camp in Valivade (Kolhapur) housed five thousand women and children in bamboo huts. Near a resort in Panchgani, situated within tabletop mountains, about sixty miles south of the city of Pune, was St. Joseph's, a Catholic convent boarding school for girls. The school received several of the Polish refugee children, Mira among them. She attended classes with a hundred other Polish, English, and Hindu girls. In the meantime, Janina worked as a Red Cross nurse at the Polish children's hospital in Jamnagar. Because the convent school was so far away from

Janina, Mira could only visit her infrequently on longer breaks throughout the school year.

The school was a finishing school, and classes were taught in English or Hindi. Even though Indian princesses attended it, on Saturdays all the girls were required to darn their own socks in accordance with the strict rules of the dour nuns, some of whom were German. The more privileged girls were permitted to keep exotic pets such as monkeys, rabbits, and tropical birds, and Mira became fast friends with many of the girls. When they were given time off, they would run up the high steps to the table-top mountain beside the school to play organized games such as volleyball or simply to go for walks. Mira enjoyed her time at the school and delighted in the much cooler climate high in the mountains. She did not like the hot, humid weather where Janina was stationed.

Adjusting to the tropical climate was a challenge for Janina, who greatly disliked hot temperatures. The rainy monsoon season was the worst. The entire roof of her barrack leaked, and rain poured in on her. In one corner of the barrack, a three-foot-long lizard made its nest in the small dry space under the roof over the toilet. During her visits, Mira said the lizard peered out at her like a dragon. She threw sticks at it to scare it away. Janina liked to watch the gentle creature with its enormous bulging eyes. "They need to live too," she would say and admonished Mira not to bother it.

Janina felt differently about the many scorpions and other biting insects. Each evening when she returned from the hospital, she carefully inspected her sleeping area for the poisonous creatures, killing several of them. One evening, she ventured out for a walk along a path to the sea while the rain had stopped briefly. She walked with her head down, lost in thought, through fields of peanuts and over a small bridge that crossed a stream. She was startled by a whip-like sound ahead of her. As she lifted her head, she saw the head of a huge black snake veering up, "at least eight feet," she claimed, but it probably wasn't that big. It was hitting the ground with its tail and looked as if it were ready to pounce on her. She turned and ran.

At the hospital, a group of boys of around seven or eight years of age killed a small cobra that had made its home under the bed of one of the boys. "They were so brave, those little children," she recalled.

Of the 350 children at the camp, 120 had malaria. About every six weeks during the epidemic, Janina also developed a fever and chills, but her case was mild. Mira, however, had more debilitating symptoms, a recurring high fever and chills that were thought to be more damaging. Janina always suspected the disease to have adversely affected Mira's brain. Mira recovered, but for the rest of her life Janina worried about what the disease had done to her.

Life seemed to settle down for Janina and Mira, and they began to enjoy their new strange but beautiful surroundings. Even the oppressive tropical heat was becoming tolerable.

After two years, Janina accepted a nursing post in a private hospital in Bombay (Mumbai), which was closer to Panchgani, so Mira could now visit on longer weekends as well. One time on a trip to Janina, Mira's bus was stopped by a crowd rioting during one of many such outbreaks against British rule in India. A sympathetic Indian took Mira in his car to the Polish Consulate for safety during the riot.

Dr. Masina, whose wealthy Parsi family had established the hospital, was a ninety-year-old full of energy, and he took a liking to Janina and Mira. On occasional holidays he would take them on picnics to historic places in the area, one of which was just north of Panchgani, where a monument marked the historic unification of India. Mira remembered signing the visitor's book and looking at Dr. Masina as he choked back tears, much to her surprise. Another time, Dr. Masina brought Janina and Mira a silver coin collection and a figure of an eagle made from shells that was mounted on top of a heavy black base.

Mira enjoyed the yearly Diwali light festival and watching the lighted clay pots float on small rafts full of colorful flowers in the nearby river. The Hindu marionette puppet shows along city streets were a special delight to her and the other children from the school and a good lesson in Indian history. On a visit to Bombay, Mira was walking with Janina hand in hand when they came across a

Hindu wedding. The couple was showered with flowers, and Mira later recalled that there was a strong scent of jasmine, which became one of her favorite flowers. Another time they visited the Taj Mahal and enjoyed the cooler temperatures and the exquisite beauty of the mausoleum and its gardens. Janina recalled sitting at the reflecting pool sipping a tall glass of cool, crystal clear water. "I never tasted such good water," she said. "It seemed surreal as the war continued, and I wondered what had happened to my fellow countrymen and to my dear guardian."

The World at War

After leaving Janina and Mira at Dzhalal-Abad, Wawrzyniec was sent to Iraq, Palestine (Israel), Lebanon, Syria, and Egypt with General Anders's forces to prepare to fight the Germans. He worked as an adjutant for the Fifth Artillery Regiment, Anti-Tank Division of the Polish Second Corps under General Bronisław Rakowski. Eventually, he ended up in Italy, in the newly formed Tenth Hussar Wołyn Regiment under Major Antoni Smodlibowski, where he took part in a defining battle at Monte Cassino, for which he was awarded the Monte Cassino cross.

While the Soviets had deported hundreds of thousands to their labor camps and murdered over twenty thousand Polish officers and others at Katyń and elsewhere, the Germans perpetrated mass killings of Jews and others in gas chambers built by the Germans in Poland, which resulted in over eleven million victims in total.

At the end of 1943, "the Big Three" (Britain, America, Russia) had their first meeting in Tehran to discuss resolution of the war against Germany. The Allies' division of Europe into zones of postwar control left Poland in a vulnerable position under Soviet influence. It was the beginning of Poland's downward spiral into Soviet Communism's stranglehold. Most Poles, including Janina and Wawrzyniec, who had witnessed Soviet atrocities staunchly maintained that Roosevelt and Churchill had sold Poland out to Stalin. It would take the West several more decades to come to the same realization, as documents kept secretly hidden away by the Soviets surfaced.

After the war ended in 1945, it took several more months for the refugees to be released so they could go back home, a home that no longer existed in Janina's case, as the part of Poland she was from had become Belarus. Those who had witnessed the daily struggles of life in the Soviet Union were reluctant to return to Poland under the new Communist rule. At Yalta in 1945, the Big Three met again, and Churchill and Roosevelt made attempts to reassert their influence over Eastern Europe by recognizing Poland's right to land annexed by the Soviet Union from eastern Germany. However, at the third and final meeting in Potsdam later that year, the Western powers left Poland to its fate with Soviet Russia.

In 1947, with the end of British rule in India, Janina's camp was closed, and she and Mira were transferred to the large camp in Kolhapur. There, Janina continued studying English, medical laboratory testing, and cosmetology. Mira continued her schooling in Panchgani at the convent boarding school.

Though the beauty of India was enticing to Janina, the hot, humid climate and the threat of malaria became unbearable. She longed for the cool climate of Poland, the embracing sound of the Polish language, the possibility of reconnecting with distant relatives and old friends, and the familiarity of her ancestral home, but she feared facing the Communists more than anything. By then, her farm was gone, as the shifting borders of Poland did not encompass that part near Grodno anymore, and in any event, having lost all her documents in the Soviet Union, she had no way to prove her land ownership. She abhorred the thought of never seeing her parents' graves or the graves of her two babies again, but she knew the deceptions of the Communists too well and feared for her life if she were to return to Poland. "Besides, I have no one left there, anyway," she tried to console herself as she discussed these matters with friends.

Stories circulated in the camp about how the Soviets had stood at the outskirts of Warsaw in 1944 simply waiting for the Germans to finish off the Polish Home Army in the uprising to liberate Warsaw. She learned of how Polish soldiers were being sent to prisons and labor camps when they did return to Poland. Since the exiled Polish government was in London, Janina felt safe going to England. Her English was getting better each day, and, she reasoned, England was not that far from Poland in case there was any change in the political climate. And so, considering herself a political refugee, Janina left India with Mira by ship in late 1947.

Janina continued to work as a nurse on the ship, and Mira stayed with her, as the living conditions for ship workers were better than those for the rest of the passengers. They traveled back through the Arabian Sea and the Red Sea and into the Mediterranean, where unusually stormy weather made everyone, including Mira, very seasick. Along one of the stops, Janina purchased a souvenir Persian prayer rug and a silver bracelet to commemorate the Polish Army's contribution to the battle at Monte Cassino against the Germans in 1944.

England

After passing through a temporary resettlement camp in Liverpool, Janina and Mira settled in Coventry. Janina began work as a nurse in a factory that made sewing needles, wheel spokes, bicycles, motorcycles, and cars. She made a good salary and tried to be content and happy. Mira, by then thirteen, attended a public high school. Both were settling into peaceful life in Coventry, which had been heavily bombed during the war. The city, like the rest of England, was slowly recovering from the wreckage.

Janina's frostbitten toes had not bothered her in the hot climate of India, but in the cold, damp weather of England, they began to burn. The pain was so excruciating that she decided to undergo surgery to have her small toes removed and to eliminate the painful bunions that had formed on both feet. After the surgery, Janina tended to walk heavily and off balance. She always regretted that, owing to the loss of her toes, she could not dance well.

In her spare time, Janina tried to locate friends from the camps. She placed an announcement with her name and address in the Polish language newspaper, especially hoping to locate Wawrzyniec, if he were still alive. Not much later, a letter from Hereford, another resettlement camp for Polish soldiers, arrived. The script was familiar. It was from Wawrzyniec.

On a day off from work, Janina went to visit him as he lay in the hospital recovering from an accident that had left him with a severe concussion. Their reunion was brief, as he was convalescing in a large hospital room full of other Polish soldiers who were likewise recovering from illness or wounds. Since Janina was not able to take off much time from work, Wawrzyniec promised to write. Though he struggled with constant dizziness, he managed to write often to Janina, motivated by his loneliness.

"My dearest Janio . . . I hope to be released soon so that we can be together . . . I miss you terribly . . . With love and affection, Waw."

Neither of them could marry due to their previous marriages, at least not in the Catholic Church. While the war was going on, Wawrzyniec's wife in Poland had become convinced he had died. After the war, when she discovered he was alive but hadn't returned to Poland, they became estranged. In the meantime, Janina connected with her husband, who was in England by then, but only to implore him to provide for Mira and later to request his agreement to a divorce. Finally, after each of them succeeded in procuring civil divorces, Janina and Wawrzyniec did marry in a civil wedding, in a dark, dingy English courthouse, an occasion about which Janina never wanted to reminisce. Wawrzyniec's wedding gift to Janina was an ornate wooden box with inlaid pearl shells and ivory obtained somewhere during his wartime travels in the Middle East.

After the wedding in early 1949, Janina, Wawrzyniec, and Mira settled into a bombed-out row house at 34 Hill Side in Coventry, and by the end of the year I was born. I visited the place on that first trip to Europe in 1976. The English taxicab driver said to me in his very Cockney accent, which I could barely understand, "I bet you're glad your parents left for America," when I observed the small, dilapidated place in the poor working-class neighborhood of the factory town that Coventry still was back then. I didn't even ask to go inside. I imagined that I would still have been living there if we hadn't left, as life in England was difficult enough for the English after the war, not to mention for foreigners.

After being discharged from the Polish Army, my father, whose English was poor, took a factory job in Coventry, as his college education was of little practical use in that struggling nation. During that time, food was limited to weekly rations of one pint of milk, one egg, and half a pound of meat for each person. The city was being slowly reconstructed, and the large hole in the bombed-out roof of our rented row house was finally repaired after months of rain and snow falling on our heads.

Life in England seemed to settle down for our new family. Thoughts of returning to Poland faded, but they were never surrendered completely. My father sent weekly packages of clothing and food from our meager rations to his ex-wife and two daughters, who were Mira's age, and to his sisters and their families in Krosno in southern Poland. Mira was able to reconnect with her father, who had been released from prison in Siberia and then went on to serve in the Polish Army. It was their first meeting since the days of the labor camps in the Soviet Union. A few years later, he died in England after we had already left for America.

My mother was always surprised at how much Mira cried when she learned of her father's death. "He didn't do anything for her," she bemoaned. She was always restrained in talking about Mira's father, as if hoping to protect her from the truth. Whatever he was, I could understand how my sister would have felt abandoned by her father. By then, my father had become close to her and supported her so that she could finish school.

When I was about three months old, my mother was diagnosed with tuberculosis when several large holes in her lungs were found on her x-rays. She was told to stop nursing me immediately and was not even allowed to hold me. I can imagine the agony my mother must have felt in being prevented from touching me, wondering the whole time if I had become infected with the disease, remembering how her sister had died from it. After a few months, she was cleared, but she was always cautious about its return, and I can remember her going for checkups with me at free health clinics even long after we came to America. My chest was x-rayed, and luckily there was no sign of the disease in my lungs.

When I was about two years old, my mother underwent a hysterectomy. In the process of healing, a blood clot lodged in one of her lungs and fluid accumulated, making it difficult for her to breathe. My father was told that my mother would most likely die, so he brought me to the hospital often, but I was not permitted to be near her. For several weeks, my father brought her fresh squeezed orange juice that he obtained by trading sugar and other food rations from his share as she struggled to regain her health. One time, the story goes, my mother saw me in the distance as I paraded back and forth in the waiting area with my new homemade toy elephant. No one else could see me from behind the curtains around the beds, but my mother raised up both of her arms and began calling to me. The nurses thought she had gone mad. My mother thought for sure that she was going to die and begged the nurses to allow me to come to her, but they would not permit it.

I do vaguely remember playing with the stuffed toy elephant in the hospital. My mother had made it for me out of my father's khaki army wool coat just before she was hospitalized. My father glued the stiff feet to a wooden stand with wooden wheels that he had made in the factory. Tied to the top and around the belly of the elephant was a colorful basket that he filled with red, green, yellow, and brown M&Ms. I can still remember carefully picking out the red ones, thinking they were more delicious than the others, and begging my father to allow me to have just one more. I still have the elephant, which I display in a glass case to remind myself of those hard times and to show my gratitude for my parents' sacrifices.

My father recalled how he worried about what would happen to me if my mother died. Several weeks passed while she stayed in the hospital. Mira attended school while my father worked, so he began leaving me in a nursery during the day. In the cool autumn weather, among the dozens of children, I quickly developed a cold, which later turned into pneumonia. During my illness, my father pretended to have an injured knee so that he could stay home to take care of me. Supposedly I almost died. My father was eventually able to find an older English woman to take care of me while my mother remained in the hospital recovering from the surgery.

Early in our stay in England, my father applied for us to immigrate to Canada, but we were denied permission due to my mother's poor health. Then we were finally granted permission to come to the United States. On February 2, 1952, we arrived in New York on the British ship, *Mauritania*, with fifty dollars among us. My father was almost fifty, my mother was almost forty, my sister was eighteen, and I was two. As we passed the Statue of Liberty, my mother said she found it daunting to express her gratitude, to finally be reaching a land that not only promised freedom but exuded it in every way. She was determined to make America her beloved country, and she brought with her the same patriotism that had been imbedded in her in Poland.

My mother often recalled how as a child during World War I in Poland, she ate the sweet, cinnamon-flavored white rice that President Wilson sent over after the war had ended. Every time she made that rice dessert when I was a child, she recalled President Wilson.

"I never expected to see America," she would say. "It was a long and desperate journey to my second homeland."

The Land of White Rice and Cinnamon

As a child in America, I lived with my nose buried in my father's photo albums. The war photos he took and developed drew me like no toy could. We would sit together for long hours going through the black and white photos. As he carefully turned the pages of the album, he described the strange places and exotic peoples he had captured by his inventive camera techniques. There were three blue suede leather-covered albums with his Polish Army insignias firmly glued to the covers. Those albums contained early photos of the primitive Polish Army and civilian camps that had been hastily constructed in the cold winter of 1941–42, after Soviet Russia had just released thousands of army prisoners and civilians from the camps.

The tan leather albums had embossed, colored Arabian and Egyptian symbols and contained photos from the Middle East. There was page after page of military gatherings that he had photographed. Late into long nights, he had labored to develop these prints in the faint light of his makeshift darkroom of his tent. As desert sands swirled outside in the wind, he meticulously preserved the memory of their Middle East encampment. There were picnic scenes and official army celebrations, especially Catholic masses celebrated on simple field altars. There were photos of local women in full burkas, local men on camels, and hundreds of scenes from the surrounding lands, mostly swirling sand hills with beautiful clouds in the background captured in black and white. Clouds were his favorite subject outside the interesting old, hardened faces of the local people.

"I bought cameras and photographic supplies while my friends invested in rich luxurious Persian rugs that they later sold for great profit," my father laughed. I often wondered if he really did regret spending the little money he had on his important hobby. It seemed that he derived far more pleasure from that than the return on selling a rug could have provided.

I grew to love geography through my father's many tales of foreign lands traveled during the turmoil of the war. On occasion, I was allowed to sit with him late into the night, way beyond my bedtime, in our cramped kitchen, which he transformed into a temporary darkroom. I watched in awe as the imprints of his photos came to life in the vinegary odor of the developing chemicals that filled the room.

"Show me again where you've been," I would beg him as I spread out a world map of Europe and Asia. Tirelessly, he pointed to these strange names from a world halfway around the globe. At the age of six or seven, it seemed like a great adventure to me.

"Here is Poland where I lived, though now the borders are different again," he said, pointing as I listened completely absorbed. "Here is Lithuania, where I was captured in 1939. Here is Russia, where I was imprisoned. Here is Persia, where we trained, and Palestine and Syria, where we received more training, and then Egypt, where we fought the Germans. Here is Italy and Monte Cassino, where I fought, and here is England, where I became a war refugee and where you were born," he explained.

I did not sense any sadness in him. Though those had been sad times, he always maintained a positive outlook on life. As an adult, I realized that he had saved me from the sadness that had engulfed my mother.

On his lap, I learned history as few children could in America. One time, he went on to tell me the story of how he had almost been killed.

"During one attack at Monte Cassino, I ran from one doorway to another. Suddenly, there was a loud bomb. I couldn't hear any more sounds. I saw only explosions all around. Then, a flash of light streaked across the side of my face. Something hot pressed against the back of my neck. Expecting to see blood, I reached for my neck and grabbed a hot metal object. I found pieces of a bomb and brick in my hand. The shrapnel had struck the brick wall behind me, bounced off, and nearly severed my jugular vein. I've

kept it all these years to remind me of how close I came to death."
Then, he showed me the piece of metal.

Sometimes, I open my father's army field altar, a curved
wooden box with a cross embedded in the lid and a place for two
candles. I take out the piece of shrapnel that lies alongside his
various medals, including his Monte Cassino cross. I run my fingers
over the hard sharp edges of the molten piece that have not
changed with time. I ponder how without this one irregularly
shaped metal object, my mother's and sister's lives would have
been different and how I might not have been born.

My own education in America during the 1950s and 1960s was
nothing like my sister's disjointed education, which began in the
labor camp, where she spent most of her time alone, and continued
in Central Asia and India in the temporary resettlement camps
and orphanages. As my mother and the other Polish women settled
into their newfound freedom, they tried to establish a sense of
routine for their children. My mother worried about Mira's education all the time. By the time they reached Tehran in 1942, Mira
would have been in second grade. At the labor camp, my mother
did not have time to teach Mira reading and writing. Whatever
Mira learned had been almost by accident as she sat with the other
older children who were fortunate to have their mothers with
them while their fathers or other family members worked in the
forest to fulfill their work quota.

Years later, my sister often lamented how hard it had been for
her to obtain an education. She blamed her poor beginnings. "I
didn't have a good foundation," she would say, sadly looking into
the distance as if trying to recall those early days. "But you! You
better study hard!" she admonished. She never mastered reading
well and lacked confidence in her ability to keep up with assigned
school work. At one point, she was almost dismissed from the
university because of her poor grades. Determined to make something of herself, she approached her advisor with her dilemma.
Normally shy and reluctant to speak to strangers, my sister mustered up the courage to protest her grades.

"I had to learn from books that were shared by several students.
In the desert at the settlement camp, the sand blew for hours into

our faces and we had to hide for days at a time covered up in the tent. We moved often. What I learned in one camp, I had to re-learn in the next. I never got the connections. I was always sick. I almost died." When she had finished telling her story, the advisor granted her an extension to finish her schoolwork.

Having spoken only Polish with some Russian thrown in, the English language was a stumbling block at every turn for my sister. English is a difficult language to master for a Slavic-speaking person. She and my father would often have pronunciation con-tests with just the *th* sound, where my father could only produce a weak version of the correct sound. "Father, just put your tongue curled up against your teeth and blow," she would repeat as she demonstrated, but his poor results frustrated her. Sometimes, I think he just wanted to tease her, for she was very serious about this one matter. He ended up laughing every time and never did master the sound. "Really, Father, you learned five languages and you can't get this one thing right?" she would scold. "Maybe it's my mouth full of dentures," he answered in his defense with a twinkle in his eye. She never did relent.

It was that quiet stubbornness that ultimately allowed my sister to finish school. She obtained a degree in chemistry from Roosevelt University in Chicago in 1958. I remember her talking about her long hours of study into the night. Though she was a talented artist, she said, "I picked science because there wasn't so much required reading and writing."

Life in America became a stable refuge for my parents and sister, and I thrived in the stimulating company of a family and commu-nity who had gone through so much, even though it was confusing to me until I learned Polish history well. With my sister's help, I managed to finish my undergraduate studies, my mother's voice about the importance of my education always in my head.

When I married, my mother waited patiently for me to have children but gratefully never pushed the idea. I dreaded having a daughter for fear of having the same poor relationship that I had had with my mother. My mother often stated her strong opinion, even before I had children, that children should never be put into childcare. I struggled with that decision after my first child, a boy, was born. I was in a well-paying professional position after having worked hard for several years to obtain my master's degree in engineering. Could I just walk away from all that? It was the early 1980s, and most career women like myself hired nannies for their children as they embarked on nontraditional career paths. At that time women comprised only about 3 percent of all engineers, and many men in the profession were not especially welcoming of women. Executive women were just hitting the glass ceiling, and more often than not they had to give up family life if they wanted to get off the "mommy track" in the corporate world. I thought of my mother, who had made her choice clear when I was a child. I stayed home, being able to do so with my husband's support. I began to write.

Forever the Farm

How did my mother's longing for a simple life become so complicated? She liked to say that she felt as if she were sitting in a darkened movie theater watching her life unfold on the screen, so vivid were her tales.

It seemed to have all started with farm life—the birth into farm life, the pursuit of the dream of farm life, the actual living of farm life, the reading about farm life. As a teenager, I spent weeks in the summer at the Wisconsin farm helping prepare it for my parents' retirement. My mother would sit and read aloud to me in Polish her father's favorite lyrical poem, *Pan Tadeusz* by Adam Mickiewicz, the Polish or Lithuanian or Polish-Lithuanian writer, depending on one's perspective. This long and difficult-to-understand 1811 poem is the epic tale of two feuding noble families and of the love between Tadeusz, who is from one family, and Zosia, who is from the other, against the background of the revolt against the Russians who were occupying Poland at the time.

While I installed wall tiles in the kitchen, she was uncannily at peace as she read, and it was a rare occasion that I actually enjoyed her company during those tumultuous years of my American adolescence. I was growing up with half of me in Poland, locked in some faded memory of my parents of a life that was full of tradition and that clung to the past, unable to reconcile itself to the suffocating Communist presence, and the other half in the 1960s culture of free America, full of raging rebellion against the establishment and tradition.

On breaks from work on the house, my mother managed to persuade me to help out in the garden. With only a couple of years until my father's retirement, they had already planted rows upon rows of raspberries, which needed to be watered, weeded, and picked. More than any other crop, the raspberry field reminded my mother of the farm she had to leave behind in Poland.

My mother introduced many such reminders of the life she left behind, ever more of them the older she became, and in the most unexpected ways, like in the kind of dogs she had. I was never fond of small dogs, but my mother insisted on having these female Chihuahua-like mixes around at the farm. They always had the same name: Figa. When one died, she would find another. I asked her one time, "Why do you keep naming them that?" As the small dog licked her face, my mother giggled and gave her tidbits from her dinner plate. Her answer was always the same. "She reminds me of *my* Figa." And, of course, that led to another retelling of how her Figa had jumped out of her arms that fateful day of her arrest and deportation and how she was never to see the dog or her farm again.

Sometimes, my mother asked me to sit by her on the couch in a quiet moment. One time, with my sister at her other side, she began gently rubbing my scalp. It felt relaxing as she twirled her fingers around locks of my hair and massaged my scalp, and she seemed to enjoy it. "You have such beautiful hair," she'd say, and I would smile, relishing the rare moment. It wasn't always so bad, I reminded myself—my mother's touch, that is. I told myself that a mother's touch should feel welcoming, anticipated, appreciated, loving. Most of the time, hers was pragmatic, as if she were clearing away dishes from a table or pressing an iron to some wrinkled clothes. So, when she began that soothing massage of my scalp, I didn't react the way I usually did when she touched me. It was a relaxing touch, but she always seemed to be searching for something. Had I known that she was on a quest for lice, I might not have enjoyed it so much, but then I didn't think much about such things. I had not yet comprehended what she and Mira had been through.

In winters at the farm during Christmas break, we would often take long walks in the late afternoon along the quiet unpaved road near the farm or into the woods along the tracks made by my father's tractor, which he used to pull huge logs to the house for firewood. After a heavy snowfall in this remote farmland, I could imagine the desolate vastness of Siberia, and I began to look forward to hearing my mother's stories, much to my surprise. The fields before me would be still in an eerie kind of way that was almost painful to my ears, and I could imagine my mother's trek back in Siberia.

Sometimes, the snow was so deep I struggled with each step as my leg sank almost to my hip. My mother and sister often accompanied me on such walks into the woods or on the desolate road. When we returned to the house, we sat around the wood-burning stove warming ourselves and more stories would emerge. Mostly, my mother spoke and my sister and I just listened, but on occasion my sister added a few words here and there. Sometimes, my mother spoke of how beautiful her own mother had been. I remember wishing that I could've felt the same about my mother. Then she was quiet and sad and I dared not ask more about her. I hadn't realized that her mother had been a hero in her own right. I wished that I could have at least seen a photograph of her.

Five years after they had started the working farm, my parents sold off all the farm animals, realizing that it was too much work for them. My mother became an avid reader. My father, on the other hand, continued to expand their vegetable garden, growing zucchini the size of baseball bats and weeding rows of cucumbers, potatoes, beets, and carrots. He taught himself to use the zucchini to make sweet bread with cranberries and walnuts, although he did ask me how to remove the baked bread from the pan to keep it from sticking. I was amused to be advising him for once. He gathered bushels of pickling cucumbers that my mother made into sour pickles without using vinegar, and he shredded cabbage for delicious sauerkraut that my mother later used in her special hunter's stew, *bigos*. They canned hundreds of jars of beets, carrots, and green beans, which lasted for months in their cellar. They seemed satisfied with their life on the farm, but there was always that occasional surprising comment about one day returning to Poland.

Perhaps, with all the reading, my mother was trying to catch up with the education to which she so aspired as a young woman but that always seemed to be just out of her reach. My mother insisted that my sister or I go to the Polish library in Chicago and bring back dozens of books that she then devoured. The farm meant peace and quiet and time for such luxuries. Living in the city was difficult for my mother—it was hard for her to shut out the noise, the people, and all their distractions. Living in the country was simple—merely satisfying the need for food, shelter, and clothing left time for contemplating the *philosophy* of life. My mother discovered philosophy for perhaps the first time when she became absorbed in the works of Proust, Balzac, and many Polish writers. She tried to engage my sister and me in discussions about her readings, but neither of us was literary, and by that point in our lives we were too tired for philosophical bantering with our mother.

My mother had time to ponder these higher thoughts, which she did more for her amusement than for any practical application such speculation might have to her life. She had returned to the simple peasant's life of which she had always dreamed. She became the well-read farmer intellectual, like her father, and yearned for like-minded people with whom to discuss these newfound insights—only those sorts of people mostly lived in the city.

"Only in the country will it be safe if war should erupt," my parents would say to me. This was one of their reasons for wanting to live outside a large city as Chicago. I listened to those words with a cautious sense of disbelief, nervously laughing to myself, secretly fearful that even in America, we could be subjected to the kind of devastation they had experienced. Their conviction was that strong. My father often spoke of war erupting in the Middle East. By the time of the terrorist attacks of 9/11, he was already slipping away from life, and I was grateful that he was not aware of what was happening.

It was a sad day for all of us when my parents could no longer manage to live independently on the farm and had to sell it. I came up with my children to visit just before the auction that would dispose of the many things that reminded my parents of their joys and hard work on the farm. I had long thought of the farm as a refuge for my family, but with one-year-old twins and a four-year-old, I was engrossed in childcare and so sleep deprived that there was nothing I could do. My father had a severe case of

Lyme's disease, caught from a tick on one of his many treks into the woods for firewood, and my mother was slowly deteriorating from congestive heart failure.

It was time to move them into assisted living.

Reconciliation

M y mother deserved better than what she got during the last few days of her life. I had been planning on moving her from the nursing home in my neighborhood to one with Polish-speaking workers that, unfortunately, was located much farther away from my house. I knew it would be an ordeal to visit her there, considering how hard it was to get my father ready every day and into the van. He moved slowly with his bad knee, which he had injured chopping wood years ago, but I couldn't stand to hear her complain anymore about how "they hit me," as she told me each time I visited her. I looked for bruises on her arms and body but couldn't find any. I knew she was prone to accusations of maltreatment, but I did think she deserved to be somewhere where at least the attendants understood the language of her birth, to which she had exclusively reverted. And then, they had pumped her up with Haldol, the antipsychotic drug commonly used to calm unruly patients in nursing homes. After all, by their account, she was "crazy."

I received a call from the nursing home around ten o'clock at night on February 23, 1998, and even before the nurse said anything, I knew it was the end. I had tried to imagine that moment. I could not cry, at least not at first, just as my mother had not been able to cry when her sister and then her brother died. It felt like a vise had gripped my chest, and I found breathing difficult, but I had to rouse my father, call my sister, get dressed and face what I had been dreading for weeks. It would be my first encounter with the death of someone who mattered to me.

I let the kids sleep. The morning would be early enough to tell them. After my sister arrived, we left with my father for the home, which was only a few minutes away by car.

In those past few weeks, while I struggled to regain my sister's house, so much had happened that I barely had any time to visit my mother, who bounced between the nursing home and the hospital every time her heart teetered on the verge of stopping. Then she developed a urinary tract infection, and I remember struggling with her, trying to steady her onto the toilet when she begged to use it every few minutes. She couldn't use a bedpan and could barely stand up, let alone walk to the bathroom. No sooner had she gotten back in bed than she thought she needed to use the toilet again. Sometimes we went through this routine several times in an hour. When I was not there, the nurses' aides would just let her lie in a wet bed. During the last hospitalization, she had developed pneumonia, but she was returned to the nursing home, too stubborn to die.

And now, she had died, and I had to see for myself. I didn't want to believe it. It would have been only a few more days before I could have arranged to move her to the Polish nursing home. That is, after I got my sister's house situation under control, after I dealt with my older son's anxiety attacks, after I attended to my daughter's burnt hand, after I got my father to his oncologist for yet another appointment, after I breathed. In retrospect, my mother's ordeals in life had prepared me for my own, though I had not yet recognized it.

"I pray for a heart attack," my mother used to tell us abruptly during those dinnertime conversations woven with tales of her ordeals during the war. When I looked puzzled, unsympathetic teenager that I was, she assured me that "that's the best way to go. Quick. No lingering." I never knew what to say when she talked about death and just dismissed her as "crazy" again.

I realize now that all that talk about death and dying did not really prepare me for what I was about to encounter at the nursing home, but in some unexpected way, I felt comfortable with the *idea* of death. I accepted death as part of life, but I dreaded to find out if I could accept it as part of *my* life.

When I first started recording my mother's story, she would often drop her head down and stare into her hands, which had become red and thick from work and wrinkled and blotched with brown spots. "Once I had beautiful hands," she would lament as she had so many times, and I sensed her tiredness with life. And then she added, "It's time to die." That would startle me. I sat unable to say anything, trying to deny that I'd heard her. I was torn between agreeing with my mother, who had lived longer than even she could have imagined, and wanting to have her around for me a while longer, hoping to make peace with her.

Everything seemed to come too late in life for my mother. She was thirty-seven when I was born, and she always seemed old to me. I was thirty-seven when my twins were born, but I felt young, a product of a good nutritional upbringing in war-free America. Back then, I tried to finish writing her story as I chased after my three-year-old and cared for my newborn twins. In all of that commotion, I finally learned to empathize with my mother as a mother. I learned to appreciate the joy and agony that must have overwhelmed her as she tried to raise Mira under those impossible labor camp conditions.

I entered the darkened room in the nursing home that my mother shared with another woman who also spent all her time in bed. A curtain was drawn between the beds and the whiteness of the fluorescent light above my mother's head glared into my eyes as I tried not to avert them from her face. No one had prepared me for what to expect.

There is a hauntingly beautiful painting in the National Museum in Kraków entitled *The Death of Ellenai* by Jacek Malczewski from 1883 in which a very young and beautiful woman rests outstretched on a cloth-covered divan, propped up with a pillow of hay, her eyes closed as if sleeping, her long blond hair flowing out from her pale thin face as she lies in her white dress, her legs covered with a fur throw on top of which rests her slender, delicate arm, as if she had just finished caressing the softness. Her sad male companion sits at her feet staring downward toward the floor, lost in thought. I learned that the painting symbolizes the failed 1830 November uprising of the Poles against the Russians. I was drawn to the painting in a strange way, and I stared at it too long for my liking when I returned to Poland. I tried to imagine myself lying there with my long blond hair flowing out, my family sad at my side. Would death be like that for me? Elegant and dignified, my body prepared with just the right dress, just the right arrangement? I expected to find my mother in this manner.

The first thing I noticed was my mother's mouth gaping open. I had the odd impulse to go up to her and to push her mouth shut. A white cloth band was tied from under her chin around to the top of her head. She was propped up slightly with the hospital bed raised so that her head was almost eye level with me as I entered the room. This should not be how I should encounter my mother! It should be like Malczewski's painting, I thought. Then, a very strange thing happened. I looked at her closed eyes. They were the most peaceful I had ever seen. Her forehead was relaxed, not furrowed like I had been accustomed to finding it. I stood silently staring at her in awe. I was relieved. She had died peacefully.

I asked the nurse the purpose of the cloth band, and she told me it was to keep her mouth from falling open further, a common thing in death. I tried to look only at her eyes. I looked at my poor father, who sat staring at my mother. My sister stood next to me. I was too mesmerized by my mother's strange peacefulness to think about them. After a few minutes, my father said, "So, we go now. It's the end." I wanted to linger. I really didn't know how to behave, but I respected my father's wishes and we left.

My mother had always told us that she wanted to be cremated, much to my father's dismay. On the way to the funeral at my friend's Polish Catholic church, I picked up the urn with her ashes from the funeral parlor. My father and sister were with me. It felt surreal to be transporting this small square bronze urn with the remains of my mother's body. I was surprised that the priest allowed it for the service. I had always thought that Catholics were supposed to be buried, not burned after death, but then my mother was not very Catholic, and she had never been to that church. By then the Catholic Church was more relaxed and embraced many different people, and it was a Polish priest, after all, who conducted the services.

I had prepared the eulogy, which I had written late into the night before, wiping away tears that seemed to flow too easily. Who was this person I was so bold as to eulogize? Would she have chosen me for this task? I didn't even think about asking her. My mother was never one to belabor decisions about such things anyway. "Just put my ashes in the ground. It doesn't matter," I expect would've been her pragmatic answer. I'm sure she would've preferred that we donate the money for the funeral expenses to charitable causes, like the orphaned, starving children of the world.

So, with all the strength that I could gather, I began my eulogy with the story of our arrival in America, with how my mother had instilled Polish patriotism in me but also fierce loyalty to America, "where I never had it so good," as she liked to say. "*This* is my country now," she would declare, but I always sensed her longing for the Poland that was no more, the Poland that had raised a generation of staunchly determined people who remained loyal to the country no matter where in the world they ended up. She had sacrificed much to bring me up in that tradition, spending all of her Saturdays, her one day a week free from her job, dragging me across the city to Polish school and Polish Girl Scout meetings and events, until I resigned myself to attending school six days a week and could take public transportation on my own.

She was the frugal, defiant survivor, and perhaps the greatest lesson she taught my sister and me was the importance of obtaining the education that seemed to always elude her, of "becoming *somebody*," as she liked to repeat. Referring to a husband whom I might someday have, she would expound, "He could die, get sick, or leave. Then where would you be, raising children on your own? With a good education, you can be independent, free! Nobody can take your education away from you. You can be poor, but nobody can say you are not somebody."

As I read the eulogy, my sister stood on the altar steps next to me, both of us in tears. My mother's stylish portrait made by my father in the early days of our American experience stood next to the urn with her ashes. The urn did not seem large enough to contain the power and worth of this mother. Mira and I tried to comfort each other, lost in thoughts of our very different experiences of the woman who had raised us. I had asked my sister if she wanted to say something at the funeral, and at first she declined in her usual demure manner that often left me wondering what thoughts lurked in her mind. Then to my surprise, she produced a short eulogy in Polish, which I translated:

"What can I say to truthfully value you? I am at a loss for words, both in Polish and in English. But, as the saying goes, a picture is a thousand words. When I think of you, I see a mother cat carrying her young and protecting them from danger. I see a person who is very sympathetic toward human beings and sincere, who in her truthfulness could seem even to lack tact and who was always the best friend there ever was. You lived for many years, but there was little fortune or calm in your life. There was the horror of the First World War, then the horror of the Second World War, and at the end, the torture of a Siberian-like nursing home in America. You, Mother, were always the Siberian hero."

I ended my eulogy by acknowledging my mother. "I thank my mother for sharing herself with me and reliving those excruciating experiences. In listening to my mother, I have come to see the fine line between sanity and insanity. My mother and I had finally come to terms with each other in our very different worlds—mine of privilege by *not* growing up in war and hers of always reckoning with the past. In having her story told, she at last could be at peace and had stopped talking about the torment. She had let go and gradually succumbed to the inevitability of death, knowing that her memory would not be forgotten. I honor your life, Mother, *Mamusiu*. It was not for nothing. It was for everything."

King Takes Rook

Before my mother's death, my father had always been vivacious and engaging, a charming gentleman, eager and able to converse on any topic, reading various newspapers with political stories that could still arouse him into heated debate. Well into his eighties he enjoyed playing his beloved chess with each of my children, often winning even as my sons became excellent players.

After my mother's death, all that had mattered to him no longer seemed important, and he spent most of his days sleeping. I used to recall how he would always be sleep deprived as I was growing up. He worked two jobs so that I could have some semblance of comfort and then in his off time fixed up our two-flat building in Chicago and the farmhouse in Wisconsin, and then after he retired, he maintained the ten head of cattle for milk. It seemed he was always busy, always moving, always working on something. "I'll sleep when I die," he would joke.

In the business of taking care of him and the children and fighting to regain my sister's house, I hardly noticed how little interaction my father and I had anymore. I missed his respectful questions about what was going on in my life, his precious insights into what ailed my children, his intelligent conversation on politics, history, current affairs. When my mother died, I lost my father as well. I lamented the loss of the times of my youth. I had missed him so much after he had moved to Wisconsin, and I thought I would never regain those carefree childhood days with him. I had always tried to reestablish those times—on rare occasion he would dance with me or we would go ice skating and dance around the ice rink at Rainbo Arena on the north side of Chicago. People would stop to ask how old he was, and he would laugh and tell them his real age. Everyone thought he was at least ten years younger, and this continued well into his late eighties. I finally took away his ice skates when he fell and hit his head on the ice. He had that infectious joie de vivre that made me laugh, and I eagerly looked forward to spending time with him. But after my mother died, that joie de vivre just evaporated.

How many times have I heard that it is the journey, not the destination, that matters in life? Yet I rushed along a path in life to get things done, to move toward the time when I would finally be able to do what I really wanted to do, only I didn't really know what that was. How many times did I miss some small but significant moment to cherish, either with my children, or with my father, or even with my mother, in that mad dash to some undetermined destination?

Four years after my mother's death, in the midst of doing way more than I should have taken on, I was finally stopped. My cancer diagnosis led me to reset my priorities in the midst of constant thoughts about death. I understood my father's reaction to his own cancer diagnosis. Suddenly, I was thinking about myself in a very real way, like there may not be a tomorrow. With great sorrow, I put my father into a nearby nursing home, then I moved my father-in-law there as I underwent my treatments. When my younger son was diagnosed with cancer, my father lay dying at the nursing home. I didn't have the heart to tell him that his grandson was so ill.

It was determined that my father could no longer swallow. This explained why he had aspirated some liquid into his lungs and developed pneumonia. There is no cure for this age-related condition. When the doctors started discussing feeding tubes, I realized that this was the beginning of the end, and I told them, "No, he wouldn't want that." I looked at my father's thin bruised arms, and it was hard for me to believe that this was the same man who could lift two-hundred-pound items, a man who at eighty years of age rebuilt our front porch, who at eighty-six still chased after my children when he watched them for me while I worked, who at ninety was still driving his car and picking my kids up from school.

I rushed between doctor and hospital appointments for my son and the nursing home and back again. When they started talking hospice care for my father, I knew that meant the end was near. I called my friend to get the name of a Polish-speaking priest to come visit him. I began preparing for the funeral with a veteran of the Polish Army who had kindly offered to attend the services and salute my father. I called my other half sister, Luta, to come up from Florida and take turns with me and Mira sitting at my father's side. I was determined to be there at the end, holding his hand just the way he had held my hand all those days when I was ill as a child.

I was better prepared for my father's death than for my mother's. When the moment came, I was holding his hand as his favorite music played from a bygone era. The voice of the Italian opera singer Caruso filled the room with an eerie clear tone. I had just taken over holding his hand from Mira when I noticed how limp it suddenly went. The hospice nurse examined him to confirm the end. I fell over onto his legs and bawled to the point that Mira had to tell me to stop. I wasn't even embarrassed.

Those few moments turned out to be my only real mourning in the chaos of dealing with my son's cancer.

My father was my savior, my guardian, as he once had been my mother's. He showed me how joyous life could be by teaching me to play chess, dance, ice skate, ride horses, do photography, love dogs, garden, paint, be his committed workshop helper. He was a doting father who wanted a son and got me instead, but I never felt unwanted. He was a man of supreme integrity. He was a skillful student of human nature, and I could confide in him like in no one else. He was a man of his word, a man who respected tradition and who demonstrated loyalty and commitment to family, country, and to his fellow human beings—a gentleman like no other.

"At age ninety-three, he finally succumbed to cancer and reluctantly gave up his independence," I concluded my eulogy at his service. "The father I had missed so much finally came back into my life full time. Yet, even during those few frail years, he gave of himself, which was the greatest gift of all. I was fortunate enough to be present to this great soul, to hold his hand and stroke it the way he had once held and stroked mine, and that privilege is the greatest gift he has given me—to be complete with him and myself. *Tatusiu, kocham cię* (Daddy, I love you)."

Both of my parents are buried in the special section of Maryhill Cemetery dedicated to Polish World War II veterans and refugees—she as *Sybiraczka* (Survivor of Siberia) and he as *Obrońca* (Defender).

There is one plot reserved for Mira next to them.

Epilogue

On Being a Mother

My initiation into parenthood with my first son was both welcome and frightening. In spite of all my formal teaching education, mothering was a daily challenge that completely unnerved me. It was learning by fire, but somehow I mastered the basics of taking care of a baby, even though I did not have any other relatives in America as role models. At first I rejected anything my mother had to say on the matter of parenting, but slowly I began to accept her advice. I became more confident in my abilities to parent, and when my daughter arrived with her twin brother some three years later, I was thrilled to be having a daughter, along with the bonus of another son. The concerns I had had about having a daughter dissipated, and I no longer fretted that my relationship with a daughter would result in the same difficult one I had had with my mother. I was eager to see what would develop.

Throughout the writing of my mother's story, and what reluctantly turned also into my story, I had avoided one crucial question. So what kind of a mother had I become? I had tried not to become my mother, whose hysterical ways of expressing her displeasure with me as a child and teen and her anguish whenever she embarked on a particularly distressing story from the war or whenever she faced a challenge in life had so unsettled me. I often pondered about what kind of a mother she would have been had the war not happened. Trying to separate the mother I experienced as a result of the war from the one that might have been kept me from facing up to the reality of my own mothering—how much of her war experiences really did influence me?

I only know that I had made a conscious effort to be different from my mother. I read every parenting book available, attended parenting classes, and joined new mother support groups. I took on motherhood as a profession, as an American mother, not as a refugee Polish mother. Of course, at those times when I was completely exhausted from lack of sleep and was feeling disconnected from the working world I had grown to love and that I had left to take care of my children, I didn't always apply all that I learned from those books. I began to resemble the parent I vowed not to become. I raised my voice, insisted that things be done my way, lost my patience, and even spanked my children.

I wanted to control every aspect of my children's lives to protect them from the world where danger lurked either physically or psychologically, just as my parents had wanted to control every aspect of my life when I was growing up. I would soon learn that I could not control everything in their lives. In the meantime, I did what my mother had done for me—cooked from scratch, sewed special outfits, especially for holidays, made sure they got plenty of outdoor play and, kept a regular sleep schedule, monitored who their friends were; in other words, I made sure all of their physical needs were well taken care of. Like my father had done with me, I read to them, played with them, engaged them in many activities, sent them to good schools, and talked to them. Fortunately, like my mother, I was able to stay home during their formative years with my husband's support. That became particularly important during their teenage years, especially when my younger son was undergoing cancer treatment. To our great relief, he has survived, though the tumor is still there, a constant reminder of the damage it caused and the stress it continues to cause. Yet each day is precious, a gift not to be squandered. Like the trauma of war, this trauma too leaves us forever changed.

How much of my mother's war experience affected me in my parenting is hard to determine, and I would probably need to spend hours on a therapist's couch to figure it out, but I do know that those experiences did affect me and were reflected in the way I parented. Part of it was cultural—that embracing, protective hovering over and control of children. When I was a child it was not unusual for my father to scold another child, unsupervised on the street, for doing something wrong, much to my huge embarrassment. This was common practice in Europe. When I attempted to correct other children's behavior, my children protested loudly. In other subtle unconscious ways, I incorporated my own upbringing into my children's lives. Whenever I had left food on my plate, my parents would both reprimand me and remind me of the many starving children in the world. In a similar way I insisted on my children not wasting food by taking only what they could eat, and I often pointed out to them how other children they knew threw out lots of food. They seemed to accept my direction on that matter. It was much more of a challenge when it came to other matters.

I often wonder what my children would say of my parenting, but I am afraid to ask them. They have not yet lived enough, nor do they have children of their own. My mother never really talked with me about her parenting until I became a parent because she assumed I wouldn't understand, and I think my children likewise would not understand me. As they progress through adulthood, our relationships continue to develop, but glimmers of their thoughts about me as a mother perhaps can be found. Is the answer reflected, for example, in the many Mother's Day cards they prepared for me as children expressing love and gratitude and sometimes even apologizing for their misbehavior? Can it be seen in the small gifts that they proudly presented to me at various occasions? At those times, I was careful to show my appreciation, remembering how little my mother seemed to care about such things when I was a child. I am sure my children love me, but I imagine they find my ways too controlling, much like I found my parents' ways too controlling. By the time I reached adolescence, my mother had become exasperated with me. She gave up trying to monitor my behavior and handed this responsibility over to my father. I remember the day she announced to me very dejectedly, but firmly, that "from now on, you are now going to deal with your father for anything you want." I was surprised but relieved. In my mind I had prevailed with all my argumentativeness. Had I known that I would face the same kind of challenges with my own teenagers, I may have been more forgiving of my mother. I finally came to understand how difficult it had been for my mother to parent me.

I deliberately avoided talking to my children about the War and how it had affected my parents and only mentioned it in passing when they were growing up. I did not want to burden them like I had been burdened, weighed down by an inconsolable sadness that seemed to permeate every aspect of my life. By the time they were old enough to understand such things, my parents were too old and sickly to talk about the war, and Mira never wanted to talk about it without prodding. I wanted to consign it all to the past. Only in writing my story have I come to realize that it is nearly impossible to escape the effects of war, no matter when the war has occurred.

Writing this book helped me resolve many issues with my mother. I was able to forgive her for all her craziness that confused me so much as a child and for all the guilt she laid on me in insisting that I be responsible for my older sister. I began to see her as my sister had seen her—as a friend who related to me as an adult, as a painfully truthful person whose lack of finesse now seemed oddly amusing and less hurtful, as a basically good person who always tried to do the right thing. I regret that we never were able to connect in the way that I thought she and Mira connected, though I admit I was a challenging child, not the quiet, acquiescing one that my sister had been. Secretly, I took satisfaction in the fact that as a mother I had something to share with my mother that my sister never had—Mira never had any children of her own, though many times she took care of me as if she were my mother. I finally accepted that my mother and I came from two different worlds in two different times and that our relationship could never be the kind that I expected or craved.

Through my mother's stories of her experiences during the war—the intertwining tale of a mother who saves her child and lives to have another—I realize that I did learn to survive, even to blossom, as a mother. As much as I resisted becoming my mother, I recognize myself in her in the good ways. And as for my own now adult daughter? Recently on Mother's Day she wrote in a card, "I love you so much. You are the Momma bear to our tribe. I love your support and knowing you'll fight for me whenever I need you."

Notes

Part I. The Generation between the Wars

9 "one of several hundred thousand civilian Poles deported from eastern Poland." The exact number of those deported is still controversial in the consciousness of the Polish diaspora. It is often claimed that more than one million were deported, as this number was supplied by Polish authorities in 1944. Suspicion of any information disseminated by the Communist government, either in Poland or the Soviet Union, adds to this controversy. The Soviet Communists only allowed access to NKVD documents after 1989 with the fall of the Communist government in Poland and later in Soviet Russia. The figure may be as low as 320,000 and as high as 800,000, counting all the deportations through June 1941 for all groups, including soldiers in prisons and prisoner-of-war camps. Today's historians have accepted the 320,000 figure, admitting that more investigation is needed. See Jolluck's *Exile and Identity*, Snyder's *Bloodlands*, Kochanski's *The Eagle Unbowed*, and Porter-Szűcs's *Poland in the Modern World*.

13 "the distant hills of the Niemen River valley." My mother often recalled the river around Grodno near her farm, which she visited and which I visited in 2008 on a trip to Lithuania, but most of the descriptive details here come from Eliza Orzeszkowa's epic tale in *Nad Niemnem*.

14 "Janina considered Roman Catholics to be Poles." How ethnicity was, or is, defined is highly controversial in the context of accounts of post–World War I Poland. For my mother, "true" Poles were those who adhered to Catholicism, recognized the new government that was led by Józef Piłsudski's political party, and were patriot freedom fighters like her brother; the people who had lived in what became eastern Poland near my mother's farm near Grodno considered themselves either Belarusians, Lithuanians, or Jews. See Porter-Szűcs's *Poland in the Modern World*.

15 "NKVD commandos." The Naródnyï Komissariát Vnútrennikh Del, or People's Commissariat for Internal Affairs, was a secret police force that operated more or less without oversight and was notorious for arresting people without cause at all hours of the day and night.

15 "As a landowner." Many people like my mother were sent to Siberia without explanation because they were landowners. Being the wife of a Polish Army soldier who fought in 1920 to free Poland from the Soviets was another reason for her arrest. See Gross's *Revolution from Abroad* and Jolluck's *Exile and Identity*.

16 "Stefan Starzyński, mayor of Warsaw." Starzyński tried valiantly to encourage resistance and to comfort the citizens of Warsaw and the country and to keep them informed at the start of the invasion by the Germans, but after many days of fighting Warsaw was defeated. My mother's recollections of what she heard on the radio that day are similar to what has been documented, but they are not the exact same words. See Bartoszewski's *1859 Dni Warszawy*.

22 "'I see you have already forgotten your Polish!'" This is an example of the kind of remark my mother would make that would later make her a target of the Soviets, especially in the labor camp.

24 "Marshall Józef Piłsudski." Though somewhat of a controversial figure, Piłsudski was instrumental in securing Poland's freedom following World War I. For a detailed description of Piłsudski, see Reddaway's *The Cambridge History of Poland*.

30 "Adam Mickiewicz's *Pan Tadeusz* (*Mr. Thaddeus*)." *Pan Tadeusz* is a famous long lyrical poem with a story similar to that of Romeo and Juliet, but set in the early nineteenth century in a part of Poland that was near my mother's farm near Grodno. The translation here is from the Everyman's Library edition.

31 "as a European power and a defender of Christianity." At one time the Polish-Lithuanian Commonwealth stretched from the Baltic to the Black Sea and beyond. See Davies's *God's Playground*.

34 "the official non-Communist-produced Polish history book." At the time I was attending Saturday Polish school, I was not aware that the children in

Poland were not taught an accurate history of World War II. It was not until later when I visited Poland after the fall of Communism and spoke with my family that I discovered the propaganda that was fed to children in Poland during the Communist era following World War II. This also came to light during my many conversations with Poles who had immigrated to the United States in the 1970s, 1980s, and 1990s. It should also be noted that the Communism referred to in this book is that of Soviet Communism and not the type that became popular in the communes of the rebellious 1960s and 1970s in America.

35 "'My, Pierwsza Brygada,' the Polish Legion's song." This song was written by Tadeusz Biernacki in around 1915; it was included in the Polish Girl Scout songbook that I received in the 1960s. The translation here is my own. The words were written as a patriotic tribute to Piłsudski's Legions who fought for Poland's freedom during and after World War I.

36 "acceptance of [Poland] as an independent country at the end of World War I was not widespread." For an in-depth discussion of conditions in Poland between the World Wars, refer to Davies's *God's Playground*.

36 "words from patriotic songs, such as 'Jak Długo w Sercu Naszym (As long as in our hearts).'" The White Eagle refers to the Order of the White Eagle, the highest decoration a Polish officer or civilian can receive. The translation here is mine.

46 "'the first king of Poland was a peasant!'" According to legend, the first king of Poland is alleged to be Piast the Wheelwright (c. 850 AD). The first documented king was Mieszko I (c. 963–992) from the Piast Dynasty. See Davies's *God's Playground*.

Part 2. Russia and Siberia

75 "the threatening presence of Germany at Poland's doorstep." See the discussion of this neglect in, for example, Kochanski's *The Eagle Unbowed*.

81 "bitterly cold day on the tenth of February 1940." The first deportations were especially brutal, as they took place in the middle of a very cold winter. See Gross's *Revolution from Abroad* and Jolluck's *Exile and Identity*.

84 "'Boże Coś Polskę (God thou hast Poland, or God save Poland).'" Poland's defining religious hymn was composed by Alojzy Felinski in 1816. We sang this religious national hymn, which appears in my Polish Girl Scout songbook, at almost every ceremony and during Catholic masses. The translation here is from an unknown source. The connection between the Catholic Church and fighting for freedom in Polish history is reflected in songs, music, literature, and art. See Olszer's *For Your Freedom and Ours*.

86 "In 1830 and 1863, there were bloody uprisings in Poland against the Russians." These uprisings in 1830 and 1863 were a constant reminder to Poles of their subjugation by Russia, in particular during the 123 years of the partition. This fueled much resentment and instilled staunch patriotism among Poles. See Davies's *God's Playground*.

90 "the old Polonia, near downtown Chicago." Poles who had immigrated to the United States during the years of Poland's partitions, when education was squelched by either the Russians, Germans, or Austrians, tended to be poorly educated and were mostly simple peasant farmers. My parents were part of the *new* generation of immigrants who had fled Communism; they had been well educated in Poland between the wars. While the new Polonia strived to maintain their Polish heritage, the old Polonia had by then lost even the language. Abhorrent to my father was the slaughtering of Polish words, as in *"niech Pan idzie za kornerem* (Sir, go around the corner),*" whereby the English word "corner" was turned into an abstract Polish word. Whenever I mixed English with Polish at home, my parents would immediately chastise me by saying, *"Nie gadaj za kornerem* (Don't talk in *kornerem*),*" and we would all laugh. I would immediately correct myself in Polish. I was never allowed to speak English at home so that I would become proficient in Polish. See Jaroszyńska-Kirchmann's *The Exile Mission* for further descriptions of life in America for Polish immigrants.

93 "The Polish anthem, 'Jeszcze Polska nie Zginęła' ('Poland Has Not Yet Perished')." This extremely patriotic national anthem was written by Józef Wybicki circa 1797, just after the Third Partition of Poland, which erased Poland from the world's maps.

94 "the international conspiracy of silence to cover up the atrocities." See Paul's *Katyń* and Adamczyk's *When God Looked the Other Way*. Adamczyk's father was one of the officers murdered among the more than twenty thousand.

119 "Her elation spurred her on to sing a favorite song." This is most likely a version of a poem—compiled from memory by one of the refugees—by Juliusz Słowacki, one of the major Polish writers and poets of the nineteenth century, whose work was stylistically similar to the romantic poets Keats and Wordsworth. It could also be a verse adapted from Mickiewicz's *Pan Tadeusz*.

Part 3. Choices and Destiny

170 "secret additional protocol to the Ribbentrop-Molotov Pact of 1939." Most of the West was not aware of Poland's historical enemies' secret plan to

divvy up the country. Roosevelt and Churchill did not consider it a good political strategy to anger "Uncle Joe" Stalin while they were trying to defeat Germany. All of this is well documented today and is reported in the historical literature; see, for example, Davies's *God's Playground*.

170 "'granting amnesty to all Polish citizens.'" Frequently referred to as *po amnestji* (after amnesty) by Poles, it was a significant turning point during World War II for those Polish citizens who had been deported to the labor camps and the remaining Polish officers and soldiers imprisoned in Siberia. These documents are part of the Yalta agreements.

172 "the Polish Army did accept all who requested help." There was much propaganda about what happened in the turmoil after amnesty and how matters were handled by the Polish Army and the British and whether the Soviets in fact did what they had agreed to do. See Kochanski's *The Eagle Unbowed*.

182 "'My country with whispering forests.'" This poem is most likely loosely based on one by Juliusz Słowacki; the translation here is mine. Deportees would not have had books and probably put this together from memory so the words would not have been exact.

195 "'Only this narrow passage to the Baltic!'" The new borders of Poland after World War I left only a very narrow passage to the Baltic. This was a constant lament I heard many times, not only from my parents but also from my Polish schoolteachers and others. It was one of the main reasons Poland had so much difficulty establishing itself economically and militarily after World War I and why it was not militarily well prepared for the invasion by Germany at the start of World War II. See Davies's *God's Playground*, Kochanski's *The Eagle Unbowed*, and Snyder's *Bloodlands*.

Part 4. Bittersweet Lessons

252 "he took part in a defining battle at Monte Cassino." Very little is mentioned in English history books about the role of the Polish Army in this battle, yet the Polish losses were great. Most of the historical references have passages about this battle.

252 "Roosevelt and Churchill had sold Poland out to Stalin." Churchill tried to advocate for Poland but in the end acquiesced in order to end the war. See Davies's *God's Playground* and Kochanski's *The Eagle Unbowed*.

References

Historical Sources

Anders, Władysław. *An Army in Exile: The Story of the Second Polish Corps.* London: Macmillan, 1949.

Applebaum, Anne. *Gulag: A History.* New York: Anchor, 2004.

Bartoszewski, Władysław. *1859 Dni Warszawy.* Kraków: Wydawnictwo Znak, 1974.

Davies, Norman. *God's Playground: A History of Poland.* Volume 1: *The Origins to 1795.* New York: Columbia University Press, 1982.

———. *God's Playground: A History of Poland.* Volume 2: *1795 to the Present.* New York: Columbia University Press, 1982.

Gross, Jan T. *Revolution from Abroad: The Soviet Conquest of Poland's Western Ukraine and Western Belorussia.* Princeton, NJ: Princeton University Press, 1988.

Grudzińska-Gross, Irena, and Jan Tomasz Gross. *War through Children's Eyes: The Soviet Occupation of Poland and the Deportations, 1939–1941.* Stanford, CA: Hoover Institution Press, 1981.

Jaroszyńska-Kirchmann, Anna D. *The Exile Mission: The Polish Political Diaspora and Polish Americans, 1939–1956.* Athens: Ohio University Press, 2004.

Jolluck, Katherine R. *Exile and Identity: Polish Women in the Soviet Union during World War II*. Pittsburgh, PA: University of Pittsburgh Press, 2002.

Kochanski, Halik. *The Eagle Unbowed: Poland and the Poles in the Second World War*. Cambridge, MA: Harvard University Press, 2012.

Korbonski, Stefan. *The Polish Underground State: A Guide to the Underground, 1939–1945*. Boulder: East European Quarterly, 1978.

Koskodan, Kenneth K. *No Greater Ally: The Untold Story of Poland's Forces in World War II*. Oxford: Osprey Publishing, 2009.

Olszer, Krystyna M. *For Your Freedom and Ours: Polish Progressive Spirit from the Fourteenth Century to the Present*. New York: Frederick Ungar, 1981.

Paul, Allen. *Katyń: Stalin's Massacre and the Triumph of Truth*. DeKalb: Northern Illinois University Press, 2010.

Porter-Szűcs, Brian. *Poland in the Modern World: Beyond Martyrdom*. Hoboken, NJ: Wiley Blackwell, 2014.

Przybylski, A. *Wojna Polska, 1918–1921*. Warsaw: Wojskowy Instytut Naukowo-Wydawniczy, 1930.

Reddaway, W. F., et al. *The Cambridge History of Poland: From Augustus II to Piłsudski (1697–1935)*. New York: Octagon Books, 1971.

Snyder, Timothy. *Bloodlands: Europe between Hitler and Stalin*. New York: Basic Books, 2010.

Szkopiak, Zygmunt C. *The Yalta Agreements: Documents prior to, during, and after the Crimea Conference, 1945*. London: The Polish Government-in-Exile, 1986.

Literary Sources

Mickiewicz, Adam. *Pan Tadeusz; or, The Last Foray in Lithuania*. Everyman's Library. New York: Dutton, 1966.

Orzeszkowa, Eliza. Nad Niemnem. Warsaw: Gebethner and Wolf, 1888, rpt. Warsaw: Czytelnik, 1971.

Podalak, Tadeusz, ed. *Wrócimy Tam: Zbiór pieśni polskich*. Detroit, Michigan, 1952 (handbook used by Polish Scouts in the 1950s and 1960s).

Słowacki, Juliusz. *Ojciec Zadżumionych w El-Arish*. N.p.: n.p., 1936–38.

Memoirs

Adamczyk, Wesley. *When God Looked the Other Way: An Odyssey of War, Exile, and Redemption*. Chicago: University of Chicago Press, 2004.

Czapski, Józef. *The Inhuman Land*. London: Polish Cultural Foundation, 1987.

Mikosz-Hintzke, Teresa. *Six Years 'til Spring: A Polish Family's Odyssey*. San Jose, CA: Author's Choice Press, 2001.

Obertyńska, Beata. *W Domu Niewoli*. 2nd ed. Chicago: Nakładem Grona Przyjaciół, Dziennik Związkowy, 1968.

Rybczynski, Witold. *My Two Polish Grandfathers: And Other Essays on the Imaginative Life*. New York: Scribner, 2009.

Tarnowski, Andrew. *The Last Mazurka: A Family's Tale of War, Passion, and Loss*. New York: St. Martin's Press, 2006.

Topolski, Aleksander. *Without Vodka: Adventures in Wartime Russia*. South Royalton, VT: Steerforth Press, 2001.

Index

Page numbers for illustrations are in italics.

Britain, 75–76, 149, 170–77, 187–89, 233–34, 250, 253–59

Canada, 258

cancer, 202–5, 211–15, 241–46, 277–79

Catholicism, 14, 26–27, 30–32, 90–91, 182–85, 256, 260, 288–89

Chamberlain, Neville, 75–76

Chardzhou, 189, 192–201

Chicago: Polonia and, 33–34, 46–49, 90, 267–68, 276–77, 290; Wisconsin farm as escape from, 25–29, 54–58, 65–70

Chicago Sun-Times, 244

Chicago Tribune, 244

Christmas, 78–80, 266–67

Churchill, Winston, 252–53, 291

Ciot, Józef, 224

Communism: Cold War and, 93–94; justice system of, 81–89, 97, 130–34; labor camp policies and, 95–99, 103–8, 116–23, 139–44; in Poland, xi, 252, 265–66, 287; propaganda of, 14, 60, 64–65, 289; religion and, 126–27; Russian poverty and, 86–87, 107–8, 133–34

Coventry, 255–57

Cud nad Wisła, 43

Czechoslovakia, 111

Darek (Donna's cousin), 112

Davies, Norman, xii

The Death of Ellenai (Malczewski), 272–73

deportations, 9–10, 60–61, 65, 81–89, 184, 219

Donna Solecka Urbikas: birth of, 256; cancer battle of, 202–5, 277–79; father's relationship with, 54–58, 78–80, 92, 134–37, 146–48, 190–91, 241–46, 260–64, 267–69, 276–79, 285–86; husband of, xiii, 70, 110–13, 124, 136, 202–5, 212–13, 218, 226, 230, 244, 264, 284; interviews of, xi, 3–4, 18–20, 38–40, 271–72; Janina's relationship with, 4–6, 10–11, 18–20, 48–49,

124–25, 146–51, 241–46, 263–75, 283–86; Mira's relationship with, 226–31, 242–46, 270–71, 286; as mother, 38–40, 182–85, 202–5, 211–15, 230–31, 241–46, 263–64, 272, 283–86; photos of, *161–62, 164–66*; Poland visits of, 109–14, 124–25; Polish Girl Scouts and, 10, 33–34, 93, 100–101, *166*, 289; Unitarianism of, 91–92, 182–85; Wisconsin farmstead and, 25–29, 54–58, 65–70, 101, 134–37

Dowbór-Muśnicki, Józef, 41–42

dysentery, 236

Dzhalal-Abad, 216–25

Dziennik Związkowy, xii, 33

Egypt, 261

England, 255–59, 261. *See also* Britain

Fergana Valley, 221

Figa, 15, 63–64, 83, 118, 266

Free Public Library of Kaszewo, 31–32

Germany, 13–17, 35–37, 59–60, 73–76, 222–23, 252

Girl Scouts, 10, 33–34, 93, 100–101, *166*, 289

Górny Ślask, 36

Government-in-Exile (of Poland), 170, 179, 189, 247, 253–54

Grodno: Janina's escape to, 13–17, 21–24, 287; Janina's farm in, 4, 13–17, 62–65; Jews of, 184; Soviet attacks on, 59–65; Walenty's land near, 45, 200; Wisconsin farm's recollection of, 28. *See also* Belarusians; Niemen River

health. *See* mental illness; *specific diseases and people*

Hitler, Adolf, 13, 16, 76, 179

Holocaust, 184, 252

India, 247–51, 253–54

Iran, 232–37, 261

Iraq War, 40

White Russians. *See* Belarusians

Wilson, Woodrow, 35, 259

World War I, xi, xii, 11–12, 14, 23–24, 30–32, 35–37, 73–75, 246, 288

World War II: Germany and, 13–17, 73–76, 222–23, 252; mental health and, 227–31, 283–84; Polish Army in, 4, 75–78, 190–91; Soviet Union and, 9–12, 59–65, 222, 252–54

Wybicki, Józef, 290

Yalta Conference, 253

Zimmerman, Janina. *See* Janina Zimmerman Solecka

Zimmerman, Rudolf. *See* Rudolf Zimmerman

Zorko, Nikolay, 120–22